A Most Irregular War

SOE Burma, Major Trofimov's Diary 1944-45

A Most Irregular War

SOE Burma, Major Trofimov's Diary 1944-45

This edition first published in the United Kingdom in 2023 by DevonPress and 'The Trofimov Literary Estate', c/o Brethertons Solicitors, Franklins House, Manorsfield Road, Bicester, Oxon OX26 6EX United Kingdom.

PB ISBN 978-1-7394402-0-6
HB ISBN 978-1-7394402-1-3
Ebook ISBN 978-1-7394402-2-0

© The Trofimov Literary Estate, 2023

The rights of this work have been asserted in accordance with the Crown Copyright, Designs and Patents Act 1988.

A CIP catalogue record of this book is available from the British Library.

Publisher: PWN Honeywill
Editors: GH Bennett, R Duckett and P Trofimov.

All rights reserved. No part of this publication may be reproduced, stored in a retrieval system or transmitted in any form or by any means whether electronic, mechanical, photocopying, recording, or otherwise, without the prior written permission of The Trofimov Estate. Any person who carries out any unauthorised act in relation to this publication may be liable to criminal prosecution and civil claims for damages.

Cover: Crossing of the Sittang River with their distinctive Slouch hats.

Historical content courtesy of The Trofimov Literary Estate.

Typeset in Adobe Garamond Pro 11/13.2pt. Printed by Print on Demand.

Unless stated all images are copyright The Trofimov Literary Estate. Maps are older than 50 years and require no reproduction notice in accordance with OS UK Adanac Drive, Southampton, SO16 OAS, United Kingdom.

To retain as an historical record, all three diaries are transcribed as written.

Following our late father's express wishes found in correspondence amongst his many papers, we dedicate this book to his grandchildren and great-grandchildren, some of whom were not born at the time of dad's passing.

Contents

Acknowledgements.. 8
Foreword: *Richard Duckett* 12
Introduction: *GH Bennett* 18
A Tin Trunk, A Diary and A Journey into Our Father's 32
Past: *By his sons Mark and Paul Trofimov*

Diary Codenamed "Mongoose Green" With Force 136 and 46
the Karen in Burma January-September 1945

Diary

Diary I 11th February – 25th March 1945 47
Diary II 25th March – 4th June 1945 70
Diary III 2nd June – 27th September 1945 114

Albums

Part I Original Mountings 144
Part II Training in Ceylon 146
Part III People 154
Part IV Life among the Karens 166
Part V In the Bush 174
Part VI Resupply by Air 182
Part VII Air Operations 190
Part VIII The Japanese Dead 204
Part IX Sports Day 208
Part X Final Parade 214
Part XI Final Pay Day 218
Part XII Farewell 222

Maps Force 136 230
Operation Character

Appendix I 266
Codenamed "Guy": With the Jedburghs in France June-August 1944
Appendix II 272
Post-War Report by Major AAE Trofimov on "Mongoose Green"
Appendix III 286
Liberation By Saw M. Shwin, BA, BIL Superintendent, Shwegyin Karen School, Shwegyin, Burma (17th July 1946)
Appendix IV 304
Karen Platoon Lists – Pay (March-September 1945)
Appendix V 312
Letter to Girlfriend in England (Unposted), 6th March 1945, Describing Parachute Drop into Burma
Appendix VI 316
Itinerary of Character/'Mongoose' Operations from February 1945 to September 1945 in the Karen Mountains
Appendix VII 322
Original unedited photographs
Appendix VIII 376
Maps

Biographies
AAE Trofimov 378
Richard Duckett 380
GH Bennett 380
Clive Bassett 381

Index 384

Acknowledgments

Our journey towards publication began with a father – daughter relationship. On a chance listening to Radio 4's author interviews in October 2019 with Keggie Carew[1] about her book entitled *Dadland* (published in 2016)[2] about her life-long relationship with her father, Tom Carew,[3] a former 'Jed' and SOE[4] agent, I was subsequently put in contact with Keggie via her literary agency in London.

My brother, Mark, and I had already had the privilege of meeting Tom Carew as we had been introduced to him on a couple of occasions of SOE reunions during the 1990s and I had the fortunate opportunity to meet his daughter, too, at one of these events. Keggie was most helpful in providing me with a variety of suggestions for possible publishing routes, one of which was to put me in touch with Richard Duckett in early November 2019 (*see* biography page 378) who has published two books on the Special Operations Executive in Burma. Richard was most helpful, too, in putting me in touch with various publishing houses as well as introducing me to his website,[5] The Special Operations Executive in Burma 1941-1945, in which Dad features within 'the Men of SOE' section. I maintained contact with Richard over progress with my dad's diaries since 2019 and it was again by chance that in September 2021, he emailed me to say he had been contacted by Harry Bennett of Plymouth University (*see* biography page 378) as his father Roy was at school with ours in the 1930s and he apparently had a few memories of his time at school with our father that he thought we might be interested to hear.

I followed this up directly with Harry Bennett via email and Harry responded by return and very kindly forwarded my email to his father (then aged 93) whom he said remembered our father 'pretty well from their days at Queen Elizabeth's Grammar School' in Derbyshire. Shortly afterwards I received a lovely email direct from Roy Bennett in which he very kindly shared his memories of being a junior at Queen Elizabeth's Grammar School in 1938 as a 10-year-old boy at the time when our father was a senior pupil and Prefect of the School (aged 17). We share a couple of Roy's memoirs here:

> Of all the prefects, Aubrey Trofimov's strange name made him a special case. He was a boarder, while most of us were day boys from the local area. He seemed able to chat effortlessly in French with our French teacher and also with his dog. We believed all sorts of rumours that he was actually a Russian Prince who had been brought out of Russia as a child to save him from the fate of other members of the Romanov dynasty. There was never the slightest whisper of Trofimov's exciting and distinguished war record behind enemy lines in Europe and Burma until the details appeared in his obituary (2006) published in the press. I had ended the war as a 17-year-old merchant seaman whose ship happened to be in Calcutta on VJ day. I had carefully inserted in the flag hoists decorating my ship one which spelled out the motto of Queen Elizabeth's Grammar School – 'EN BON ESPOYR'.[6] What strange fate had brought the prefect and the new boy of 1938 halfway round the world to face Japan, one in the hills and jungles of northern Burma [southern – in the Karen mountains] and the other in the waters of the Bay of Bengal and the River Hooghly.

Then in further correspondence with his son Harry he asked to see a transcript of our late father's war diaries and it was from this that he later agreed to provide an introduction and contextualisation for the diaries in their original form and we have collaborated since in assembling the evidence from our father's original diaries, maps, photographs, platoon lists and other documentation both during and post-war in preparing a manuscript suitable for publication. In this regard Harry, as a historian and highly accomplished author himself with a variety of publications to his name[7] (see publications page of his university listing), put me in touch with Paul Honeywill by email stating: 'Paul Honeywill runs his own publishing company which works with the Britannia Royal Naval College on a series for which I am one of the editors'. Paul later confirmed to me that: 'I am gradually building a naval brand for the Britannia Museum Trust Press, based at Britannia Royal Naval College, Dartmouth but as BMTP only publish Naval Military History, so if you wish to publish with me, it would be under DevonPress which is me as an independent'.

Major Trofimov's kit on display at the Harrington Museum. Donated in 1990.

So, we are truly thankful it all came together with Richard Duckett agreeing to do a Foreword, Harry Bennett agreeing to do the Introduction and contextualisation for the diaries and Paul Honeywill undertaking the publishing through his independent publishing company, DevonPress.

My brother and I would also like to acknowledge Clive Bassett's[8] considerable support over many years. Clive has been very closely affiliated with the 'Jeds' and SOE agents attending most of their reunions and through his friendship with our father developed over the 1980s and 1990s up to his passing in 2006, he has looked after many of our father's war memorabilia including weapons and other SOE equipment which are on display at the Harrington Museum.[9] Known as the Carpetbagger Secret Warfare Museum in Harrington, Northamptonshire, it is where B24 Liberator aircraft took off from the airfield on an Operation Carpetbagger mission to drop secret agents and supplies to resistance groups in occupied Europe during World War II. Clive was also involved in putting together the text for our father's obituaries from the information he had gleaned from father of his war career, and which were published in the obituary sections in *The Times*, *The Telegraph* and *The Observer* shortly after his passing in 2006 for which we remain ever grateful.

In recognition of the considerable support that we have received from Richard, Harry, notwithstanding his own father, Roy's input as without him this connection may not have occurred, Paul and Clive in getting to this publication of our father's war diaries in Burma in 1945, we shall be arranging with Richard for full access to all father's war photographs and other documentation. This will include the original Karen platoon lists for inclusion in his website, The Special Operations Executive in Burma 1941-1945. We will also provide continued support to Clive in ensuring that the SOE display at the Harrington museum is maintained with as much encouragement given as possible for this to be a lasting legacy of the SOE and in recognition of the small part that our late father contributed to this irregular warfare in WW II for the benefit of future generations and so that their story is never forgotten.

Thanks go to Mary Masters (a well published author) for her assistance with the proofreading in the final stages and noting, too, her own father's connection to Burma.

A special thanks goes to Lorraine and Leon too, for all their advice and support.

---

[1] www.keggiecarew.co.uk

[2] 2016 Costa Book Awards – Biography Award Winner for *Dadland* by Keggie Carew.

[3] Lt. Colonel Thomas Carew – Personnel file: HS 9/268/5 IWM interview – Team *Camel* (December 1944 – February 1945) and Team *Weasel* (March 1945 – May 1945). Both parachute drops into Burma were part of the *Billet* operation https://www.thetimes.co.uk/article/lieutenant-colonel-thomas-carew

[4] 'Jed' and SOE – refers to Jedburgh Teams – part of The Special Operations Executive – *see* Introduction.

[5] https://soeinburma.com/

[6] In Good Hope.

[7] https://www.plymouth.ac.uk/staff/harry-bennett

[8] *See* Biographies (page 379).

[9] https://harringtonmuseum.org.uk/

Foreword

Richard Duckett

When I first started researching the Special Operations Executive's war in Burma back in 2001 for a Master's thesis, I soon realised that there was a massive haul of important historical research that, for some reason, barely anyone had bothered about. I knew there was a PhD thesis waiting to be written, but I had to sit on it for the next seven years until I was in a position to do something about it. Those seven years between completing my MA and starting a PhD were crucial. While I hoped that nobody would choose to start researching SOE in Burma, I was too busy getting my teaching career started to carry out interviews with many of the SOE Burma veterans that were still alive. Consequently, I missed out on meeting men like Major Trofimov, 'Trof', who passed away in 2006.

'Trofimov' was a name I already knew when I finally started my research with the Open University in 2008. There were some names that had stood out immediately with just a casual sweep of the archives when I started looking in 2001. He was also mentioned in the official history of SOE in the Far East, written by Charles Cruickshank and published in 1983.[1] It was readily apparent that it wasn't the unusual, non-anglophile, surname that marked him out. Here was a man who, along with a few other names – such as Colin Mackenzie, Major Saw Torry, Honorary Lieutenant Kan Choke, Lt. Col. Edgar Peacock, Major John Hedley – seemed well respected within the archival record. It will always be a regret that life made it difficult for me to meet many of these men while I still could.

It is therefore the next best thing to now be in a position where I have been invited to write this Forward for a book which Trof seems to have wanted published, and on which his sons feel such a sense of responsibility to follow through. The weight of family and historical responsibility is often a heavy one, so it is right that Trof has his diary made available for the growing number of people who are interested in SOE's war beyond Europe. SOE was a truly global organisation, and I hope that this book can contribute to a broader assessment of what I think was a remarkable part of the British war effort.

The diary is gritty. It immerses the reader in the day to day reality of fighting a war behind the lines in unfamiliar and difficult territory, where there was much more than the enemy to consider in order to survive. Trof wrote candidly of his boredom on some days, and how he admonished himself for his self-introspection on others. He writes of falling head over heels in love almost at first sight while on leave in Calcutta, and his joy at receiving news from the outside world after weeks of isolation in the Burmese jungle. He also writes about the ghastly nature of war, of spies and treachery, of ambushes and death; then he'll be writing with humility about concerns for his dog, 'Pagoda', and his fears for the health of his officers and men. By the end of the three sections of diary, if you, the reader, are anything like me, you will have ridden the highs and lows of Trof's eight month roller-coaster, and disembark with a sense of wonder for his fortitude and courage in the most stressful of endeavours. You will also marvel at the tender young age at which he did all this.

Trof was, as I have shown in my book, part of what can be considered SOE's most impressive military operation of the Second World War.[2] Operation *Character* as a whole raised approximately 12,000 men who were trained, armed, and then fought on the flank of the regular army's advance on Rangoon. This meant that General Slim had the equivalent strength of a division of guerrillas (in terms of numbers) attacking the Japanese lines of communication. By setting ambush after ambush on these roads and jungle tracks, not only did the *Character* teams prevent the Japanese from regrouping in central Burma at Toungoo, allowing Rangoon to be taken before the full onset of the monsoon, they also prevented the Japanese from regrouping in the southeast of the country in July 1945. An estimated 50,000 Japanese troops had been cut off in Burma once Rangoon had been reclaimed on 3rd May, and in July they attempted to break out. In this fight, known as 'The Battle of the Breakout', the Army acknowledged that SOE was killing more Japanese than they were, and it was to take part in this battle that Trof was urgently summoned towards the end of the diary. By the end of the campaign, Force 136 guerrillas in Burma claimed a total of 16,279 Japanese killed in what was gruesomely called 'The Game Book'.[3] A further 995 are recorded as wounded and 285 were captured. Add to this the 11,000 Japanese who surrendered to Mongoose in September 1945, and in terms of numbers of Japanese, it can begin to be surmised that SOE acquitted itself well in Burma.[4]

These results would not have been possible were it not for the indigenous races of Burma. To the extent that these ethnicities are known, the Karen have received the lion's share of attention. Indeed, most of the 12,000 recruits for Operation *Character* were Karen, but in Burma, Force 136 recruited somewhere in the region of 20,000 Asiatic personnel. As my 'Men of SOE Burma' research reveals though, recruits included men from across almost all the races represented in Burma - Lahu, Chin, Kachin, Burman, Arakanese, Gurkha, Shan, Indian, Chinese, as well as Anglo-Burman, Shan-Burman, Indo-Burman, Shan Palaung, Shan-Kadu.[5] In Appendix III, Saw Marshall Shwin writes that only Major Lucas had Burmese parachutists with him. While this might be true of the *Mongoose* officers, it certainly wasn't true of many other SOE teams in Burma, including other parts of Operation *Character*. While we have to be careful in our consideration of how Force 136 was, without any doubt, multi-ethnic in its composition, a historically sour – and sensitive – debate about the extent to which British officials and men of SOE Burma made promises to the Karen regarding independence after the war has persisted since 1945.

Just as in 2021, some British officials and many British soldiers and officers felt a huge duty of responsibility to their Afghan interpreters, many of the men who served with the Karen in Burma agonised over what unfolded in Burma after 1945. Just like in 2021, it was felt that the Karen were abandoned by a country that should have done more in recognition of their wartime services. What happened in Burma, however, needs to be seen in the context of a new Labour government in Britain in 1945 elected to provide the 'New Jerusalem' of the Beveridge Report; of the grim aftermath of the Second World War and the rise of the institutions of Global Governance such as the United Nations; the Cold War; of the era of decolonisation after the total loss of British prestige across the Far East in 1942; and specifically in the melee of nationalist movements, but in particular in India and Palestine.

Trof and many other British soldiers and colonial officials never gave up appealing and lobbying for the Karen all the way through the subsequent decades, into their old age. Privately held papers that I have had the privilege of seeing, such as the contents of Trof's Tin Trunk, the papers of Captain Tony Bennett of V Force and the recently discovered pristine treasures preserved by Major Freddie Milner,[6] as well as books such as the *Changing of the Kings* by Leslie Glass – all reveal the sadness and anger caused by a perceived betrayal of the Karen. The Attlee government, by leaving the Karen to be included in a Burman dominated government of an independent Burma in 1948, caused anger which is still manifest in some quarters to this day.[7]

While war rages in Ukraine and atrocities are splashed across our TV and our social media feeds, the Karen continue to be persecuted in the country now known as Myanmar in a civil war which has now entered into its ninth decade. This latter conflict barely gets a mention in our news, and nor now does Afghanistan. Those same institutions of Global Governance which were established with such high hopes to live up to the aspiration of 'never again' in the wake of the genocides of the Second World War, those same institutions that men like Trof endured such horrors to help bring into existence, they are needed as much now as they ever were so that young men like Trof can avoid fighting in terrible conflicts all around the globe.

---

[1] Charles Cruickshank, *SOE in the Far East* (Oxford: OUP, 1986).

[2] Richard Duckett, The Special Operations Executive in Burma: Jungle Warfare and Intelligence Gathering in World War II (London: IB Tauris, 2017).

[3] The National Archives (hereafter TNA), HS 1/10, 'Game Book of Casualties', 1st January to 5th September 1945, from HQ Group A Force 136 to HQ Force 136, 5th September 1945.

[4] TNA, HS 7/106, Report of Major Lucas, p.12.

[5] *See* Richard Duckett, 'The Men of SOE Burma' [online] https://soeinburma.com/the-men-of-soe-burma/

[6] Major Frederick Stanley Milner: Born on 26 March 1916, Milner attended the Duke of York's Royal Military School from 1920 – 1934. On leaving school at 18, Milner joined the Wiltshire Regiment, with whom he served in Palestine (1936-7) during the Arab Revolt.

In 1939, Milner went to France, returning via Boulogne in 1940. Attending OCTU, Milner was commissioned into the Dorests in December 1940, and promptly recruited by SOE as an instructor.

While instructing at STS 4 in 1941, Milner was injured when a grenade splinter lodged in his neck. The Royal Surrey Hospital returned him to duty without removing it! Later, at STS 103 in Canada, Milner suffered second degree burns when the 'Silent Soldier' grenade thrower he was demonstrating spontaneously ignited.

After a spell in North Africa and Corsica during 1943 – where he 'worked well with Americans' – Milner was posted to India where he joined the Burma Country Section of Force 136.

On 26 March 1945, his 29th birthday, Milner was dropped into Burma on Operation Character where he was in charge of station Mongoose, area White. On this operation, Milner was recommended for the Military Cross twice, the second time for immediate award. This was for his work during the Battle of the Breakout in July-August 1945, when his Karen guerrillas inflicted an estimated 300 casualties upon the Japanese who were trying to cross the Shwegyin Chaung. He was described as 'A brilliant and fearless leader' who was respected by 'all the Karens.'

Personnel File: HS 9/1038/6

[7] Leslie Glass, *The Changing of the Kings: Memories of Burma 1934-1949* (London: Peter Owen, 1985). *See* Chapter 11 in particular.

FOREWORD

Military Cross.

The Burma Star.

Introduction

GH Bennett

This book constitutes a graphic insight, into a largely forgotten corner of the Second World World War. It does so through the diary and the camera lens of a young Special Forces Officer, a member of the British Special Operations Executive (SOE), Aubrey Alwyn Edgar Trofimov (7th December 1921- 6th May 2006), Croix de Guerre and Military Cross. During the Second World War he served with the Royal Artillery and later, from 1944 to 1945, with British special forces in France and Burma as part of the Special Operations Executive. In 1946 he resumed pre-war studies to be an architect at Manchester University later practicing in London, Newcastle and France. He passed away on 6th May 2006 in London University Hospital after being taken ill at a Special Forces reunion the previous day at the Bonnington Hotel in Bloomsbury, leaving behind his wife Jean and their two sons. Like many men of that generation the stories of his wartime endeavours might have been lost at that point but, as will be recounted later in this book, his sons (Mark and Paul) on clearing the family home found a large metal trunk. The trunk contained diaries, photographs, maps and other paper ephemera to allow us to glance back to the world of 1945, and the struggle to defeat an Imperial Japanese Army that had unleashed devastation across much of Asia from 1931 onwards. Collectively, the papers give us a remarkable insight into "Trof's" war and that of the Karen people, who he fought alongside in the closing months of the conflict. For them the war would not end in 1945, but it would continue as a struggle for self-determination, on-going to this day in the Karen resistance to the military dictatorship of Myanmar.

Upbringing and Army Service

For Trofimov the road to the Karen Hills in 1945 was anything but straightforward. Born on 7th December 1921 to Edgar Morton (1898-1973)[1] and Mary Morton (*nee* Woodcock, 1901-1982), who had married in 1919, AAE Morton was adopted at age 12 by Professor Michael V. Trofimov who had married his mother on 29th October 1925 following the breakdown of her first marriage. Michael Vassily Trofimov had been born in a small village near Archangel in North Russia, eventually attending the University of St Petersburg. His political views got him into some difficulties with the Czarist authorities and he eventually arrived in the United Kingdom, lecturing at Liverpool University and King's College London.[2] In 1919 he had been appointed Professor of Russian Language and Literature at Manchester University after lecturing in the Department of Slavonic Studies at King's College

London from 1916 to 1919.³ The marriage between Michael and Marie also broke down by 1940 so that they were leading largely separate lives, with Michael petitioning for Divorce as a result of abandonment in May 1943. During their short-lived marriage, Trof attended the junior school at the College de Sacre Coeur, Menton, France after his mother moved there. He would later attend the Lycée in Nice. He learned to speak French fluently before returning to the UK and attending Queen Elizabeth's Grammar School, Ashbourne Derbyshire to complete his education. Later, and attracted to a career in architecture, in 1939 he began his studies at Manchester University. They were, however, to be disrupted by the war and he was called up to the Royal Artillery in 1941. Demonstrating an aptitude in signals, his qualities meant that he was sent for officer training in 1943. He was commissioned at Catterick in September 1943. A few weeks later the young officer, now with 148/170 Regiment Royal Artillery at Glynde in Sussex, saw a mysterious invitation on a noticeboard in barracks. It asked for 'volunteers … with a sound knowledge of French and experience in signals prepared to work behind enemy lines'.⁴ Intrigued "Trof" volunteered. For several months he heard nothing, with him being sent to Northern Ireland as part of an advance party for 175/180 Field Regiment Royal Artillery. However, in January 1944 he was called to London for interview and for tests. That process lasted from 13th-19th January with the outcome being that he joined the Special Forces, proceeding to Milton Hall in Peterborough for intensive training. Here he was trained to be part of a Jedburgh three-man sabotage and resistance team to be dropped into occupied Europe to support the Allied advance after D-Day on 6 June 1944. As Trofimov later wrote, while at Milton Hall:

> There followed an intensive period of training covering every aspect of guerrilla warfare, comprising sabotage, use of explosives, enemy identifications, military operations, silent killing techniques, organisation of networks, dropping zone drill, wireless telegraphy, Morse code, parachute training, training on Eureka and two-way S-phone larynx sets.⁵ Because of my earlier training in Signals, the wireless and Morse code came very easily to me. We eventually formed into Jed teams, comprising either an English or American Officer, with one French Officer and a radio operator.⁶

Operation Jedburgh

The purpose of the operation which Trofimov was being trained to take part of was a fascinating collaboration between the British Special Operations Executive (SOE), the American Office of Strategic Studies (OSS) and the Free French Bureau de Renseignements et de Action (BCRA), with the participation of the Dutch and Belgian armed forces.[7] The multinational nature of the operation, in planning and development since May 1943, saw the first major collaboration between the SOE and the OSS, and it was intended to facilitate close co-operation in support of the Allied invasion of Western Europe between Allied special forces and resistance groups. Around 300 "Jeds" were selected after several weeks of extensive training starting with commando training in the Scottish Highlands (not explicitly identified by Trofimov in his account) before moving on to Milton Hall in close proximity to the airfields from where they would depart. After landing in France the purpose of the Jedburghs was to provide assistance to local resistance groups, along with expertise, leadership (if required) and, above all, a means to call in arms and supply drops as and when required. In April 1944, following the formation of the individual teams SOE set about orientating the men to conditions in occupied France: 'Several agents were taken out of France by Lysander (aircraft) to deliver lectures on precisely what Jedburgh teams could expect to find when they landed, what never to do, and how far to trust the locals. They were sobering occasions'.[8]

Naturally enough, given the unpredictable and rapidly changing tactical environment in which they operated, they were expected to improvise and go beyond their expected mission parameters, if the situation merited it, in the interest of assisting allied forces in their advance against the Germans. Given inter-Allied political sensitivities, and the key operational area, on 9th June General Eisenhower handed over control of the "Jeds" to De Gaulle's command.

Operational Deployment in Normandy

Some 93 teams comprising some 268 men were to be dropped into France following the invasion.[9] They were typically armed with American M1 Carbines and Colt automatic pistols, together with a considerable sum of money (around 100,000 French Francs and 50 US dollars), along with Type B (Mk.II) radios and cipher gear. "Trof" and fellow team members (Captain André Duron and Lieutenant Roger Groult) of the group codenamed "Guy" were dropped on the night of 11th-12th July into Brittany, a vital hinterland for the Allied bridgehead in Normandy, especially as it expanded out to the South and West.¹⁰ It was perhaps in the fighting in France that Trofimov's military talents (both orthodox and unorthodox) really began to flower. As *The Guardian* newspaper later recorded:

> His French assignment was particularly fraught, as there had been betrayals among the resistance in the Mayenne area of eastern Brittany into which he was dropped, leading two French officers in a group codenamed Guy. Almost knocked out by his own weapon as he landed by parachute, one night he ran into a German patrol in such a disguise, with a concealed American automatic pistol that would have got him shot on the spot if found, and had to impersonate a vomiting drunk. But he found allies among the local resistance groups and helped the Americans to capture a town with almost no casualties.

Fortunately, through Trofimov's own writings, and wartime records, we can understand some of the detail of a very eventful operational deployment.¹¹

One day after the landing in France SOE Headquarters received word via another team "Gavin", which had landed at the same time and place as "Guy", that the latter's radio had been "smashed" in the landing.¹² At the same time team "Guy" also lost their three carbines. A reception committee of local resistors was waiting to receive them on landing. In the days that followed the team faced considerable difficulty ranging from local rivalries and antagonisms between resistance groups, the impossibility of moving their equipment in daylight given its weight and the number of vigilant German units in the vicinity, and the fact that they could have been landed closer to their intended area of operation. As the team leader complained in his report: 'When you have to consider the weight of the equipment to be carried and the fact that walking at night we covered about an average of 2.5 miles per hour, it can readily be seen that moving 75 miles is a slow and tedious process'.¹³ It was on 30 July at Gorron, during this long and difficult transit to Mayenne, and after the purchase of a car using some of the funds allotted to the team, that an encounter took place with the Germans. It was during this encounter that Trofimov became separated from the rest of his group.

The encounter began with their car breaking down and being forced off the road by a group of German vehicles. The group split up and moved away as a passing German patrol began to pay the occupants of the car too much attention.¹⁴ While they all escaped detection, and most of the occupants of the vehicle were able to regain it and continue their journey, Trofimov found himself alone. On returning to a safe house previously occupied by the group, after two or three days 'Trof' decided to change into civilian clothes. This was an interesting move. The vast majority of "Jeds" remained in military uniform, such was the fear that if captured they would be shot out of hand under the Hitler commando order (Kommandobefehl) given by the Oberkommando der Wermacht (OKW) on 18th October 1942, following the Dieppe Raid. That "Trof" should find it easier to do his job in plain clothes was understandable, but he did run significant risks, and went against prevailing thought within the "Jeds", in doing so. Provided with false papers by local resistors 'Trof' began to carry out reconnaissance work in and around Gorron to monitor units and equipment falling back from the front against Allied forces, and to make note of the development of local defences (manned by around 500 members of the SS, together with tank support). "Trof" sent the information gathered to an advanced American headquarters as US forces headed towards Gorron and later guided an American unit into the town (it emerged later that his information had only reached Headquarters of the US 1st Infantry Division after the town had fallen to them). It was for his efforts in Gorron that "Trof" was later awarded the Croix de Guerre.¹⁵ With Gorron and much of Normandy and Brittany in American hands "Trof" could move freely and was able to rejoin his team at Combourg which similarly had fallen to the Americans. Here, and more widely in Ille et Vilaine Department, they played a role in organising local resistance groups to provide rear security for American units and to help mop up small groups of Germans on the loose behind the lines. After several weeks in the field, and with Allied units continuing to race through France and Normandy, Team "Guy" returned to the United Kingdom on 23rd August 1944 by Landing Craft (Infantry).

Burma and Force 136

Perhaps surprised by his own abilities, and the extent of his own successes in France, as the war in Europe was drawing to a close in late 1944, "Trof", and a number of other "Jeds", volunteered for another hazardous operation. This time in the jungles of South East Asia. In 1941, SOE established two missions in the East, one based in Singapore and the other in India. After the Japanese successes during 1942, the India Mission absorbed what was left of the Oriental Mission. Initially its cover name was the innocuous GSI(K), but from March 1944 it became Force 136. Its primary goal was to assist local resistance groups fighting the Japanese and to engage in sabotage operations with or without local forces as appropriate. While most of the command leadership of Force 136 was British, most of the field operatives were indigenous to Burma, Malaya, Indo-China etc. While some British officers were infiltrated to lead operations behind the lines, others had been left behind during the retreat to organise local resistance forces such as Freddie Spencer Chapman in Malaya and Hugh Seagrim in Burma to assist the organisation of local resistance forces and to provide support and expertise in major operations. It was as part of Force 136 that "Trof", in the closing months of the Second World War in the Far East would find himself parachuted into the Burmese jungle, after training in Ceylon, to engage in a vital campaign to recruit, train, arm and bring into combat, and sustain through a major logistical effort, a resistance force in Southern Burma.

Operation Character[16]

Trofimov's training and deployment was part of Operation Character: a major effort to raise a resistance force, and to engage in sabotage, guerrilla activities, and potentially assist regular military operations against Japanese troops in the Karen Hills in Southern Burma.[17] The operational area for Character lay between the Salween and Sittang rivers between Loikaw in the North (Kayah State) and Bilin (Mon State) in the South. Character was further subdivided into four neighbouring operations running from North to South between the two rivers. These were codenamed Walrus, Otter, Hyena and Mongoose. Mongoose was under the command of Major (later Lieutenant Colonel) Ronald A. Critchley an officer for whom 'Trof' would have considerable respect) and had an initial complement of around 11 British officers and NCOs, together with a small number of officers and NCOs (around 8 initially) drawn from Burmese Army Units.[18] Critchley, born into a military family in 1905, was an experienced officer who, fresh from Sandhurst, had joined the 13th/18th Hussars in 1925 as a 2nd Lieutenant. He was also a special forces veteran. In 1940 he had become part of Mission 101, a highly successful attempt to encourage Ethiopian resistance against the Italian occupation of their lands. Decorated for his service in Ethiopia, in 1942 he had moved to Delhi to help the development of SOE's operations against the Japanese.[19] With extensive experience of unconventional warfare operations, and considerable time in theatre, Critchley was an obvious choice to command one part of Operation Character. Rather like the "Jed" set up in Normandy and Brittany, with Character small teams of British Special Forces were to be inserted into Southern Burma, in the Karen Hills, and along the likely route of Japanese forces, to assist with the Allied advance. Beyond Character there would be other operations designed to gather intelligence or otherwise interfere with the increasingly hard-pressed Japanese forces in Southern Burma. The strategic logic of the operation was obvious, but much would depend on the Karen who had suffered at the hands of the Japanese and the Burman majority.

The Karen and Operation Mongoose

The Karen, a loose ethnic-linguistic group residing primarily in Kayin State in the South of Burma, and comprising the second largest group in the population of Burma, had long had an association with the British, unlike the Burman (Bamar) majority. During the late nineteenth century British missionaries (primarily Baptists) had converted a large number of the Karen to Christianity. This meant that the colonial authorities tended to favour Christian Karens over the Buddhist and folk-religion practising Burmans. That in turn led to tensions between the majority Burman population and minority groups like the Shan and Karen. In the midst of the Japanese occupation after 1942 the inter-ethnic tensions in Burma played out into violence and atrocity in which the Japanese took the side of the Burmans, with the minority populations looking to the British for support and liberation. As one contemporary OSS study explained in late 1943:

> Japanese military officers forced the three outstanding Karen leaders … to issue a circular dated 14th October warning that if the Karen community did not cooperate with their friends, the Japanese, in ferreting out enemy agents, the offending villages would be wiped out, guilty and innocent alike. The Karen leaders urged full acquiescence in the Japanese demands since, there was no feasible alternative … (The) Karens have provided fully half of the enlistment for the so-called Heiho Tat, or service battalions of the Japanese army. They have borne a heavy burden of forced labour and most of them doubtless hope for Allied rescue soon'.[20]

During 1944 the war turned decidedly against the Japanese in the Far East, and the background to the operation that Trofimov was about to embark on was the collapse of the Japanese presence in Burma, and the imminent victory of Allied forces. From the point where Japanese forces had battled at Imphal and Kohima (8th March to 18th July 1944), in a full-scale invasion of India, Japanese forces had been pushed back deeper into Burma by Allied forces advancing in the West from British India with the Americans coming down the Ledo Road to Myitkyina and British 36 Division. Both were able to take advantage of the fact that SOE had prevented the Japanese from occupying all of Burma, meaning the northernmost triangle above Sumprabum and including Fort Hertz (Putao) remained Allied for the entire war. The Japanese 15th, 28th and 33rd armies had been driven back steadily into Central Burma in the last few months of 1944, facing logistical difficulties, aerial attacks, and the possibility of having to withdraw to Indo-China and Siam. The launch of Operation Capital in November 1944, with 33rd Corps establishing a bridgehead across the Chindwin River and pushing into North East Burma near Mandalay, had paved the way for rapid advances in late 1944.[21] In turn, these advances would lead in early 1945 to the fall of key cities such as Meiktila and Mandalay in March 1945 and the capital, Rangoon, in May 1945. With Japanese forces under pressure throughout the Pacific, and with resupply and reinforcement of the degraded units in Burma almost impossible, the Japanese position was untenable. This would, however, not stop a determined enemy from continuing to fight with suicidal determination all the way to the Japanese formal surrender on 2nd September (and in some cases beyond).

The collapse of the Japanese position in Burma put "Trof", his fellow SOE operatives and their Karen allies at centre stage in strategic terms. From February to April 1945, they stood in the way of any attempt to reinforce the Burma front from Japanese troops elsewhere in South East Asia. As the tide of battle turned in March-April the teams operating in the Karen Hills found themselves on the line of escape for thousands of Japanese troops trying to make their way to the relative of safety of Siam. To reach that safety they would have to cross the fast-flowing rivers that cut through Karen territory. The crossing points and fords across those rivers, and the approaches to them, could be turned into deadly killing grounds, and to encourage the Japanese to retreat, isolated garrisons could be attacked.

In this deadly game of attack and ambush, mobile guerrilla units, working with SOE officers, and equipped with American-made M1 carbines, Bren light machine guns, Sten sub-machine guns and grenades, and operating in their own hills, took a massive toll on the retreating

Japanese forces, sometimes in conjunction with Allied fighter bombers. While the Japanese increasingly starved, and ran short of supplies and ammunition, the guerrilla forces in the Karen Hills were kept supplied by Allied airforces with C47 Dakotas and B24 Liberators dropping supplies from above, while personnel and wounded could be evacuated from jungle airstrips by Westland Lysander and L5 Stinson Sentinel light aircraft. This was irregular warfare at its most deadly efficient as Japanese forces were killed by the hundreds for minimal losses on the part of SOE-Karen forces. By war's end, and the completion of Operation Character, with the assistance of some 110 British officers and NCOs around 12,000 Karen had been armed and brought into action against the Japanese.[22] Total Japanese losses amounted to an estimated 11,874 Japanese dead, 644 wounded and 119 captured for the loss of 22 killed and 29 wounded.[23] Given such numbers it would be hard to take issue with Richard Aldrich's summation that Character had been 'spectacularly successful',[24] or General Slim's comment that as a result of the operation the Japanese had run into 'ambush after ambush, bridges were blown up ahead of them, their sentries stalked, their staff cars shot up'.[25]

Understanding "Trof's" Diary

"Trof's" diary and photographs document what it was like to live through, and be a critical part of, this highly successful campaign in irregular warfare waged in the Karen Hills in the last months of the Second World War. It is possible to mistake his pride and relief in the daily progress of this campaign for a certain blood thirstiness. "Trof" kept score of the number of Japanese killed by his platoon, and he enjoyed the planning and successful execution of military operations as if they were interesting intellectual problems (he later became a highly successful architect). In the diary he refers to Japanese as "Japs" (in common with the parlance of Allied forces of the Second World War), but it is equally clear that he had no love of killing, and was ready to accord surrendered Japanese the fair treatment which he did not expect to receive if he fell into their hands. It would have been remarkable if he had perceived of his duties, and his enemy, in any other way.

The war in Asia and the Pacific had been characterised by its savagery, and Western soldiers had learned the hard way that the Geneva convention simply did not apply in the treatment that they would receive at the hands of the Japanese should they become prisoner. Murder and mistreatment of non-combatants, and surrendered enemy soldiers, had been a feature of Japan's campaigns in Asia from 1931 onwards. Both the men of the SOE and the Karen knew that if they did not kill "Japanese" then they would be killed with no quarter given. An earlier attempt by SOE at irregular warfare in Burma using the Karen launched in February 1943 had ended with most of the SOE force being killed, and harsh reprisals against defenceless villages. When the surviving SOE officer, Major Hugh Seagrim, handed himself over to the Japanese on 15th March 1944 to spare the Karen people from further brutality they executed him, and eight Karen captured with him, even though he had taken pains to argue that they were acting under orders and could not be held accountable. Those men who jumped into the jungle as part of Operation Character, just five months after Seagrim's execution on 2nd September, knew exactly what their fate would be if they fell into the hands of the Japanese.

Reading any diary immediately raises questions in the mind of the reader about what kind of man was the writer. To a certain extent, as the previous paragraph demonstrates, we can get to know them from the writing and from their lives "beyond the diary". In the case of "Trof" we have photographs taken by him, and of him, which document aspects of his arrival in Ceylon for jungle training, through to his life with the Karen and the campaign against the Japanese. In addition, we have a wider body of material about his life including an extensive oral history interview gathered by the Imperial War Museum.[26] Thus the researcher can hear his voice, the description of events, the intonation, significant pauses in his speech to add a further level of understanding about the man whose experiences in the Karen Hills in 1945 are the focus of this book. We can also add to that the memories of his two sons.

Taking these various sources together we can perhaps glimpse some of the factors that made Trofimov such a capable special forces soldier. In part his qualities were determined by an apparent unusual combination of qualities, or at least the ability to present himself in certain ways. For example, to listen to Trofimov's interview given to the Imperial War Museum is to hear the voice of a man who appears remarkably humble about his wartime achievements. The tone of the diary is remarkably similar. There is also pride in achievements (keeping his wartime papers, giving an interview to the Imperial War Museum, and the post-war editing of his diary further confirm this), and satisfaction at a job well done, but the reactions are those of a modest man. In both interview and diary, even in the midst of wartime operations Trofimov comes across as relaxed and affable. The privations of the field, the grind of operations and the dangers at hand are only rarely glimpsed in the diary, even though the dangers were obvious. Trofimov, along with all those serving with Force 136 would have known what to expect if he fell into the hands of the Japanese. He also knew that even without the Japanese and the dangers of combat the jungle was a hostile and disease-ridden place that could claim his life, and yet the diary betrays little trace of worry or self-doubt. Against his affable and relaxed exterior we can also see Trofimov as a man of determination, precision, focus and care. He thought about things in great detail in order to work out how to improve performance and to mitigate the danger. He was a highly efficient army officer, a capable field operator highly skilled in the world of signals. That precision can also be seen in the fact that after the war he worked in the very precise world of architectural practice and he took effective steps to preserve his personal archive. Within the box, the lists of the sums paid to his men, and the serial numbers of the weapons distributed to each man in his group, written in pencil and brought out of the jungle by "Trof" flying out from a makeshift airstrip, show a meticulously correct approach to his duties. Only in quiet corners of the diary the man of precision, who knew that mistakes could cost lives, can be glimpsed: Little flashes of anger when things did not go according to plan – or dissatisfaction with the performance of some of those around him. This combination of relaxed and affable outer persona combined with an eye for detail made him an excellent member within a "Jed" Team, within the ranks of the SOE, and in enlisting the support of the Karen.

In Trof's papers and career we can also see his intelligence, intellectual, cultural, and emotional (the latter a particularly significant and underrated aspect of leadership). His ability to move between cultures, rugged physique developed during his education, and language skills set him apart. His background (with the exotic name, diverse education and unusual fluency in French) served in part to mark Trofimov out from his contemporaries, building self-reliance and self-confidence. Trofimov was a man used to standing on his own two feet to the point that a parachute jump into the Burmese jungle to work with indigenous personnel, against a fearsome enemy in a hostile environment, was a challenge he was only too happy to accept. His intelligence and focus meant he constantly strove to refine his tactics in the light of experience, his growing understanding of the operational environment, and the changing capabilities of the forces under his command. He was a capable and intelligent leader. At every turn, and from different sources, we get a sense of the man at the heart of this story.

And lastly, and perhaps just as remarkably, the author of this introduction also has a privileged insight into "Trof". More than eighty years ago my father was at school with "Trof" at Queen Elizabeth's Grammar School at Ashbourne in Derbyshire in the months between Neville Chamberlain's Munich agreement of September 1938 and the outbreak of war one year later. Forty years later, while I was a student at that same school, my father would tell me of his memories of his school days. Percolating through these memories were a couple of vivid descriptions of "Trofimov", the man with the unusual sounding name (at least so far as Derbyshire is concerned), and his shock of bright ginger hair, who had done something rather interesting in the Second World War. It would not be for another forty years and a chance introduction to one of his sons via social media that I would understand the nature of Trofimov's war.

[1] Edgard Morton came to Manchester University as a geology student (BSC 1922 and MSC 1924, joining the staff of the University in 1923. He was an engineering geologist, lecturer at Manchester University, consultant and businessman in Edgar Morton and Partners (Geotechnical Consultants) based in Altrincham. Morton specialised in the geological issues associated with reservoirs and dams (he was involved with the construction of 150 dams during his life), foundations and the exploitation of minerals underground. In 1963 he was promoted to Reader in Applied Geology, retiring three years later. *See* Edgar Morton Archive at University of Manchester Library GB 133 EMP.

[2] 'Professor Trofimov', *The Manchester Review*, volume 3, Spring 1942. pp.1-2.

[3] Private correspondence between Archives at King's College London and Paul Trofimov, 9th October 2008, Trofimov Archive.

[4] Appendix 1: Codenamed "Guy": With the Jedburghs in France June-August 1944. *See* also his SOE personnel file TNA: HS 9/1485/2.

[5] The Eureka/Rebecca system was a short-range navigation system designed to assist the accurate dropping of parachutists and their supplies. Eureka was a transponder system that could be activated by pathfinder forces on the ground as a radio beacon. The aircraft-mounted Rebecca transceiver would pick up the signals from the Eureka set and calculate the position of the ground signal to enable the aircraft to home in on the position of friendly forces on the ground. This would provide a reasonably precise aim point for any airdrop. The S-Phone larynx set enabled short-range air-to-ground two-way voice communication to further assist effective parachute drops, or to enable intelligence to be passed at ranges and at speeds which would make it hard for German forces to home in on the position of a ground-based transmitter.

[6] Trofimov's notes on his career before Burma, undated 1950s-60s, Trofimov Archive.

[7] On the development of the Jedburgh concept, Arthur Brown, *The Jedburghs: A Short History* (Unpublished, 1991) but seemingly widely circulated amongst former members of the Jedburgh teams.

[8] Brown, The Jedburghs, p.11.

[9] That number was comprised as follows: 47 British officers (38 radio operators); 89 French officers (17 radio operators); and 40 American officers (37 radio operators).

[10] '"Troff" Trofimov', *The Times*, 26th May 2006, https://www.thetimes.co.uk/article/troff-trofimov-g2hp3wl3wqj (accessed 28th October 2021). *See* also Major "Trof" Trofimov, *The Daily Telegraph*, 29th May 2006, https://www.telegraph.co.uk/news/obituaries/1519691/Major-Trof-Trofimov.html (accessed 28th October 2021). For date of drop see SOE Archives, File 173, TNA: HS6/519.

[11] For Trofimov's own account of his service in France, which appears as though it may have been typed up after being dictated in the 1990s *see* Appendix 1: Codenamed "Guy": With the Jedberghs in France June-August 1944.

[12] SOE Archives, File 173, TNA: HS6/519.

[13] Leader's Report, Team Guy, SOE Archives, File 173, TNA: HS6/519.

[14] 'Major 'Trof' Trofimov: SOE Officer Effective in France and Burma, The Guardian, 10th August 2006, https://www.theguardian.com/news/2006/aug/10/guardianobituaries.mainsection (accessed 28th October 2021).

[15] Croix de Guerre citation, 16th January 1946, Trofimov Archive.

[16] For Trofimov's own account of his service on Operation Character/Mongoose see Diary: Codenamed "Mongoose Green": With Force 136 and the Karen in Burma January-September 1945 and Appendix 2: Post-War Report by Major A. Trofimov on "Mongoose Green."

[17] On Operation Character see Charles Cruikshank, *SOE in the Far East* (Oxford: Oxford University Press, 1983), pp.186-90.

[18] Trofimov would continue to write to him, and meet with him, later in life.

[19] Supplement to *The London Gazette*, 24th May 1949, Number 38620, p.2607.

[20] OSS Research and Analysis Branch, *Japanese Administration of Burma*, (Washington (DC): OSS, 1944), p.32.

[21] For the background to Operation Character see Major-General S. Woodburn Kirby, *The War Against Japan: Volume IV The Reconquest of Burma* (London: HMSO, 1965). p.199ff.

[22] General Smith Dun, *Memoirs of the Four Foot Colonel* (New York: Cornell University, 1980), p.110. The same figure is also given in the chapter on Operation Character in Richard Duckett's *The Special Operations Executive in Burma: Jungle Warfare and Intelligence Gathering in World War II* (London: IB Tauris, 2018). Duckett's Book remains the best overall recent analysis of the work of SOE in Burma.

[23] Mongoose's contribution was 1,420 Japanese dead, 82 wounded and 1 taken prisoner for the loss of 3 killed and 1 wounded.

[24] Richard Aldrich, 'Legacies of Secret Service: Renegade SOE and the Karen Struggle in Burma, 1948-50', in Richard Aldrich, Gary D. Rawnsley, Ming Yeh T. Rawnsley (Eds), *The Clandestine Cold War in Asia, 1945-65: Western Intelligence, Propaganda and Special Operations* (New York, Frank Cass, 2000), p.135.

[25] Reproduced in Frank McLynn, The Burma Campaign: Disaster into Triumph (London: Random House, 2011), p.173.

[26] AEW [AAE] Trofimov interview, reels 1-5, Imperial War Museum, 24th April 1992. Catalogue Number 11760, https://www.iwm.org.uk/collections/item/object/80011503 (accessed 12th October 2021).

Hugh Dalton – appointed by Winston Churchill in May 1940 as his Minister of Economic Warfare refers to his 'special' instructions:-

"and then he (Churchill) said to me "I want you to do something else as well, I want you to be responsible for ungentlemanly warfare, for using all means secret and underground means against the enemy to break his will to resist."

A Tin Trunk, A Diary and A Journey into Our Father's Past

By his sons Mark and Paul Trofimov

Our journey with this war diary began most regrettably on the death of our Father in May 2006 and then, during the course of de-cluttering of his home ready for sale, we came across his large metal army war chest in the attic. If we had seen the trunk before it hadn't made much of an impression, but we did know that our father had kept back some material from the war. Indeed, he had already donated his M1 carbine and some other items to the Harrington Aviation Museum in Northamptonshire. On opening the trunk there were several items, including medal ribbons and letters, and an oilskin waterproof covering in which there were three, tightly packed notebooks. These contained a diary record of his entire operation as an SOE agent behind enemy lines in Burma from his departure on the 11th February 1945 until he left the field on the 27th September 1945. We knew a certain amount about our father's wartime service from what he had said and from attending SOE reunions in the 1990s, but the notebooks took us to a whole new level of detail.

Later, in going through his personal files, we found that he had a typed manuscript of these three diaries that his secretary had prepared probably sometime in the 1990s, and it was with this and the original handwritten pencil diaries – that he compiled in the field but presumably hid within the waterproof covering – which enabled us to compile this manuscript of his activities in Burma as an SOE agent, part of Force 136, Operation Character, Area Mongoose operations in the Karen mountains behind Japanese enemy lines and in support of the XIV Army advancing from the west.

There were three diaries, written up in pencil, and several loose pages found in the trunk. Also, in the trunk there were two double-sided printed silk maps of Burma,[1] with which we understood SOE agents were provided to assist with identifying where they were dropped behind enemy lines and presumably better than paper maps at withstanding the weather conditions, particularly during the onset of the monsoon season in Burma, which would occur soon after they were dropped into the territory.

Despite the inclement weather conditions, it soon became clear to those who were parachuted into this mountainous area of Burma, that these maps were of little use since many of the smaller villages where the SOE were intending to recruit volunteers amongst the local Karen people did not feature. Hence one of the first requests to the SOE HQ in Calcutta was for larger ordinance survey maps. Indeed, in our late Father's metal war chest there was a well-worn and folded paper map of this area in Burma from 96° longitude to 98°, and from 17° to 19° latitude. Even then there were many smaller villages that still did not feature, and as the first diary soon makes clear they are sending off telegraphic requests to Calcutta for larger scale OS maps, several of which, for the area classified as Mongoose south (Mewaing & Dubaw) in Force 136's 'Operation Character' and further south to Lakyokawthi and Kyowaing, aided the men in the field to plot and navigate their whereabouts with traditional wayfaring using a map and compass, to organise off-beat tracks and routes which the Japanese would be unlikely to use as main thoroughfares through the jungle and mountain passes.

We then found handwritten logs of the Karen people that were recruited in the training camps that our father was tasked with establishing in the Area known as 'Mongoose South'. As the diary later makes clear and in some of our Father's notes and recordings from post war interviews, he was fervently of the opinion that the British left the Karens to their own fate and did not honour the belief held by many Karen, who volunteered to join the British guerrilla forces harnessed by SOE and other operatives in the field to assist the XIV Army to defeat the Japanese in 1945, that come the end of the war they would be granted independence.

There were paper transcripts of messages which our father kept as it seems there was little hope of radio contact between the various SOE camps that were established under Operation Character – being split into four principal areas: Walrus, Otter, Hyena, Mongoose. So, it seems there were local Karen people that were recruited as runners to carry messages between the SOE base camps. Our father kept many of these which were also found in his trunk. Beyond the trunk dad kept meticulous records – his house was filled with files – every person he corresponded with over the years had their own file including former members of Force 136. He often talked of his love for the Karen people – he probably wished he could do more – although he did encourage his senior officers – like Col. Critchley to see what more they could do to help with their cause. This was quite a common theme amongst former SOE Force 136 personnel.[2]

One of the most interesting messages preserved in the tin trunk came from the end of the war. On 12th August 1945 our father received a message from Colonel Ronnie Critchley, sent by messenger (runner) on 12th August (1530 hrs) notifying him under the heading 'War News' of 'Russia advancing rapidly' and '⅓rd of Nagasaki… destroyed'. Also mentioned was the Japanese decision to surrender. Three days later a second transcript arrived informing them of the official Japanese surrender at 0530 hrs. SOE operatives were ordered to suspend further attacks whilst continuing to defend the territory and prevent the Japanese from trying to cross the Shwegyin Chaung, a tributary of the Sittang River. The end of the war was in sight.

Why he chose to keep a daily diary record of his exploits in Burma and not in France is perhaps because the latter was expected to be a shorter timeframe operating behind the lines in support of the Allied D-Day invasion whereas in the former they most probably anticipated a much longer duration given the Japanese occupation of Burma at the time and the complexities afforded by this type of jungle warfare. To emphasize the point, his French SOE operations under Team Guy lasted 2½ months (6th June 1944 to 23rd August 1944) whereas his SOE Burma Operation Character campaign lasted 7½ months (11th February 1945 to 27th September 1945). Moreover, we suspect there was, generally amongst the SOE Officers and personnel, a feeling that this was a very high-risk strategy coupled with the consequential risks to life and limb which were considerable given the known treatment of prisoners by the Japanese forces, especially agents and special forces operating behind enemy lines. Perhaps he felt he needed to keep a record – hidden as we suspect his diaries were in their oilskin wrapper daily and nightly after individual entries were made – in case of death or severe injury so that a brief record of his activities, limited as this may be in terms of operational sensitivity, could, potentially be of benefit to a successor in the field. Had he informed his Area Commander, Colonel Ronnie Critchley perhaps? –

as they developed a strong, mutually respectful, relationship in this period of conflict – evident too from their long-lasting friendship post-war with frequent correspondence and indeed mention of this within Ronnie Critchley's own personal papers[3] in which Dad features. Was it a common thread amongst some of those who were organising the recruitment and training camps for the Karens? We are not sure. There was considerable responsibility attached to the logistics associated with the drop zones, supplies of weapons, ammunition, and other daily needs (as the inventory records illustrate) and these were often stored in secret dumps away from the hillside camps – so the whereabouts may have been shared between the various sub-area commanders within the Mongoose Area for mutual benefit.

He clearly felt it necessary to supplement his written record when he purchased his Kodak camera during his absence on leave in Calcutta in early June 1945[4] and his subsequent recording of the many photographs in the field on his return up until the final surrender. Indeed, in one of his later post-war correspondence folders we found a typed letter dated 20 August 1981 addressed to Colonel CH Mackenzie CMG,[5] whom he had met at one of the earlier SOE reunions in which he offers up the availability of his diary transcripts, photos, and maps to help with the research for the book by Charles Cruikshank, *SOE in the Far East* (Oxford: Oxford University Press, 1983), in which Father features. In the end, we believe it was only the summary report entitled 'Mongoose Green' (included in Appendix II) that was shared with Colonel Mackenzie and not the full diary manuscript.

We found a typed-up hard copy of the diaries in one of the many files locked away in his filing cabinet at his home. He also edited part of his own story in this process – so some of the more controversial elements were diluted in text compared to his hand-written records and consequently we have tried to reflect this in our own edition of the original transcript – albeit these were taken direct from the diaries before we realised that he had made his own typed up version!

We feel quite strongly that our father intended to publicise his diaries in some form or perhaps bequeath them to a museum or the war records office but since he was bound by the Official Secrets Act for a period of 60 years[6] – which only expired in September 2005 – just eight months before his passing in May 2006, it is not surprising that this remained a work in progress on his passing. He may well have corresponded with other SOEs on his intentions during the many SOE reunions that he attended over the years since many of his associates were recording their own memoirs and some were already published. Also, they worked together on several collaborations such as *The Jedburghs: A Short History* (1991) by Arthur Brown (unpublished but circulated widely within the ranks of former "Jeds") and, subsequently in Glyn Loosmore's Postscript,[7] himself an SOE agent also dropped into Burma on the 29th March 1945 as part of Operation Character, Mongoose Blue – and evidenced through his papers and correspondence over many years. For instance, when he wrote to Glyn in October 1994, with documentation from his diary to assist with this Postscript he refers to, *'there are a number of personal remarks in my diaries, which I know you will disregard as they were never meant to be read by anyone else but myself'.*

So, we are quite confident that our father wanted to see something tangible come of his own records. It is also notable that in his recordings for the war office records, he skirts around the detail, cognisant as he was then that he had a bountiful source of the very detail of what actually happened daily in his Mongoose Area Green as part of Operation Character, Force 136 in Burma such that he most probably was keeping the best for last!

One thing we should mention is our father's life-long fondness of France and those who resisted the German occupation – bearing in mind it was the opportunity for him to be educated at primary level in southern France that enabled him to meet some of the criteria for selection into SOE; and, it was from his French SOE activities in Brittany as part of Team 'Guy', in support of the D-Day landings that meant he later was able to reunite with his former French resistance colleagues in civilian and commercial life to bring about development opportunities in association with some resistance colleagues.

Throughout his civilian life and through his architectural practice he maintained very strong links with France through language, his SOE experiences, and, as mentioned in the footnote to 'The Postscript' document, his efforts to help those gain due recognition for their efforts amongst his French Resistance colleagues.

His sadness, however, was often expressed in family life that he could not do more for the Karen people – distance, language, climate, culture and inevitably politics played their part as well as the normal pressures facing all veterans in re-entering civilian life and getting on with their careers, business, daily life, families and more. However, what we found within his post-war papers is evidence of his constant struggle with this sadness and at times frustration and anger that the Karen people had been essentially abandoned to their fate through the combined effect of continual persecution from the Burmese militia and inaction by the Allied Authorities and the UK Government in particular. He shared these frustrations in his correspondence with his Area Commander, Col. Critchley and by sharing the 'Liberation' paper by Saw M. Shwin (included in Appendix III) with other SOE colleagues, and by writing to the former head of the India Mission, Col. CH Mackenzie (2008 1981)[8] as well as to Colonel John Douglas Slim, 2nd Viscount Slim, OBE., DL,[9] (House of Lords on 29 07 1996) with reference to '*a disturbing film which was shown on Channel 3 some months ago, called 'Inside Burma – Land of Fear*'). His father, Field Marshall William Joseph Slim (1st Viscount) led the XIV Army for the recapture and liberation of Burma. In another file, as referenced in a previous footnote (no. 2), he records a copy of a petition by SOE agents at a reunion in 1991 and here I draw attention to the last paragraph of that *Times* article – entitled 'At risk in Burma' by Dr MEA Panter – and the concluding remarks: 'Will Western Governments take notice of another people whose human rights are being grossly violated and who have no voice to let their cry be heard'.

If nothing else, then the publication of his diaries focusing primarily on his Burma exploits should help to draw attention to this long plight of the Karen people having been repeatedly persecuted by various Burmese authorities since the end of WWII despite their loyal efforts to support the Allies during that crucial period. If by shining a spotlight on the failure of the Allied Authorities and their respective Governments to help the Karens, if not to gain independence, then to at least have the right to co-exist alongside the Burmese people and other ethnic minorities within Burma, without the constant threat to their very existence, then some virtue will have come from picking up where our father left things before his passing. If such could be accomplished through a process of re-engagement, belated as that may be, to help rectify a past injustice, similar perhaps to the campaign that was asserted to recognise the Gurkhas and the families of those who fought and died for this country in the same conflict, then something worthy may eventually come from this publication and others seeking a similar outcome.

Were that to happen, it would be a significant moment and make our father's legacy and all those from SOE Force 136 all the more satisfying in the knowledge that within a generation or so of his passing, albeit sadly four generations or more for the long-suffering and anguish of the Karen people, that some justice may at last prevail.

Why we chose to release his diaries as an actual transcript rather than the framework for more of a narrative is simply because in their original uncensored form, they convey to the reader a raw first-hand, factual record and insight into the day-to-day role and responsibilities experienced by a young officer and agent working as part of a dispersed team of special forces in the Karen mountains operating behind enemy lines. That insight becomes all the more tangible when taken together with some of the other contents of the tin trunk, namely the photographs, maps, messages and platoon lists (in Appendix IV). By weaving these together with the diary records of his journey through the Karen mountains and the various camps and stores that he and his colleagues established to help recruit, train, arm, equip and look after daily, the Karens who were there to serve in Area Mongoose south's endeavours and guerrilla warfare as part of their contribution to Operation Character, 'his' story comes to life. Apart from the foreword by Richard Duckett and the introduction and contextualisation provided by Harry Bennett, both esteemed historians with knowledge and expertise in this field, we feel that the transcript of his diaries, the photographs and associated documents stand on their own merit without the need for any embellishment.

In putting together the manuscript over several years we found ourselves immersed into a window on our father's past, that is both captivating and illuminating, revealing the 'warts and all' daily grind associated with such a high-risk logistical and operational challenge. In so doing we are getting to know another side to our father that hitherto we only rarely caught glimpses of from some of the SOE reunions that we were fortunate to be invited to attend and where we had the privilege to witness this camaraderie amongst the 'Jeds'. Their very own ingrained identity as a special group or *'family'* unit was clear for all those who attended as guests to see. One example that comes to mind is when attending one of these reunions at Peterborough – close to Milton Hall where they first trained as agents – was during an unnecessarily prolonged commemoration event at the wonderful Peterborough Cathedral when on the command of a predetermined coded message (a two-digit number shouted out by one of the SOEs in attendance) they, as one, got up and left much to their own families and guests' surprise. They were left sitting wondering what to do next! It soon became clear when the Jeds and their families were reunited outside the cathedral shortly afterwards that all they wanted was to avail themselves of some much-needed hospitality and enjoy their time together without undue pomp and ceremony!

The burden of responsibility passes in this context from father to sons and in bringing this record of his diaries to publication we are reminded in his own story of those Karen recruits where, in his life-long precision in keeping records, he not only records the names of the individual Karens who joined up but those of their fathers too, and the villages from where they came. We are also reminded through coincidence as Harry Bennett refers to in his final paragraph of the introduction and which we also allude to in the acknowledgements section, in that the journey to attaining the publication of his diaries relies in part on another father and son connection for which we are truly thankful.

[1] A third silk map of Major Trofimov's may be seen on display at the Harrington Museum, Sunnyvale Farm, Lamport Road, Harrington, Northampton, NN6 9PF https://harringtonmuseum.org.uk/

[2] The Trofimov archive includes a copy of a petition raised by SOE representatives at an SOE Reunion held at The Bonnington Hotel in 1991 where several attendees had signed a petition for issue to Foreign Secretary to the Government raising concerns over the plight of the Karen people some 46 years after the end of the WW.2 following an article in *The Times* dated 8th May 1991 entitled 'At Risk in Burma' by Dr MEA Panter; an excerpt of which states: 'Following 42 years of struggle for freedom and democracy, under General Byo Mya, at present many thousand Burmese forces with fighter aircraft and helicopter gunships are poised within mortar fire of the Karen headquarters at Manerplore, threatening to "destroy and eliminate" the Karen "problem".

[3] Colonel Ronnie Critchley (1905-1995) – 'The Trofimov archive contains a copy of 'A Rough Sketch of My Life from 1905-1995 Ronald Asheton Critchley in which on page 26 thereof in his recollections of Force 136 he states: 'Most of all I remember my courageous companion Trof, (Major AAE Trofimov. MC Croix de Guerre), who, despite the proximity of the Japanese, insisted on belting out 'Night and Day', on moonlight nights to remind himself of some lovely he had left behind in England! He adds: 'In September 1945 the Japanese surrendered and we said goodbye to our Karen soldiers. They were splendid people, and I am glad that they were left plenty of rifles to help them fight the Burmese for their independence'. Dad also featured in Ronnie Critchley's Obituary in the *Daily Telegraph* London November 3rd, 1999, in which it states: 'On one occasion, during the attack on Papun, his companion Major Trofimov, who was serving under Critchely and commanded the force which was entering from the opposite side, remembers being entranced by the sight of a tall figure advancing through the smoke waving his customary walking stick'.

[4] Reference diary entries for the 7th and 14th June 1945 – in the former it mentions Trofimov was interviewed by 'Q' ops and 'they got interested' in what is working and what is not in the field and 'said they would try and get him a camera'; and in the latter it states: 'Q' ops 'secured a Kodak 35 mm camera, a beauty'.

[5] Colonel CH Mackenzie – *see* Charles Cruickshank's *SOE in The Far East* – with multiple references to Mackenzie who was appointed by Dalton, the First Minister for Special Operations to command SOE's 'India Mission throughout the war' (ref. page 11). He also refers to making available his original maps from the field which he had marked up with numbering according to his locations – *see* diary entries for the 3rd, 7th and 21st March – requests for additional maps (1 inch OS) and subsequently to a larger scale.

[6] For the reader's benefit this is the period that our father mentioned to us as children he was bound by under the Official Secrets Act and I (Paul) have had no reason to question this – however on reading the preface to Charles Cruickshank, *SOE in the Far East* (Oxford: OUP, 1983), who was commissioned by the Government to undertake

this work, I see that in the third para, thereof it states: 'the introduction in 1968 of the 'thirty-year rule', which allows the use of most official records formerly withheld for fifty years, has had a significant effect on the nature of scholarly research'. So, this explains why he was having his diaries typed up in the 1980s – some 40 years or more since this 30-year ruling came into effect. Whether more sensitive material undertaken by SOE falls outside this 30-year rule, I have yet to deduce from a quick perusal of the Act!

[7] This postscript was distributed widely among 'Jeds' and SOEs and it includes part of Father's own Biography, which is included later and which refers to his post-war activities in northern France – Le Touquet and Brittany where his architectural practice was responsible for architectural services in relation to new housing and residential developments, some of which were in conjunction with former French Resistance fighters, notably one in the Cherbourg Peninsula area with Commander Louis Petri who, with his wife became the managers of the development. Noting too that Major Trofimov was instrumental in promoting Petri for the honorary award of MBE granted to him on 13th August 1946.

[8] Trofimov archive – papers and post war correspondence.

[9] Colonel John Douglas Slim, 2nd Viscount Slim, OBE, DL, FRGS (20th July 1927 – 12th January 2019) was a British peer, soldier and businessman, https://airleague.co.uk/news/colonel-john-douglas-slim-2nd-viscount-slim-obe-dl-obituary

A Tin Trunk, A Diary and A Journey into Our Father's Past

A MOST IRREGULAR WAR: SOE BURMA, MAJOR TROFIMOV'S DIARY 1944–45

Diary

Codenamed "**Mongoose Green**" With Force 136 and the Karen in Burma January–September 1945

Diary I

After his heroics in France Trofimov returned to Manchester on leave. There he was contacted by Jedburgh Headquarters at Milton Hall and ordered to report back. Here he learnt that he was being sent to the Far East to join Force 136 in Burma. Travelling to India by troopship and then by rail and sea to Sri Lanka (Ceylon), Trofimov was given a short period of jungle training before being sent to Calcutta to join Peacock Force under Major Ronald Critchley. Trofimov's ostensible assignment 'to organise DZ drill, wireless and guerrilla warfare techniques, demolitions, etc., and to organise supplies for Peacock Force' as part of Operation Character was originally scheduled to last for three months. In reality Character would last more than three times that estimate and Trofimov, with Critchley's blessing, would rapidly move beyond the roll of a Drop Zone and training officer. As he later noted: 'After organising parachute drops of arms and equipment for Peacock Force, Major Critchley and I set off with a handful of local Karens that we had enlisted, and armed, to go south to recruit and organise a guerrilla army'.[1]

The raising of that army and its combat operations was documented meticulously in the diary which now follows.

P. Force – 1945 (Peacock)[2]
Montague John Cook Montague, MC, Croix de Guerre[3]
Sell Cyril Herbert Sell, MC – Character / OTTER[4]
Guthrie Duncan Dumbar Guthrie OBE, a Jedburgh Team officer
Critchley Lt. Colonel Ronald Asheton "Ronnie" Critchley MC
Trofimov Captain AAE Trofimov, later promoted to Major during the Burma Force 136 campaign

Post War notes and commentary made by Major Trofimov regarding the diary:

> While on leave after the French Jedburgh[5] ('Jeds') SOE operation, I received a telephone call from Milton Hall to the effect that I could re-join my Royal Artillery Regiment or volunteer to join Force 136 in the Far East with a view to parachuting into Burma. I opted for the latter and duly sailed to India on the troopship Otranto together with several other 'Jeds' in October / November 1944.

On arrival at Bombay, we proceeded by train across India until we finally arrived at a jungle training camp at Horana in Ceylon. We were put through an all too brief jungle training course, which did not prepare us for the conditions in the Karen Mountains, such as the voracious insect life.

11th February 1945
We left Horana for Trinco and thence by sea on the cruiser HMS *Newcastle*[6] arriving in Calcutta on the 12th to 15th with Peacock Force. We proceeded to a camp at Jessore[7] on the 16th February. Major Critchley and several others were there.

16th February Jessore Camp[7]
Major Ronnie Critchley[8]
(Maj. Young, Maj. Howell, King, Woolf)
Calcutta Burma Country Section (BCS)

17th/18th February 1945
Briefing at Calcutta Burma Country section, the actual brief was OK but the squabbling between the three Officers of Peacock Force over who was to be in overall command was disgraceful, so I left them to it and was shortly joined by (Ronnie) Critchley who obviously felt the same.

20th February

Depart from Jessore aerodrome in a Dakota – take off time 5.45 p.m. As I have never jumped out of a Dakota, I had to have lessons during the flight!

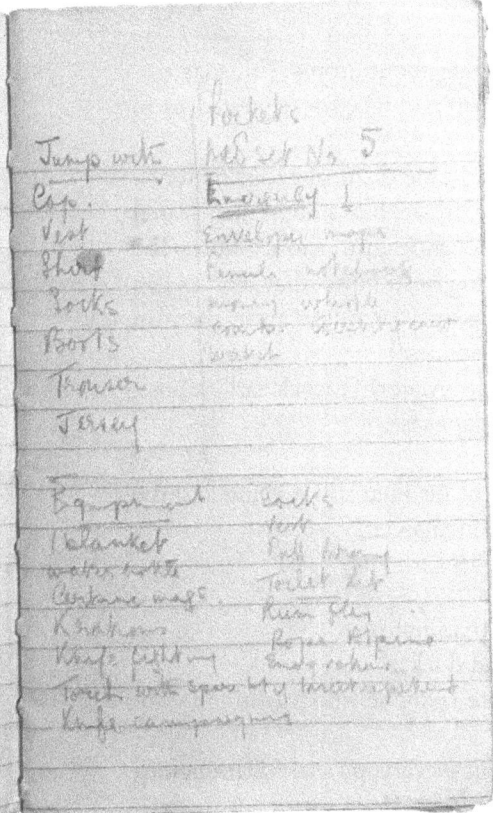

2 planes took off:
First plane Ronnie Critchley + 5 special group Burma rifles Guy Turrall.[9]
Second plane Trofimov + 5 ditto Sgt. Little[10] + 5 ditto.
Arrived over target at 10 PM.

Jump with: Cap, Vest, Shirt, Socks, Boots, Trouser and Jersey.

Pockets: Med. Set No. 5, Emergency 1, Envelopes, Pencils, Money, Comb, Watch, Maps, Notebook, Whistle and Identity card.

Equipment: 1 blanket, Water bottle, Carbine magazines, K rations, Knife fighting, Torch with spare battery, Knife campaigner, Socks, Vest, Pull throng, Toilet kit, Rum flask, Rope Alpine, Emergency rations and Insect repellent.

Dropped at approximately 2000 ft. slap bang into jungle some 2 miles or more from the DZ (*note from summary report by Major Trofimov post activities that original destination was intended to be at Pyagawpu. A much fuller account of his landing exists in the form of an unposted letter to his girlfriend in England. Both papers are reproduced as Appendices in this book*).[11] After landing through the trees, I took a step forward in the dark and fell down a very deep ravine and cut and bruised myself. I managed to collect 3 of the Burmese and by some miracle and a good deal of luck found my way to the DZ Critchley and Turrall were delighted as they had seen the drop in the far distance and did not expect to see me again for some time. Sergeant Little was missing with his 5 men plus one from my drop.

21st February Wednesday
Karens came forth – very friendly assisted us to collect most of packages. Moved off to safe RV in the afternoon about 3 miles away to the South East (near to Pawlawdo).

22nd February Thursday
Japanese came on scene by 12 a.m. knowing about drop – Thursday

Received message Major Peacock's drop had failed – requested us to plan for receiving them.

Karens helped us carry away supplies. Made cache of excess material. Contacted Headman re. people coming in on our side – they feared reprisals – as was case a year previously over Seagrim show. (Note: The reference to the Seagrim show is telling testimony that Force 136 members had a very good understanding of what might await them in the Karen Hills and at the hands of the Japanese).

Sent off message to tell them to send in (Major) Peacock earliest poss. As ground is compromised – known to Japanese.

Moved to another RV for night.

Sgt. Little came in with two men. 3 of his men still missing and the last man from my stock. Enrolled four Karen levies.

23rd February Friday
- Received confirmation of drop for that night.
- Moved camp – bought chickens and ducks.
- Request from Headman to eliminate Japanese who was still in the village.
- 7 p.m. moved to DZ in pouring rain – everyone soaked through to the skin.
- 8.45 p.m. weather cleared up. Eureka in working order.[12]
- First plane with Major Peacock came over about 9.30 p.m.
- From then on, the sky was filled with planes and parachutes.
- Went up to Capt. McLeod[13] – Who was rolling up his chute – told me he had some letters for me – 'God I was thrilled.'
- Excellent drop – most of parachutes came right onto ground – planes dropped from about 450 ft.
- Eureka worked very well.
- Received several conts. (containers) of arms, which immediately showed to Headman, effect was terrific – he informed us all the district would be with us.
- Built large fires and dried ourselves, slept between parachutes.

24th February Saturday
- Both generators now broken. Requested more (Saturday)
- Peacock recruited 30 levies armed them immediately.
- I was appointed to control entire distribution of arms.
- Organised armoury in Karen hut.
- With Joe Marlam[14] issued discs to Karens who had relatives taking down their particulars: name, rifle no. Disc no, village, Father's name, etc.
- Preparing for reception at night. Sent levies to bring up our affairs from last camp.
- Made lovely camp by riverside. Found excellent swimming in it.
- Major Turrall set off with Burmans to block routes from Papun and the west.

Reception Committee at night. Major Poles'[15] party. Bodies dropped low and heavily.

Aircraft dropped at 9.30 p.m. Found (Duncan) Guthrie[16] after much searching on other side of river. Broken tibia and broken ankle – he was in agony. I collected some Karens and with exasperating difficulties succeeded in making a stretcher from two poles and his parachute cut up.

Got him across river safely. Put his leg in splints, man was in agony – had to give him some morphine.

Casualties were high – (Major) Poles fractured rib – 3 Burman's had fractured ankles.

Large drop of arms and supplies. Frozen and wet through – went to my camp.

Took on in the morning 5 Karens for Ronnie and self to arrange cooking etc.

1). Saw Aung Wain, 2). Saw Major The, 3). Saw Maco Gay,
4). Po The and 5). Kya Uway.

Extremely difficult to make them understand.
Major Saw Butler[17] has arranged for an English-speaking Karen from Papun – though hope he comes soon!

25th February Sunday
- Established an armoury.
- Issued out 98 rifles to mobile levies.
- Allocated equal number to each of three groups.

- 7 Ambush parties set out to cover every path leading to our base – day & night ambush system.
- Arranged to feed levies & ourselves from food of the country.
- Bought baskets of rice & different vegs.

This has solved one of our major problems as one could not cope with just our K rations.

Tea, sugar & milk we sent for in large supplies.

Levies coming in in 2s and 3s from all parts of the country. We estimate that by the end of this month, we will have 200 mobile levies and 100 static for guarding DZ, camps etc. Intelligence reports developing rapidly. Japanese seem to be storing food in Papun & Shwegyin. Bringing food up from the south and sending it northwards, building reserves at Kawludo (NW of Pawlawdo), Kemapyu (North of Kawludo) and Mawchi (West of Kemapyu).

The two missing Burman's of Turrall's group returned during the night. They saw the lights of the DZ from the hillside. They had met the Japanese previously mentioned – but as he was unarmed and they were, he couldn't do anything about it.

Interesting to note two schools of thought: Jungle types ie. Peacock force all for leaving him alone for fear of compromising locals – regardless of fact that the very arming of them compromises them. Jeds all for killing him.

Reception at 10 pm. very successful drop of arms & luxury rations. 4 Liberators and 1 Dakota. Lit bonfires on lights lest the ground mist, which rises very quickly here, should surprise us. Collected another silk parachute – to endeavour to keep myself warm at nights. The nights are bitterly cold here – you need every possible clothing.

26th February Monday

(Capt.) Guthrie and (Major) Poles both very bad.

Ronnie (Critchley) recc'ed unsuccessfully a ground for landing strip as it is essential to evacuate Guthrie – his foot is a nasty mess.

Brought number of his levies[18] up to 150 mobile, 100 static.

Major Peacock arranging intelligence network of whole area by infiltration. The whole area is a veritable bastion – Japanese cannot approach without our knowing.

Levy packs proved useful for equipping mobile levies out on ambush parties. Pinched a couple of shorts for own use out of them – got local Karen girl to shorten them for me. These Karen girls are rather pretty –

though shabbily dressed. The men, too, are all strong robust & healthy.

Ronnie set off this afternoon to recce' grounds for landing strips, staying out all night.

Feeling much better now I am walking about in shorts – with just a revolver. Also, the food – more vegs. and a certain amount of pig meat makes me feel much better.

Tonight, had an excellent chicken cooked by one of the Burmese boys. (We) will have to acquire a good cook – these boys of mine don't know very much.

Tonight, there is another drop – God for a complete night's sleep! Hoping to get plaster bandage with which to set Duncan's (Guthrie) leg.

Drop successful – food and medical (supplies).

27th February Tuesday

Duncan Guthrie receiving attention from quaint native doctor – who applied lotions of herbs and spit to his leg – very successful – does a lot of pulling and twisting. By the afternoon Guthrie's leg showing incredible signs of improvement.

Further issue of arms – **Total** now at 410: – 150 mobile, 260 static[19]

Luxury drop in last reception – heavenly to have tinned milk & sliced peaches.

Ronnie returned from yet another attempt to find landing strip – successful but now it does not appear essential to evacuate the injured as they are making wonderful progress.

In the afternoon, I acquired an English-speaking Karen – Saw Wattaw[20] – if I speak in monosyllabic words he understands perfectly clearly. What a relief!

Started immediately organising camp – hygienic training of my men – cooking – individual duties etc.

Turrall still being unsure about the situation of Ronnie's eventually becoming Area Commander.

Ronnie being very decent about it all – has talked it over with Peacock and decided upon the following:

That until the situation is clarified – i.e., Japanese reaction, we will both come under the command of Turrall.

But at the opportune moment – Ronnie and myself will move off further south – we propose to divide the southern area into two – half under Turrall and the other half under Ronnie.

28th February Wednesday

Major Peacock received 5 elephants in the morning. He and his party are moving off tomorrow – leaving (Major) Poles' party concealed in the jungle – they are using the elephants – to transport a percentage of arms and food.

They are taking a number of our levies with them – as fighting force, screen, guides, porters etc.

The time is now ripe for the establishment of dumps of arms and food all over the area – to effect this we propose to establish and function several DZ's all over the country and build dumps near them.[21]

Ronnie is not entirely satisfied with our intelligence system – we must have a really good reliable man to correlate all the information from our spies.

We have sent off a message to the effect of our new decision of future policies. To further this, we have requested for: W/T complete and asked for my old wireless operator Sgt. Tack;[22] Karen English speaking Officers; one British Sgt. to deal with food and arms.

Ronnie, whilst out on his recce' contacted some of Seagrim's men, notably three wireless operators, (all of whom were) Karens. One of these turned up in the evening.

He understands and speaks English very well – (Saw Aaron).

We had an excellent meal that night – chicken cooked in butter – it was delicious!

Saw Aaron[23] the W/T brought some rice liquor concoction, which I found rather acidy.

1st March Thursday

Information received of Japanese concentration at Kyakye[24] – Necessitated sending out groups of Burmans and Levies for four-day guards and patrols in that area.

We are having big drop of arms tonight.

Ronnie and self are arranging to bring our total number of attached levies to 12 and the 3 W/T's.

We are preparing to move camp tomorrow – and go to another area where we intend to make a cache, receiving the weapons and food for it on the spot.

Saw Harry[25] and Saw Hsi Tai joined us. The latter weak from malaria.

The drop was quite successful – we had to light bonfires to keep ourselves warm – 3 Dakotas and 4 Liberators.

2nd March Friday

Made camp preparations for move – equipped the 3 W/T's properly – boots etc.

In the drop, there was some liquor – So Ronnie and I took a bottle of whisky (each). We each took 500 RS for expenses.

We estimate that to cover our expenses whilst up in the N. (northern area of operations) area – to pay 250 static levies and our own men will cost us 10,000 RS per month.

We acquired 6 further levies and sent for 10 porters. We set off on our trek across the mountains at 2 p.m. arrived at the DZ at 6 p.m. Very heavy going. However, the scenery was heavenly. We were now near the village of Pawlawdo – We sent for the Headman of Pawlawdo – he arrived with two armed men. Part of our network of Home Guard. We arranged with him to have all the tracks guarded – vegetables and meat sent to us – he has brought eggs and some pumpkins for us.

We also arranged that he should think out a good spot for our cache and a reasonable place near the village for us to camp.

The DZ is awkwardly placed in a deep valley. Very difficult to place the lights. We manned the field from 9 p.m. – 11 p.m., but as expected no aircraft came.

Ronnie and I slept in a Karen hut – and God, was it cold! – I could not sleep at all – the height above sea level is about 2500 ft. here.

3rd March Saturday

A lot of tea and poached eggs did the trick – we feel much better. Having recc'ed suggested cache – we set of with some porters the Headman had brought to our camp.

A pleasant little spot – a glen nestling in the valley – away from all tracks and just on the bend of the river.

The Karens set to and built a shelter and table for Ronnie and me – finished it in quarter of an hour. The rest of the day we spent relaxing, washing in the river.

I managed to get my maps into some order and system. Kya – my boy – seems to be enjoying himself – he cleans all my weapons and looks after me generally.

Saw His Tai down with malaria – started him on quinine – we must get him better soon. Preparing for reception tonight – we have had no confirmation from Turrall that it is to take place – but propose to man the field again.

Information received from Turrall – cancelling tonight's drop to tomorrow night.

Throughout the afternoon reports have been coming in about a Japanese movement from Papun to Pyagawpu. However, so far nothing definite has been found out.

We have organised a network of spies around – all the villages have been warned by runner of all and any information they glean.

4th March Sunday

Spent a wretched night – bitten to death by insects – had to cover myself in iodine.

The weather is fine – should be alright for the drop.

Further messages coming in – together with a Japanese letter, which was sent by the Japanese Commander to God knows where – but which fell into the hands of our men. It seems that the Japanese have not one single Karen on their side.

Several conferences with the Headmen of the surrounding villages – made out plan for reception.

Bought a tremendous pig – about 80 lbs for 30 RS. We all had a feast before the reception – all the villages helping us participated.

At 12 pm we set up the Eureka, lights and prepared bonfires – there should be one Dakota of food and levy packs and 2 Liberators of arms and levy packs.

2 p.m. picked up DAK (Dakota) – dropped off 30 packs into our valley.

Waited till 4 a.m. but although Liberator came over – they would not come down and drop.

The Karen villagers worked very hard and collected all the packages. We had them all in the cache by 5 a.m. – we distributed the parachutes between our helpers. Despatched a runner to inform Turrall of drop.

5th March Monday

After a short rest – I cooked an excellent meal for Ronnie and myself – we had four eggs each – lots of fried liver and kidneys from our pig, and beans. We are beginning to run short on the tea – tea is a great sustainer and luxury in this part of the world.

In the afternoon, we received a note by runner from Turrall stating that we can have 8 planes between the non-moon periods from 4th – 20th March.

Ronnie despatched message to effect that we now consider the time is ripe for us to move south – there is no use in us gathering together and having all our eggs in one basket – also we have asked for our wireless to be dropped here at Pawlawdo – with Sked plan.[26] Here's hoping. Meantime, we are going to sit tight and await developments. Saw His Tai is improving quite a lot.

We have found out all their particulars, (the levies) and propose to demand Calcutta of confirmation of their continued pay at base.

6th March Tuesday

Beginning to feel really ill with the insect bites – I am covered from head to toe in every conceivable kind of insect bite. I have not yet had a real night's sleep – it is just beginning to affect my nerves.

Saw Aaron went down in the morning with a very bad dose of malaria – our stock of quinine is suffering badly.

Aaron vomited and ran a terrific temperature – at about 3 p.m. he became delirious, sent for me and asked me to shoot him. I stayed up the whole night with him until the delirium subsided and I could safely leave him with the others.

In the evening received a letter from Maj. Turrall – he has agreed with Ronnie's plan and signalled Calcutta to that effect.

Also, he has asked us how the nightly drops were going – this is against all correct procedure – you never man a DZ unless RAF confirms the drop.

I sat up with the Eureka in the camp till 3 a.m. Ronnie manned the field all night. The planes never came – we did not expect them though. Sharpening up of procedure needs to take place.

7th March Wednesday

After an impossible few hours in bed – being bitten to hell – we got up. Immediately I set the men to building us bamboo beds – I (really) cannot face another night of this merciless torture – my stomach is covered in insect bites – my limbs are all scarred where I have scratched the bites. Henceforth – I am not going to sleep on the ground.

Awaiting message from Turrall. Today Ronnie and I worked out what we would need in the way of stores to set our show on the road.

A note arrived by runner stating that 50 Japanese were moving north on our old DZ at Pyagawpu and were now about 10 miles south of it.

For new moon, we are requesting:
Rifles 400 = 44 containers

Carbines 30 = 5 packages
Stens 24 = 4 containers
Brens 12 = 6 containers
Spare weapons = 1 container

Ammo Reserve
Carbine = 1 Package
.303 = 1 container

Miscellaneous
Rifle oil = 1 package
W/T = 3 packages
Eureka = 1 package
Medical set No. 3 = 3 packages
Clothes & yarn = 3 packages

Levies
1-inch map of S Area}
Papers, Books} = 1 package
Mail, toilet requisites}

2 packages money}
1 package (P x 773) Steam Generator} = 1 aircraft
25 bundles of 8 blankets}

Food
Start-up Cache = 1 aircraft
Luxury BSC No 2 = 2 packages
Tea, sugar, milk (Tinned) = 3 packages
Levy Food = 2 Dakotas
Levy packs = 2 Dakotas

Which, amounts to:
Aircraft = 6
Containers 56 = 5
Packages 19 = 5 with Liberators

Total Aircraft = 11
1 Liberator = 11 containers and 5 packages
1 Dakota = 30 packages

We manned the DZ from 12 p.m. to 4 a.m. but no aircraft came.

8th March Thursday
Slept on blissfully in our beds – first reasonable night since I arrived. Saw Aaron very bad fever – asks to be allowed to return to his village to see his doctor and remain there until better – we sent off for an elephant.

Several men came to join us – our strength is now about 20, of which still only 8 are armed.

Bought another pig as we expect Turrall tomorrow.

9th March Friday
Early rise – feeling much better now after good night's sleep.

I set off with Saw His Tai to Pawlawdo – there the whole village gathered around me and fired questions at me: "What were they to do if the Japanese came?" "Do the British rape the women;" "How soon can they have arms".

They said they thought Ronnie and me very handsome men. One of the women was smoking a pipe – she was quite pretty, about 18.

Turrall arrived in camp about 12 a.m. Definitely won't handover Havildar Charles – a man we want for our contact with Papun. He brought us 500 silver RS and promised to send us tea tomorrow. Also, he is sending off our requirements to Calcutta and arranging for a drop on the 20th. Let us pray that it comes.

Turrall is sending us a Karen Havildar[27] and a useful contact tomorrow. When he left, we started organising the camp for a move off tomorrow – sent for an elephant, which arrived in the evening.

10th March Saturday
Waited all till 3 p.m. – no signs of the men Turrall promised us.

Set off to Kaumudo, arriving there about 6 p.m. (this suggests it is about a 3-hour journey from Pawlawdo to Kaumudo). Just as we were walking to our camp – we passed the elephant – just as I drew close it turned, roared and came for me – I took one leap into some bushes and kept running. (The elephant turned out to be in musk – Post War note from Trofimov)

Spent the night very comfortably sleeping under rice shelter.

11th March Sunday
Early start – elephant still unapproachable so we had to get some porters from the village.

Some of the home guard we had to unarm and give their rifles to our men, as they were scared of going any further.

Reliable reports indicate that Japanese moving up Bilin River – which is on our route south.

The ring is steadily closing in on Pyagawpu, in a three-way thrust from Papun – Kawludo – Shwegyin. We are going to try and break through the ring and make our way south.

Hoping that the Japanese for a time will be unaware of our location.

Towards 9 a.m. we approached our first really big range of mountains, about 4000 ft. high – it was grim going – at about 12 a.m. on reaching the other side – within about 100 yards from the Bilin River, our scouts came back saying they just saw lots of Japanese moving up the River.

We found a quiet spot away from the river and kept a watch on the river.

4 p.m. we cut across the river and cut our way through dense jungle undergrowth – eventually camped in a valley.

I started terrible headache – lay in bed and Saw Watteau massaged my head and brought relief. (post war note by Trofimov: "I had been down to wash in a stream covered in mist- which turned out to be poisonous fumes from rotting vegetables. My Karens took me on to high ground and applied pressure to my head and body to relieve the excruciating pain in my head.)"

12th March Monday

Early start. Toiled through dense jungle – I fell down a ravine and broke my carbine. After laborious trek arrived at Lekawdo – Saw Aaron joined us again – bringing with him a son of a doctor from Kaukyi – he speaks English – and also an old Burma Rifles soldier.

He brought a pig, and we are now all going to have a feast!

Terrific feast – then set off for Kaumudo at about 3 p.m. These villagers are not very keen to fight at all – they are frightened of the Japanese though – as soon as we left, they all made for the jungle leaving the village deserted.

Arrived at Kaumudo – had meal and then gathered the Headman and his people together. Told them why we had come – at the end of it all, he said they were not worried about the war. They wanted yarn. This began the feeling of doubt we had been having for some time. The war had not come their way and they were not interested in it.

13th March Tuesday
Early start to Pokhido – we are giving one more try.

Arrived there with pain – my knee swollen up with all this jogging going down the mountain tracks. Exhausted. Had lunch at Pokhido – villagers not keen. Apparently the area we intended to go to is a doubtful one as Shans and Burmans come into the area. So, we decided, after carefully considering the situation, to go back towards Dohedo (SE of Pawlawdo). We set off and trekked back to Kaumudo – it was a grim walk but walking with just my revolver and a villager carrying my pack and carbine, I managed it.

14th March Wednesday
Early start arriving in Lekawdo to find village deserted at 9 a.m. Aiming to trek hard and make the crossing of the Bilin early.

Crossed Bilin River without any incident and started that merciless, heart-breaking climb on the other side. How I made it in the heat of the day – I swore I would never do it again – little did I know how fate would turn. Camped on the other side of the mountain.

15th March Thursday
Badly stung by poisonous caterpillar – arm up like a balloon in no time – (Saw Harry applied hot poultice of cooked rice in between leaves, which eventually worked).

Arrived Pawlawdo – found Turrall was nearby.

Ronnie went to see him – returned with following information:

> Turrall had been attacked by Japanese – four of which they had killed.
> The area very sticky – we must get out tomorrow.
> Calcutta have changed our role to information on … (*redacted line as it was operationally sensitive information*) side watching …

Also, he brought down with 15 more men – our number is now 40 – all armed. We have also acquired a non-descript Jemadar.[28] We worked till about 1.00 a.m. Making preparations for an early departure.

16th March Friday
Early start – walked to that bloody same mountain and toiled up its cruel heights – then once again across the damned Bilin River – we are to have a reception on the hillside for our W/T on the 20th at Kaumudo …

(*redacted line as it was operationally sensitive information*).

Exhausted and weary, we camped the other side of the Bilin.

17th March Saturday

Trekked through the jungle, arriving at Lekawdo village (NE of Kaumudo) at about 12 a.m. Just about to have lunch when two villagers came and told us that the day before the Japanese had gone through that way – to Pyagawpu – and said that 100 Japanese would quite likely be along at any minute. So, we went up stream into the jungle and finished our meal. In this area now all villagers are living in the jungle and have hidden their rice.

We made one villager guide us up to one of the hideouts – the only pleasant spot I have seen yet. It is right up on the southern side of the Bilin River about 3500 feet up. It overlooks the valley of the Bilin and to the north the Pyagawpu valley.

We made our camp in a little Karen house – in front we had made for us a table and a chair – overlooking this magnificent view.

I then took names of our new men – we are now 40 in strength. The organisation is on a platoon basis with 3 sections under the command of our Jemadar – each section is commanded by a Naik.[29] We now have 21 rifles, 7 carbines and 2 stens.

In the evening Ronnie and I had an excellent meal – having bought a pig earlier on.

18th March Sunday

Ronnie took two men – to set off and recce a ground south west of here for personnel – at a place called Thauthekhi (grid ref. 5100/8100 corner of map page 239, caption 7). Accompanied by Aaron, I recc'ed the DZ for the 29th just north of Kaumudo. It is going to be difficult as it is to be on a slope with a gradient of about 50 degrees.

Ronnie expects to be away 4 – 5 days. So, I am now left to run the whole show. God! How I'm longing to see those parachutes in the sky.

The moon is up now so it should be alright by the 20th.

Moving in this country is grim beyond all powers of description – the sun is cruelly hot – the paths are dangerous – and the undergrowth is relentless.

It is now 4.30 p.m. I think I'll have some tea.

19th March Monday
Early rise. Drilled men then started preparing our list of requirements for following drop after first drop.

Beginning to long for that first drop hoping wildly that all will go well.

In the evening, I was sitting on a ridge above the camp when the Headman of Pokhido saw me and came (over) to me – he was heading to join us at Pawlawdo thinking we were still there. He brought me three new men, one a Havildar Major from Burma Rifles and two other men who had been with Seagrim's party.

Arranged with Headman of Pokhido to have 3 elephants at hand – also sent him off to collect 2 more Burma Rifles'[30] men and rice, pigs etc.

20th March Tuesday
Anniversary of my first month in the Karen Mountains. Hope to celebrate it with a first class drop tonight.

In the morning, I held an inspection of the men, the improvement is astonishing: all the rifles were shining, the men were smarter, already jumping to orders.

Conference afterwards with Aaron, Hsi Tai, Jemadar, and Havildar Major,[31] arranging plan for tonight's drop. I do not think I have longed for anything quite so much as I am longing for the drop tonight. There is now a rather strong wind, which I find rather worrying. I hope it drops by tonight.

5.30 pm. – set off with all my men for the ground (DZ). Set out lights on mountainside – set out fire squad and warning squads – spotters etc. Waited for an hour – suddenly she came – all lights went up – she dropped – what a thrilling sight to see all those parachutes coming down all in a bunch. We worked like slaves until 1 am. but only found 9 containers and 3 packages, only the steam generator and spare parts for W/T. We returned to camp. Slept for an hour, arriving back over that dangerous mountain track.

21st March Wednesday
Set off at 5.30 a.m. for DZ. Men found 2 remaining containers and the spare W/T but no signs of the W/T to be used immediately. Searched all morning.

Sent for elephants and had most of the stores taken up to camp from the cache in the jungle.

The drop comprised mainly rifles, food, and luxury drop for Ronnie and me – whisky and rum – bulk tea and sugar – 4000rps – Maps of our area (larger scale). W/T equipment.

Started changing battery of spare set – this will cause considerable delay in first possible transmission. Worked hard all day – built shelter for dump of stores in jungle. Sorted out medical equipment and maps.

In evening party with His Tai, (Saw) Aaron, Jemadar Robert Dee – felt much better. Slept like a log!

22nd March Thursday

Early rise – got wireless steam generator working.[32] Charged battery. By 12 a.m. it was registering correct current.

Ronnie arrived back lunchtime, looking very weary and ill.

Prepared two messages and coded them. Came up on 3.0'clock Sked – but nothing from Base – W/T working wonders. Got news perfectly on it.

Paid Headman of Kaumudo, who acted as a guide to Ronnie, 100RS.

Ronnie's news both good and bad. All ex-Burma Rifles soldiers taken by Japanese for transport troops. Southern area dangerous because of Burmans[33] and Shans[34] who come up to certain villages to trade in salt fish.

Also, quite thorough Gestapo activity in our area by JMP (Japanese Military Police). Usually one Japanese and several Burmans.

Ronnie contacted a man 'X' who was a lawyer in Shwegyin and tortured by Japanese – must report every fortnight. He is going to organise a complete network of intelligence for the South – also when the time is appropriate i.e. the battle of Toungoo[35] is in full sway, then he will recruit for us and direct levies to us for arming and training. But offensive activity before this time might result in severe repercussions on villages and levies' families.

Ronnie brought with him a SHAN who was tortured by Japanese and consequently hates them – he will be useful as most of the boatmen on the Sittang and Salween Rivers are SHANS.

Ronnie proposes to go off with a few men and W/T and get back news quickly to 14th Army. Leaving me to run training, organising of dumps, etc. This is excellent idea.

23rd March Friday

Issued orders to Kaumudo Headman to build a new camp for us above Kaumudo, nearer DZ.

Ronnie had very bad night – in bed today, very ill – temperature, unable to eat.

Managed to repair steam generator, which broke down yesterday. It would appear that a great fault of the generator lies in the fact that there is no really effective cooling system. Consequently, parts expand and seize up. Seized up again today.

11.30 a.m. Sked – after half an hour heard from Base QSA 4 but they were sending too fast and unintelligible signals. Will have to try in afternoon Sked again.

24th March Saturday

10.30 a.m. Morning Sked managed to pick them up clearly but they were still sending ridiculous speed and unintelligible signals. Wireless is my only interest these days – it is exasperating to have such a complete lack of co-operation from Calcutta.

Sent off Jemadar with all the baggage early in the morning to our new camp above Kaumudo. After Sked, I left with wireless for the camp – leaving Ronnie behind with a dreadfully swollen foot – to await the arrival of an elephant to transport him.

Arrived at new camp – right up on hillside – lovely stream – had a glorious shower.

Afternoon Sked was a repetition of morning Sked.

Designed myself a bamboo house – which is being built. Ronnie arrived 7.30 p.m. with remaining party.

25th March Sunday

Good night's sleep. House to be finished today.

---

[1] Trofimov's notes on his career before Burma, undated 1950s-60s, Trofimov Archive.

[2] 'Lieutenant Colonel Edgar Henry William Peacock, DSO, MC and bar (1893-1955) had served as Deputy Conservator of Forests and Game Warden in Burma before the war. Serving with SOE in Burma he made a parachute jump with the first wave on 20th February 1944 taking command of the Otter section of Operation Character. He was awarded the MC for repeatedly crossing Japanese lines in order to save the life of Captain J. Gibson who had been wounded by a grenade. The citation for the MC (TNA: WO373/34/230) read: 'Major Peacock was in command of a special force of Burmans and Karens which, shortly before the Japanese advance started, was sent on 13th March 1944 to watch the approaches from Yuwa into the Kabaw Valley. On 23rd March 1944, the day before this long-distance patrol was due to withdraw, one of his officers, Captain J. Gibson, a very heavy man, was very seriously injured by a grenade, and had to be carried back over very difficult country by slow stages. On arrival at his old camp site at the Yu river crossing Peacock, whose wireless had failed to function for

several days, discovered that the enemy were in possession of Tamu and Hesin, and between him and Moreh, and was uncertain how far out his own troops had withdrawn. It was imperative to get assistance quickly for Gibson who was left hidden at the Yu River crossing with food and water while Peacock and his party, by now considerably exhausted, made their way through the jungle via the northern flank of Moreh to Sibong where he contacted our forces again. In spite of his considerable exhaustion and the effects of heatstroke from which he was suffering, Peacock's sole concern was the safety and rescue of Gibson. He wasted no time in going to Moreh and after consultation with the commander of the Moreh garrison, left Moreh the next night with an escort of Gurkhas and two Karens to fetch in Gibson. At this time considerable enemy forces, including tanks and guns, were in the Nakala, Tamu and Hesin areas, but no exact information was available. Without thought for his personal safety and knowing that speed was vital to Gibson's safety, he took this party successfully under cover of darkness straight through Tamu and Hesin villages to the Yu River crossing, and the same night safely brought back Gibson who was still alive. It was entirely due to Peacock's dogged determination, drive, unselfishness and great courage that Gibson's life was saved.' He received the bar to that MC for ambush operations against the Japanese. The citation for the award (TNA: WO373/41/10) read: 'For his SOE personnel file *see* HS9/1158/1. In 1947 he was awarded the DSO (*See* TNA: WO 373/104/88). The citation for which read: 'During the period under review this officer, who parachuted with a party into the Pyagawpu QB 63 area in February 1945, has been in command of Operation Otter operating on the Toungoo Mawchi Road which has raised local levies who have killed 2,743 enemy troops and destroyed 94 MT. Besides giving much intelligence of great value to 14 and 12 Army HQ, Lieutenant Colonel Peacock has displayed leadership, organising ability and tact in handling the locals, worthy of very high commendation. The outstanding courage and resource of this officer within two months turned a small hunting party into the controlling force over a wide area.'

[3] Captain John Cook Montague, MC (1913-1995), jumped into the Ardeche as part of a "Jed" unit after previously served as volunteer in the Russo-Finnish war, and then with the Royal Tank Regiment. A transcript of an interview given by Montague after the war was uploaded to the BBC People's War Website in 2005 *see* https://www.bbc.co.uk/history/ww2peopleswar/stories/63/a7171463.shtml. *See also* TNA: WO373/104.104 for the citation for his MC and HS 9/1052/6 for his SOE personnel file.

[4] Captain Cyril Herbert Sell – recruited as a "Jed" in the summer of 1944 he headed team Chrysler. February 1945 parachuted into Burma as part of Operation Character (Otter). In September 1945 he was awarded the MC. The citation was signed by Lt-General Stopford (GOC-in-C) 12th Army, 16th September 1945. It read (*See* TNA: WO373/104/105) read: 'This Officer, who parachuted into the Central Karen area in February 1945, has displayed conspicuous powers of leadership and organisation. He has commanded his Levies with firmness mingled with tact and understanding, which has enabled him to extract the utmost from them. Even under appalling weather

conditions in June and July, and while suffering himself from dysentry, his infectious good humour and determination that the enemy should be harassed at every available opportunity maintained the morale and fighting efficiency of his Levies at a very high level and I recommend him strongly for an award of the Military Cross'. For his SOE file *see* TNA: HS9/1340/2.

[5] Jedburgh (Jeds) – *see* Appendix I (page 266): Codenamed "Guy": With the Jedburghs in France June-August 1944.

[6] HMS *Newcastle*, Town Class light cruiser.

[7] Note original diary refers to Jessau but is meant to be Jessore – this was later corrected in some of Trofimov's post war writing up of the diary.

[8] Major Ronnie Critchley later Colonel Critchley – *see* introduction.

[9] Major Rupert Guy Turrall MC, DSO (1893-1988), A veteran of the First World War, having served with the Royal Engineers, in the Second World War Turrall joined the Intelligence Corps serving in North Africa. Joining the SOE he was involved in operations on Crete. In 1945 he joined Force 136, later commanding operations in the Hyena section of Operation Character. *See* TNA:.HS 9/1493/8 for his SOE personnel file.

[10] Second Lieutenant Samuel M. Little (1918-1945), joined Gordon Highlanders in July 1939, Served Operation Character (Hyena), February to September 1945, and killed in air crash in the Karen Hills on 7th September.

[11] *See* Appendix II (page 272): Post-War Report by Major A. Trofimov on "Mongoose Green" Pyagawpu is also confirmed as their intended drop zone in Trofimov's photo album. *See* Appendix V (page 312): Letter to Girlfriend in England (Unposted), 6th March 1945, Describing Parachute Drop into Burma.

[12] *See* footnote 5 of the Introduction.

[13] Major John Macleod joined the regular Army in 1943, later serving as an instructor with SOE in Sri Lanka. In February 1945 he was parachuted into Burma as part of Character (Otter). *See* TNA: HS9/968/2.

[14] Captain Joseph Marlam, multilingual Anglo-Indian, employed as an SOE interpreter given suitable training, commissioned and dropped into Burma as part of Operation Character (Hyena). Later won the Military Cross for ambush operations against the Japanese. *See* TNA: HS9/991/4.

[15] Major William Eustace Poles made his way up through the ranks from being a Sergeant in the King's African Rifles in 1941. Joined SOE in April 1943 working with Henry Peacock in Burma along the Chindwin River until the 1944 Japanese offensive forced a withdrawal. Subsequently parachuted into Burma as part of Operation Character (Ferret). Later won the Military Cross for ambush operations against the Japanese. *See* TNA: HS9/1198/7.

[16] Captain Duncan Guthrie – had served as a civilian volunteer with the British volunteer force to Finland in 1939-40, later joining the Duke of Cornwall's Light

Infantry, before moving on to SOE in 1943-44. Served as part of "Jed" Team Harry in 1944 before joining Force 136 in 1945. *See* Duncan Dunbar Guthrie interview, reels 1-5, Imperial War Museum, 2nd December 1992. Catalogue Number 12345, https://www.iwm.org.uk/collections/item/object/80012088 (accessed 23rd October 2021). Imperial War Museum Documents Archive 12840. Carried on training levies despite his injuries until he was airlifted out of the bush Later wrote *Jungle Diary* (MacMillan, London, 1946).

[17] Major Saw Butler DSO, MC – Karen Officer, served North Kachin Levies in Burma and later SOE. 2nd in Command Character (Otter). On his promotion to the rank of Major in late 1944 it was noted that during 1943-44 he had commanded the forward troops in the main road sector … (displaying) 'initiative and leadership of a high order. He has lead offensive patrols against the Japanese and personally killed four and he has conducted ambushes which have resulted in some 100 casualties to the enemy', *See* promotion approval, 16th August 1944, in TNA: WO 373/104/103. In September 1945 he was nominated for the DSO. His citation read: 'This Officer, who parachuted into the Central Karen area with a Force 136 party for which there was no reception at the end of Feb 45, has acted as second in command of Operation Otter. He has shown consistent devotion to duty and, on the numerous occasions in which he has been in action, high qualities of leadership and a cool courage which has been an example to all ranks. A Karen of great influence, he has contributed more to the success of this operation than any other single Officer except the Commander, and I recommend him very strongly for the Distinguished Service Order', signed Lt-General Stopford (GOC-in-C) 12th Army, 16th September 1945, *See* TNA: WO 373/35/129.

[18] Levies – local unit raised for local purposes. A military practice going back to at least the Roman Army.

[19] Mobile Levies were for operations in the field whereas Static Levies were employed to protect the camps, Drop Zones and stores/dumps. The differentiation was based on considerations of the relative reliability and mobility of the individual Levy. The static Levies were very much a last line of defence.

[20] Saw Wattaw – named on Platoon Lists as 'NK' Wat Taw from Village of Dapawdar recruited Feb-Sep 1945, Trofimov Archive.

[21] Strategic decision presumably to minimise risks associated with drop zones and stores/dumps being compromised by Japanese finding and destroying these. Additionally, with units potentially finding themselves on the run from the Japanese, and having to move rapidly away from an established base alternative and dispersed points of re-supply could become vital.

[22] Sergeant Gordon Tack, Apprentice Dockyard Worker Devonport Dockyard, 1939-41. served with Royal Armoured Corps, before joining SOE in 1943, part of Jedburgh Team 'Giles in Brittany', from SOE Team 'Giles' dropped 8th/9th July Finistere, Northern France, Part of Team Pig, Force 136 March to May 1945, and then Team Galvanic Slate, Force 136 in Serendah/Selangor area, Malaya, July-August 1945, Gordon Hugh Tack, interview, reels 1-5, Imperial War Museum, 1996, Catalogue

Number 16699, https://www.iwm.org.uk/collections/item/object/80016165. (accessed 10th October 2021).

[23] Saw Aaron – Served with Burma Royal Navy Volunteer Reserve, before joining SOE, his SOE file TNA: HS 9/1318/4 (Closed until 1st January 2025).

[24] Possibly Kyaukkyi – SE of Toungoo.

[25] Saw Harry – Platoon lists refer to a Jemadar Harry who served from February to September 1945 in Platoon 'A' Operation Character (Mongoose).

[26] Short for schedule. It is a pre-arranged system of check-ins via radio. Failure to check-in on time indicated that a problem had arisen.

[27] Havildar – equivalent to Sergeant in the British Army.

[28] Jemadar – equivalent to Lieutenant in the British Army.

[29] Naik – equivalent to Lance Corporal in the British Army.

[30] Burma Rifles – founded 1917 as a regiment within the British Indian Army. By the time of the Second World War the regiment had expanded to a size of 14 battalions. Many recruits to SOE's guerrilla force came from former Burma Rifles.

[31] Jemadar Saw Aaron, His Tai (W/T) Jemadar Harry and Havildar Major James – reference in Platoon Lists in the Trofimov Archive.

[32] Wireless steam generator – a device to charge batteries where hook up to an external electricity supply was impossible, by pairing a pressurised steam boiler, fed by small pieces of dry wood, with a dynamo. Steam pressure was used to drive the dynamo with the resulting electricity channelled to a battery. The device could be somewhat problematic since they were less than silent and in the conditions of Burma rubber seals sometimes failed.

[33] Burmans – the principal ethnic group of Burma who largely sided with the Japanese during their occupation of Burma, unlike many of the minority ethnic groups such as the Karen.

[34] Shans – ethnic group located largely in Shan State, but also in other parts of Burma (Myanmar) including Kachin and Kayin State and in parts of China, Laos and Thailand.

[35] Toungoo – 18° 56' 23.406" N, 96° 26' 3.7032" E.

Diary II

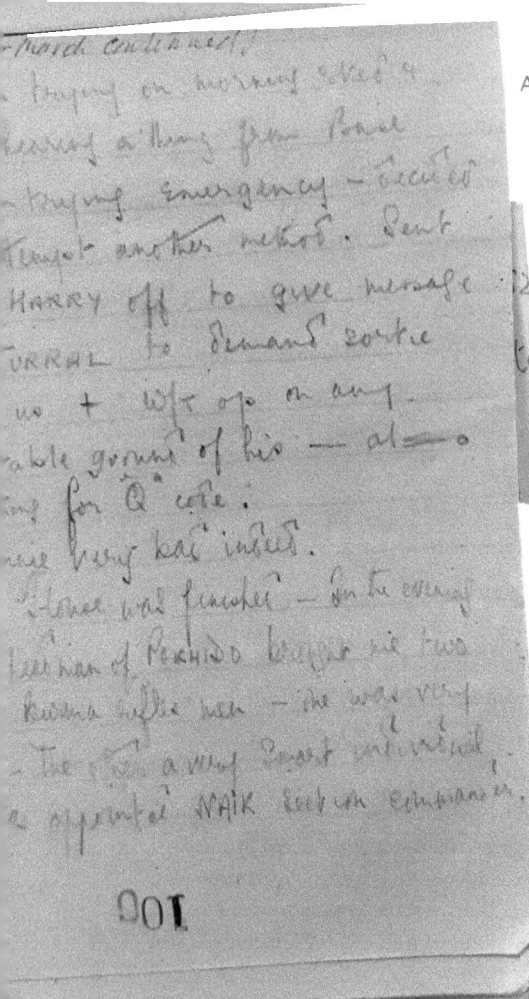

25th March Sunday

After trying on morning Sked and not hearing a thing from BASE and then trying 'Emergency' (code) – decided to attempt another method. Sent Saw Harry off to give message to Turrall to demand sortie for us and W/T operator on any suitable ground of his (unreadable) also asking for "Q" code.

Ronnie is very bad indeed.

The house was finished. In the evening, the Headman of Pokhido brought the two ex-Burma Rifles men – one was very ill; the other, a very smart individual, was appointed NAIK section commander.

26th March Monday

Early rise – recc'ed whole area of D2 for package PX771 – nothing doing. Returned to camp – recc'ed dump for food away from camp.

Sent Jemadar off to recce an alternative camp should we be surprised.

Made a stretcher for Ronnie – his foot is horribly swollen – he is off his food and generally run down.

Wireless broke down on morning Sked – receiver not picking up CW, appears to be the BFO[1] knob, which puts the set out of action.

Sent Saw Harry off to attempt to locate Turrall – with a message for Calcutta asking for a big drop on the 31st March: W/T, weapons, food, mail, everything. It will be great to get some mail – I keep wondering what is happening to Marie and Yvonne. I wonder if Yvonne is still thinking of me.

27th March Tuesday

I sent Headman of Lekawdo off to try and locate Turrall's whereabouts, which is now of very great importance to us as he is our only means of contact with India.

There is just one hope – that as was pre-arranged at BCS[2] on the 11th day after dropping our W/T (ie. on 6th March), they would make a daylight recce of our DZ and then send us a new W/T and food.

Ronnie is, if anything, worse than ever. Tried wireless in evening and found it was working again – obviously, it had shorted with the extreme dampness of this place.

28th March Wednesday

Put wireless out in sun – endeavoured to come up on morning Sked – having chosen a new site for the wireless. No results. Tried again in the evening – started by about 5.30 p.m. At 6.00 p.m. picked them up again, quite a moderate signal – but hellish interference. Anyhow, after two hours' solid work I received and sent off a message.

The message read – that they wanted to know if our DZ was suitable for personnel as they had for us – 2 JED teams and one W/T operator, plus 2 Karen Officers. We prepared a message to the effect that it is not a suitable place – but to drop in the W/T and 2 Officers further north – As for the Special Group and 2 JED teams – the time is not ripe for them – and we cannot receive them here as we dare not risk bursting the bubble here and having a repeat of Pyagawpu.

Several men are down with malaria. I took the training in the morning – PT[3] preceded by Carbine instruction – in the afternoon I held an exam for Section Commanders on the stripping of the Carbines.

29th March Thursday

Early rise. – Attempted morning Sked – fiasco! – Nothing doing from the other end. Beginning to have doubts as to the accuracy of my watch's present reading. Making arrangements to move Ronnie to Lokhi,[4] where he will lie up and also have a camp ready for me to move into as soon as the drop is over.

Afternoon Sked – very bad interference but managed to get off my message and get in two. These were to the effect that the aforementioned special group, two JED teams, a signals Officer and W/T all on their way with Saw Harry here – having been dropped to Turrall 3 days away to the west in the Kyaukkyi[5] area. This at any rate obviates our compromising this area – but God damn them for sending this bloody special group –

having just escaped from one here we get another one thrust down our throat. It will be interesting to see what they have all come for.

30th March Friday
Woke up feeling very ill – have lousy throat, sort of lump at the back – very painful to swallow. Took M & B – recc'ed camp lower downstream for special group – prepared house for JEDS in our camp. After that went to bed feeling very ill.

> **NB**. First thing in the morning the Jemadar reported that two men had deserted overnight. I had a long talk with the men – informing them of the penalty of desertion – and how stupid it was as we had all the men's names and villages, they came from.

Throat getting increasingly worse as the day goes on.

Lot of wireless traffic on both Skeds – Base asked us to prepare for further personnel – also sent message confirming our drop on the FIRST.

They want to effect a dusk drop but this is not suitable for 3 planes over this area.

31st March Saturday
Woke up feeling bloody – got around during the day though. Ronnie received notification from Calcutta that during operations he is appointed acting Lt. Colonel Area Commander, which rather implies that we will now have to establish a HQ for the area.

Ronnie's foot improving. He is able to walk around – but still unable to see properly with his eye. I give him drops every few hours.

Spent the day very quietly – began to improve a little towards the evening.

Shwe Ma[6] made an excellent dinner in the evening – chicken broth – fried chicken and beans.

1st April Sunday
Feeling decidedly better – throat greatly improved. Began to give out my orders for drop at 12.30 tonight. Receiving 2 Liberators and 1 Dakota. Contents roughly:

> 54 carbines, 2 Bren's, Stens and grenades; special weapons, explosives; Spare ammunition then lots of food. Packages of wireless and shoes for men, etc.

Wireless now working properly – traffic through in every Sked. Sent off requirement for next drop. Getting in all the men from Kaumudo and Lekawdo to help me with the drop. There is still no sign of the so-called 'special party'.

Message came in stating that our special group etc., would be delayed several days.

Had to be on ground at 5.30 p.m. as BCS made a bungle of one of their messages. Nothing doing though. In the evening, we went down and manned the ground – at 11.00 p.m. had all the men from Kaumudo and 10 from Lokhi on the DZ. All men were acting as spotters on all hills and slopes.

Dakota came over at 12.15 p.m. and proceeded to drop 30 packages all off the ground but in the area below our camp.

Then the Liberator came taking no notice of the lights – at an incredibly ridiculous height – flew across the valley towards us – dropping 17 parachutes into the valley. The second Liberator we heard but she did not drop.

2nd April Monday

We then worked until 4.00 a.m., then we all broke off and slept for an hour. Started at dawn – worked like slaves all day. Recovered all the parachutes and got them into different dumps. We now have 5 wireless sets; 2 containers of carbines broke open whilst in the air and their contents, in all 36 carbines, were shattered on the ground.

Manning the ground again at 5.30 p.m. in case the other plane that failed to find us last night tries again tonight.

3rd April Tuesday

In morning, very early received message from Headman of Lekawdo to effect (say) that new party was arriving. I set off with about 20 men to meet them. The party consisted of Major (Capt. JP) Lucas, Captain Clark(e) and Special Group. Major Milner and Captain Bourne and W/T's Captain Ford, his Sgt. W/T, also an IO Captain Woolf[7] and Signals Officer Mr. Van Kyte [Kett].[8]

I brought them into the camp, settled them in and made them comfortable. Their news was: Colonel Howell[9] – the man I disliked in Jessore is now Area Commander of Hyena – Turrall and him are not getting on at all!

The new party had a hell of a time being used day and night from the moment they dropped doing Howell's drops – patrols etc. Also, their food allowance was run on starvation lines by a Doctor with Howell.

At 5.30 p.m., all my men were at the DZ. We built large fires and made plenty of smoke. The Liberator came over and dropped after circling around for hours – dropped most of the stuff in the jungle – we recovered everything and had all stores in the jungle dump by 8.0pm.

4th April Wednesday

Ronnie set off for Lokhi on elephant early. Special party had to be given rations for five days – allocated carriers and levies preparatory for move off to next camp tomorrow. Recovered from special arms container my Mossberg .22. Handed over all signals stuff to Mr Van Kyte (Kett), the Signals Officer – what a load off my mind.

Contacted one of Wili Saw's men from the Kadaingti[10] area who it appears has an organisation of men there numbering a minimum of 50.

Taken on at least 17 new men – had to appoint Saw Gay, Section Commander. Our strength is 60 – organised into HQ Section and Sections I, II, III and IV. Section I, making it into a Bren Section.

Capt. Woolf and Lt. Van Kyte are attached to our HQ.

5th April Thursday

Moved off early – after splitting up Sections throughout the various groups. I got mad with the way people used and overlooked my men. There is going to be trouble from me I can see.

Arrived at Lokhi camp. Well organised by Ronnie with raised platforms for us all to sleep on.

Ronnie, who by the way is now hobbling about and with his eye very much better, briefed Major Milner and I (me). Despatched them with all necessary money, 2000 RS and food and porters for their area.

6th April Friday

Major Milner made an early start. My men busy bringing in stores from head dump to our camp. Also, building dumps. Killed a 15 (vingt) (stone) Pig and distributing to my men and special group. I may be going South with (Capt. Dennis) Ford to help him receive his partner Williams[11] and our new 2nd i/c poor fellow! Coming in at this stage!

In the evening reorganised my men, have now got a couple of Brens into action. The teams are being trained tomorrow. Also, issued to Section Commanders, 2 grenades each.

7th April Saturday
Men on the Bren (guns) being trained. Training of .38 pistol with my Officers and NCO's.

NB. yesterday recc'ed a DZ at Lokhi for reception on the 8th.

Spent afternoon very quietly, not feeling up to scratch. Message from Calcutta that Burne[12] and Williams would be dropped to us on the 9th.

We decided therefore to leave the next morning, go light and make for Metkyihta.[13] I am to take Ford down – get in Williams and then send them off south Kadaingti way to organise and arm levies down there.

We arranged that I would take in two drops at Metkyihta. Now in contact with ASH 14th Army, they have agreed to Ronnie's plan and think it is excellent – they also say that the Northern groups are fighting so they get priority on drops. We are given our D-day the 'vingt-cinq' (25th) – by which time all our groups and Jed teams are to be in situ and ready to fight.

Metkyihta and Tazi is in British hands so should not be long now before the bubble bursts.

8th April Sunday
Early start. Set off with Harry who we have now appointed to Havildar – the Havildar Major Tun Shin's Section – Ford and his party – incidentally, I have had to give Ford one of my interpreters – Robert Dee.

We walked like slaves – up and down these bloody mountains – the going from Lokhi to Khauchi[14] was grim – from then onwards we hit the main track. Arriving at Leklede[15] in the evening – walked into the old village – suddenly my men started shouting and looking down. I looked down, about turned my men and left the place – and walked into the river – for my legs were black with hundreds of fleas. (Note: Karens typically moved villages every 3 to 4 years when the rice fields are no longer productive – as their livestock live under the houses this could lead to a plague of fleas or other vermin). Found a suitable camp – contacted the Headman of Leklede, who produced an elephant and some more porters.

9th April Monday
Early rise. Walked right through blazing mid-day sun arriving at Metkyihta at 12 p.m. Contacted the Headman Palatoo – a very good man – had a camp built and gave out orders for the drop. Had to pull out

the pungyis – sharp (smoke-hardened) bamboo stakes (of one to two feet in length) stuck in ground – by villages about a month ago – during the Pyagawpu days.

Arrived on ground at 4.45 p.m. Started pulling up pungyis, directing fires etc. Whilst this was (going) on a plane was heard – we managed to get the fires going – she came in at 5 pm and dropped her load beautifully on the DZ.

Second Lib(erator). dropped (Maj.) Burne and (Capt.) Williams right up on the hills – Burne joined us later and received a cup of tea, which was waiting for him as the plane came over.

Set about getting all the stuff in, recovered all the containers and packages.

10th April Tuesday

(Maj.) Burne – Cuthbert nice fellow – older than most of us – had lived in Papun eight years ago – knows all the area very well. Should be very useful to us. Sent off Ford and party. The Havildar Major's Father, the Headman of Mewaing, came to see us – a charming man – delighted to see British back again. He and Pa La Too promised me 50 mobile levies and quite a number of static levies. Our aim is to recruit another 50 for (Maj.) Burne – to act as defence for HQ and bring my party up to strength. As for the HQ, we aim at having a solid wall around us and at the back of the outgoing parties.

The Headman of Mewaing also informs us that Arthur Ta Pi, the township Officer of Papun, wants to come out and join us. I have sent word through the Headman of Mewaing to get him out to us – such a man with our party would electrify the whole situation.

We are having another camp built further upstream – as this place may not be healthy after a while. We had a report that the Japanese are moving up and down the Bilin River – resting at a place called Nankhukhi[16] – right on the aeroplanes' run – so this place may be compromised now.

Message from Ronnie in the evening to say that he is moving into a camp at Dubaw,[17] just up the same river that this camp is on

Sgt. Loosmore[18] arrived in – wanting A3 set Sked plans but so far none have come in.

11th April Wednesday

Headman of Pokhido brought me 5 more men in for my army – which brings my total of recruits up to 12 new men – then kept coming in throughout the day.

Several headmen came – all bringing presents and mobile levies.

I now command an area of something like 500 Villages – one Headman commands over 400 villagers. Then I have all the Mewaing villagers' – under my control.

Had news from Ronnie – he is moving into Dubaw – directly west of this place. Asks me to send him up food – and Burne – he is joining me on the 12th. Also warns me for a drop on the 12th.

One of the villagers is making me a hammock out of parachute cord.

As regards food – presents come in every day – rice – I can have enough to keep my men fed very well indeed.

12th April Thursday

Have now organised a complete network of spies around my area – men coming in during the morning. 2 more ex-Burma Rifles came in – one brought by the Headman of Pokhido – our staunch old friend.

The drop is to be at 4 p.m. During the drop, Ronnie arrived looking very much fitter indeed. One plane came over – dropped quite well – very few arms – mostly gym shoes, soap, chillies, curry powder and such like.

I asked Ronnie to send off an emergency message asking for 300 rifles and 100 carbines. Ronnie was very pleased with the developments here.

13th April Friday

Handed over Saw Dannier's Section plus 10 men to (Maj.) Burne and the Jemadar and C (commander) TE. Recalled Maw Gay and Wattaw. Promoted Harry to Havildar and the Havildar Major to Jemadar.

Started organising new men – very difficult as most of them have very little idea of soldiering.

Started building rifle and Bren Gun range.

Ronnie spent day sizing up the situation – we formed our plan – which is to arm as many HG as quickly as possible - also to bring up our fighting strength to about 100 men. Headmen came in throughout the day bringing presents of sugar cane, toffee, eggs, chicken, rice, Karen cakes, lemons etc.

Manned the DZ again as there was some doubtful arrangement made with Calcutta. No drop made however.

14th April Saturday

Ronnie left to go and see the Headman of Mewaing. Started firing on ranges – shooting went on all day. Very good results from Tun Shein's Section.

My own carbine and Bren shooting have greatly improved. Out of 45 new men, 25 proved good shots with the rifle; this should mean that they would be first class shots with the carbine. Most of the men now equipped with shoes.

New one-eyed cook doing very well indeed.

15th April Sunday

ATP[19] – very important man came to see me. I immediately sent off a runner telling Ronnie to come down and see me today as ATP must be back at his post tomorrow.

Received message from Burne confirming drop at 3.30 p.m. to expect 3 – 4 aircraft. Also, making necessary arrangements to call in all the Home Guard.

Appointed headman of the area, Jemadar over the Home Guard.

Drop at 4 p.m. very successful – about 300 rifles, many arms etc.

Ronnie met ATP, heard his proposal for the attack on Papun (capital of Karen Mountains).

During the morning, I had gleaned some very useful information on Japanese movements in the area.

Some of the Liberators dropped beautifully from about 500 ft. right on the fires – 1 Lib however dropped at well over 2000ft and caused a lot of trouble to recover material.

16th April Monday

We now have about 400 rifles for HG (Home Guard). Sent out messages to bring them in. Spent rest of day organising new levies into Sections, appointing new NCO's. Getting two Bren Sections working.

We now number some 120 mobile levies, of which at least 70 have to be trained.

We keep on sending up stores for the dump at Dubaw HQ.

17th April Tuesday

Home Guard coming in from all around the area, we arm them, let them shoot on the range – send them off with their orders – No action until we give the order etc.

Continued with range practise all day long. Another drop tomorrow – mostly carbines and levy packs.

18th April Wednesday

Excellent drop – Dakota dropped 30 packages of levy packs and 3 containers and 1 Liberator load of carbines – plenty of cigarettes, a bottle of rum for me. 6 Jed set receivers – one of which is for me. I was able to hear news from London on 9.30 broadcast. It is a great luxury to hear the outer world again.

19th April Thursday
Issued out 80 carbines and 70 packs to the men. Getting ourselves into fighting trim.

HG coming in rapidly, all from excellent strategical positions ie. all down the Bilin Road and north along the Bilin track.

20th April Friday
Home Guard coming in in large bunches of anything from up to 40 men. We now seem to be getting in a solid block right across to the Yunzalin[20] (river). I should say by now you could walk anywhere in the area – the Japanese though still fighting are plumb scared. News is excellent. Van Kyte (Lt. Van Kett) picked up 14th Army Tank crew conversation – to the effect that they were mopping up at Pyinmana.[21] Also, there is news that Turrall has captured Kyaukkyi[22] but was wounded there. We sent off a congratulations message.

The morale of the men is very high indeed – their shooting is very good. My own shooting is better than ever before on the 25^x range. I can always get 12 out of 12 shots in the bull in about a 1-inch group.

4 p.m. Manned the DZ Dakota came in beautifully – did the best drop I have ever seen at about 450ft.

At 5.30 p.m. a Liberator came over and dropped a Karen Officer and Sergeant – Captain Ohn Pe and Havildar Wilson.[23]

21st April Saturday
Darlington from Papun bringing over 100 men here to be armed – this more or less completes the block from Shwegyin to the Yunzalin (rivers). Further mobiles came in – and as the drop consisted entirely of compos[24] – 72 carbines, 99 rifles and levy packs, I am able to equip the men as they come in.

Hope to be fighting the Japanese within the next few days.

The mobiles now number two Platoons of 50 each, comprising 4 Sections and a Bren in each.

Gave another lecture to all men on the use of carbines. Gave instruction to OHN PE in carbine and taught him to shoot.

22nd April Sunday

Mango rains are on – periodical downpours. The men are all using parachutes as tents, and very effective it is.

Ronnie has had quite a relapse; he looks much thinner and very pale – I am very worried about him – he has been ill now for over a month.

Still more mobiles coming in – got the men organised into two platoons, A & B. Each with a Bren section.

In the afternoon, we had a scheme on the DZ; we did ambush procedure(s), line up for an attack – then a glorious final dash – roaring at the tops of their voices.

The men are now all equipped with carbines and uniforms. Shooting has now reached a very high standard indeed. On the 25^x range it is very rare that one of the lads fails to get a 1-inch group in the bull.

23rd April Monday

Now starting plans for the big attack on Papun. Arranging air support – Darlington's men attacking from the east and we will attack from the west side. Darlington brought in a further 100 men to be armed – this brings our HG. strength up to 400, all armed, and all capable of firing quite accurately.

Mango rains still ongoing – very unpleasant indeed.

In the morning, I recc'ed the DZ with (Maj.) Burne – to see if it was possible to make a landing strip – would involve however far too much work – we will have to make one in the Mewaing area.

Presents simply roll in here – honey, eggs, rice, watermelons, chicken, bread, and vegetables – and so far, we have not been able to pay for a single thing!

(Burne came over to discuss plans on 22nd for the attack.)

24th April Tuesday

Held practise on instinctive shooting for the men. In the afternoon, gave lecture to the NCO's on the 75, 82 and simple demolitions.

Presents came in from different Headmen – two whole pigs today!

Cancelled attack, as Mango showers still on and without air support attack would be a complete failure.

Preparing for a move south. D-day has been given to us from the 14th Army as from tomorrow – thank God – offensive action at last.

25th April Wednesday

I am continuing in retrospect from the 29th for obvious reasons. Message came from Base saying that we must go through with the attack on the 28th as arranged. Obviously, whoever was dealing with Character Operations at 14th Army was too damn scared to get and cancel the show with RAF. Furthermore, the man must be quite mad not to take the word of the people actually on the spot. We made hasty preparations, called in about 50 HG and set off to Tahulaw,[25] near Mewaing (east of) where we met with Burne and his three Sections.

There we picked up 50 HG from Mewaing and a further 40 HG from Schweti. We left all our heavy excess baggage in the rest house and at about midnight we set off for Nankhukhi. En-route we had to cross the Bilin River, which was approximately chest high deep – very unpleasant indeed. I will always remember the Bilin!

On arriving on the Bilin Road, Ronnie decided we were making far too noticeable tracks, so we branched off from the road and went up to the Karen village of Nankhukhi, where we had food and removed the leeches from our legs – my first experiences – obviously, the result of the mango rains. God knows what it will be like during the rains.

26th April Thursday

To resume, we picked up a further 30 men from Nankhukhi, set off and arrived at Bawbaw (see page 242 with route indicated due east of Nankhukhi, south west of Kuseik) in the evening. We spent the night there tired and exhausted on the journey up – the heat was ghastly, I felt sick and weak most of the time.

> **NB**. on the 25th before turning off the Bilin Road we sent Ohn Pe up the road to contact Darlington and his men and tell them to meet us at Hkhlerko.

27th April Friday

Left for Hkhlerko (name corrected) arriving there after 2 hours walking. Here we met Darlington who had with him about 120 men.
Our combined force now consisted of the following:

- A Platoon 50 men
- B Platoon 50 men
- C Platoon 30 men
- Darlington 124 men
- Mewaing 35 men
- Shwehti 40 men

- Nankhukhi 54 men
- **Total** 383 men

We killed 4 pigs and ate lots of food. Then prepared the final details of the plan for the attack on Papun.

Zero Hour was to be the following morning at 6.30 a.m. When light fighter planes were to come over to bomb and strafe the east side of the river for half an hour then the west side – afterwards, they were to fire (a) very light and keep on flying overhead. We divided the men from Shwehti and Nankhukhi up amongst the Platoons bringing each Platoon strength up to 90. Then made the plan as follows:

Incidentally Ohn Pe still had not joined us. What he was doing we could not imagine.

There were to be two phases:

First phase attack Papun from the east side: Darlington with our old Jemadar plus C Platoon, altogether some 150 men were to attack with Darlington in command Observation Hill where there were some 15 Japanese, then sweep down taking on a further 20 Japanese south of the football ground north of the Observation Hill; then make for the bridgehead, which was to be the rallying point. When the second phase would start.

Darlington's starting point was to be north of the Kaukpok Road behind Observation Hill.

'A' Platoon under the command of Ronnie and Saw Aaron were to line up just south of the Kaukpok Road.[26]

'B' Platoon with myself in command and Saw Harry were to line up on the left of 'A' Platoon. The Jemadar – our new one – the Headman of Mewaing's son was to act as reserve Platoon with the Mewaing party – they were to line up behind us ready to reinforce the line when we wanted to extend.

'A & B' Platoons would sweep over Pagoda Hill on which there were an unknown number of men, 2 AA guns and a Bren. Then they would go through the town, A Platoon looking after the area in the centre of the town, B Platoon would swing round to the south of the football pitch taking on, on the way, 20 Japanese at the bottom of Pagoda Hill. Then we would all rally on the bridgehead and decide on the best way to attack the Japanese on the west bank – about 70 in all.

The garrison comprised about 200 Japanese; 70 to 80 on the west bank and about 60 on the east side; the remainder were out at Kyunbin Sakan to the west of Papun on the Bilin Road.

To continue with the events in their correct sequence:

Ohn Pe did not arrive before our departure.
In the afternoon, a Ghurkha came and gave us information, which caused us to change our original plan to the above-described plan.
The rest of the day we spent sleeping.
At 4.00 p.m. Ronnie briefed all the NCO's whilst I gave the Japanese situation. We gave the order to move off at 10 p.m.

We left all our heavy baggage at Hkhlerko and set off at 10.00 p.m. After about one-hour walking Ronnie called a halt, this caused a panic amongst the HG – in front of my Platoon, they thought we had met trouble, so they turned and started running back. All my men rushed into the jungle, GNA Paw, my bodyguard stood firm ground behind me. This business took about half an hour to sort out, collect the men back again, even so when we actually did move off, several of the men were missing. However, we moved off and eventually reached the Yunzalin River about 100(ft) wide and about waist deep. Having crossed to the other side, I suddenly found myself going round in circles – then the Sections in front stopped. I discovered that they had not been able to keep up with the others. This left me with about two-thirds of the force. I sent a man on in front, but he came back and reported he could see nothing at all.

Fortunately, one of my ex-Burma Rifles Section Commander knew the Papun area very well indeed. He started off in front and by 4.30 p.m. got me into a position in the jungle – about 1 mile from the Mayeki track. Here I settled down and let the men rest for an hour – Moses, my guide – I sent on to see if he could contact Ronnie. He returned at 5 a.m. having failed to do so.

28th April Saturday

I then set to about 5 a.m. to get my plan worked as though Ronnie was not in the show. Knowing Ronnie though, I knew he would go through with the attack – and I also was quite confident that he knew that I would get there somehow.

I decided to attack Pagoda Hill with my Platoon – and I ordered the Jemadar Thadin with his 2 Sections and about 50 of Darlington's men –

to capture Observation Hill and then sweep down and join me in the town itself.

At 5.30 a.m. we set off – tired, weary and cold with resting in our wet clothes. After a while we came across some recently made tracks leading off the main track. Ronnie's footprints were clearly defined. So, I gathered he must have moved in already. We came on to the track – and went down it expecting to meet the Japanese at any moment. Then we turned off up Pagoda Hill.

At 6.15 a.m. I was within a ¼ mile of the actual line up position. I decided to wait for the planes – and move into position under cover of the noise they would make.

NB. An important omission – when we were at (H) Khlerkho on the 27th (April) we learnt from the Gurkha two things:

That the Japanese had been warned that Darlington and his men had crossed the Bilin Road, through the medium of a Shan spy from Kyunbin Sakan. So, they were on the "Qui Vive" (alert) expecting some trouble from him, and …

Our Gurkha also reported that the Karen District Commissioner and Arthur TA PE had left PAPUN on the 25th saying they were afraid of the bombing, which was to take place on the 27th. From this, only one conclusion could be drawn, only one man besides ourselves knew of this proposed bombing and that was Darlington. He must have given the whole show away by carelessly talking to a friend.

With the comforting knowledge that the Japanese would be waiting for us, we sat there awaiting the aircraft. My thoughts were many and varied, I wondered to myself what would happen if Ronnie had not been able to make it. However, it was too late to think about such possibilities.

6.30 a.m. I sent Moses up the hill to see how close he could get without being seen by the men on the gun sites.

6.35 a.m. the faint but sure drone of engines – I gave the order to advance. We moved into position within one hundred yards of the Pagoda.

There followed 25 minutes of sheer hell! – we were directly in the line of bombing and strafing – bullets dug up the ground 50 yards in front of us.

7.00 a.m. the strafing ceased but I could not see the very light – I decided to chance it "Advance" – we rushed across the open ground to the Pagoda. Just then another plane dived towards us – my heart sank, I thought we were going to be strafed by our own planes. Fortunately, it flew over. We reached the top – I ran round to the magazine room – 3 Japanese inside – I fired straight in the head (of one); then my men fired and killed the other two. One was an Officer. At that moment I caught sight of the Jemadars' party swarming over Observation Hill. It was a wonderfully cheering sight – we cheered across at each other. Then leaving Maw Gay and his Bren section on top, I led on down the hill – suddenly to my great joy I caught sight of Ronnie's men swarming down the Kaukpok – Papun Road. We drew level in the centre of the town. Ronnie then turned north-west and I turned south. The whole show became a shambles – the men just were not able to keep in line – and one Section after another disappeared. Suddenly I found myself with my Platoon Sergeant Harry, Moses, Kya, Wataw, Mg Mu (my honey man) and a handful of Darlington's men – who were all bloody scared.

Whilst going round to the football pitch we suddenly came under fire from our left – Harry, Wa Taw and I fired back and silenced the guns. Then we moved left, stood out in the open discussing where the Colonel had been last seen. Suddenly bedlam was let loose all around us. We crept into the bushes, laid down – a bullet hit Moses a few feet from me, right through the brain. He started snoring horribly – there was nothing we could do for him. The firing continued – I borrowed Harry's Gammon grenade and lobbed it into the slit trench from where four rifles were firing at us – 3 ceased to fire. Then I tried to get the handful of men – all that was left with me – to follow me – but they were scared stiff and lay crouching behind a tree. I turned my gun on them and forced them to follow.

I then decided to move down to meet Ronnie, I thought he might head for the east bank bridgehead – he informed Aaron was badly wounded in 3 places – through the chest and leg. Ronnie after great difficulty managed to get some men together to carry him.

Suddenly – there was the most ungodly machine gun fire in all directions – covering the road – it was impossible to work out where it came from. (Trofimov later described this as 'horrendous … Each man for himself … A shattering experience for the Karens').[27]

Ronnie gave the order to withdraw up the left side to Observation Hill – this meant I had to cross the road and I had gone over to the right side and started firing at a place I thought I could see puffs of smoke coming from. I got across followed by Kya, Mg Mu, and a few others. I crossed a bridge – and, as I afterwards learnt, a Japanese soldier under the bridge raised his rifle aimed at my chest – but Mg Mu behind me, got him first thereby saving my life.

We then got into a riverbed – thinking all was safe – once again bullets splattered all around us. I went right, Ronnie gave the order to go to the left – again I had to cross over a fence we went into an open space about 500 yds. long with big trees here and there. Here Ronnie and I came under intense machine gun fire, from every direction, we had definitely been spotted. I rolled into a ditch and forced my way through some bramble bushes to the base of the hill. Here I had to cross clear ground up about an incline of 45 degrees.

The Japanese spotted me – bullets splattered all round me – I dived headlong into a bush – followed by a HG who landed on top of me. I crawled up amongst the bushes – made a dash for it – got into dead ground. One final difficult open bit lay ahead – as I came into sight, they opened up with everything they had – once again I dived into a valley with bushes in it. The bullets clipped the top of the bushes. I crawled, my heart pounding, exhausted, my throat parched – one final dash and I had reached safety and joined the others. Here I flopped to the ground exhausted.

Ronnie gave me some water. It was wonderful. We then cut through the jungle to a stream where, by degrees, many of the men joined us. Here though the water was muddy, we all drank it madly with thirst and exhaustion.

I began then to remember Moses and Aaron. Kya and Gnapaw carrying my sack were missing – I felt sick and weary with it all. Suddenly Kya and a whole crowd appeared, and I leapt up with joy. You see I love all these boys individually (changed in the post-war edit by Trofimov to read 'I was filled with utter relief as I like each of my Karens individually'). I feel such a personal contact with each of them. **NB.**, I forgot to mention that when we were heading back to meet with Ronnie, I crossed a space with scattered houses around – suddenly all the men flung themselves to the ground and fired at a heap of bamboo leaves. Suddenly up stood a huge Indian – his knees shaking - he ran across to me – gathered my hands in his and kissed them, so great was his relief.

To resume, we then set off still missing many of the men – including my Bren Section whom I had shouted at from Observation Hill to withdraw.

Then followed 6 hours of the grimmest walking I have ever done –

the guide took us an abominable way (a)round. Every river I gorged myself with water – then I told Ronnie I was too weak to go on. We stopped, had a cup of tea, and rested – it put me back on my feet. We kept on walking and about 4.00 p.m. we crossed the Indian Quarters south of Papun. All the Indians came out to Salām[28] us and offered to bring us milk.

Once across the Yunzalin we stopped for a cup of tea. I noticed that we had gathered most of our force together again. Maw Gay had rejoined us – after leaving Pagoda Hill. Tun Shein was looking very pale indeed from a flesh wound on his arm.

The two Jemadars, however, were still missing – 3 NCOs and about 18 men.

Harry was also missing – he had gone back when I went to look for Ronnie – to see if anything could possibly be done for Moses – Imagine our joy on arriving at Hklerhko when we found Harry there – he had brought Arran whom I had given up for dead. Harry had found Moses who was dead, so he went and found Aaron who was left with Aung Main, our ex-cook, who fought gallantly and bravely throughout the battle and Mya Thein. Between them and with the help of some Indians they got him out led by Darlington – to Hklerhko.

I got my medical kit out and went to see him expecting to find the worse. He was in great pain – so I made him as comfortable as I could. I pulled back his shirt and to my intense relief found that his chest had only been badly grazed by an exploded Bren magazine. These wounds I cleaned up and plugged with M&B 693 powder and covered up. Then I looked at his thigh. There was a horrible gaping round hole – the bullet had lodged in his bottom – but Harry had got it out for him. I cleaned and plugged the hole with M&B 693 powder. Then I gave him a morphine injection.

Ronnie sent off a runner to warn Cuthbert to get the details of the landing strip he had made tied up with RAF and arrange to have Aaron evacuated at the earliest possible occasion. I had to have some tea, as I was feeling a little sick after dealing with Aaron's wounds. Then I had to deal with Tun Shein, my No. 1 Section Commander. His wound was right through the fleshy part of the arm. After this I lay and slept heavily, weary with the whole business.

The two Jemadars' were still missing and 18 men – including 3 Section Commanders.

Now to relate the story that I gathered from different NCO's.

When I had captured Pagoda Hill, the Jemadars' and some Home

Guard from Mewaing, and Maw Gay were left there to hold it. Unfortunately, about 25 Japanese crept up inside the jungle and got on the hill slope above the Pagoda and fired on them from trenches already made there. They kept this up until 4 p.m. when they ran short of ammunition. The Jemadars' party managed to kill one officer and two men of this party. When the Japanese ran short of ammo my men got away with no casualties.

When I led the attack down from Pagoda Hill to the town, Tun Shein went left at the bottom of the hill and came across about 100 Japanese in an ammunition dump – a lot of them fled; whilst so doing my men killed 4 of them. There ensued a short battle in which 4 of their officers were killed. Afterwards I then realised that the Japanese who took up a position above Pagoda Hill were also able to cover the ground, which Ronnie and I had to cover on Observation Hill.

Any points I have missed out I will cover later.

Conclusion

The Japanese were definitely waiting for us and had an excellent crossfire plan and snipers plan worked out. Throughout the battle we came under machine gun fire and mortar fire from the west bank of the river.

The battle itself lasted 2½ hours. We held the eastern bank all this time.

Reasons for withdrawal

Our levies were alright in the initial attack – they were magnificent – but under strain of the severe machine gun fire, which ensued they lost heart and many fled - others were too scared to show themselves and fight against an enemy, which we could not see.

Ronnie and I, after the first impetus, found ourselves left with no more than 20 men each – all very reluctant to carry on with the battle. The battle through the dispersal of our troops got out of hand – we were not able to do a systematic but slow mopping up of all the pockets of resistance.

The Japanese had far too great a preponderance of automatic firing weapons. They had a definite plan worked out.

To take this town, it would have taken regular troops a long time. Because the targets were all so dispersed and with low brushwood throughout the town thus permitting them to withdraw without being seen.

The only way to take the place would be to occupy both hilltops and the slopes above them with a whole company on each – armed with mortars and machine guns.

Then advance slowly keeping in line – blasting every fox hole and trench – burning down all houses and keeping up a constant crossfire of machine gun fire on the bushes in front of the advancing line. And, doing it sector by sector slowly and methodically making quite sure that everything was destroyed.

But with 'guerrilla' untrained troops – they are alright on a 'smash and run' raid but quite the wrong thing for attacking fortified positions. They have all the disadvantages.

A few points against such an attack with guerrilla troops:

- Inability to control through language problem.
- Troops do not do the right thing as trained troops would under given support.
- Lack of supporting fire.
- Lack of adequate medical supplies and complete lack of medical staff.
- Lack of foreknowledge as to leadership of NCO's.
- Reaction of guerrillas to intense fire conditions.
- Lack of support by heavier mortar and machine gun fire.
- Lack of BO's and key men.

Results
We killed 7 Officers, 28 men and several more wounded.

For the loss of 1 NCO Moses killed in action, 2 HG and two men wounded

Tactical Results
The Japanese evacuated east side and went over to west side – and are preparing to leave PAPUN – having loaded up their bullock carts.

Air Support was puny – only strafing on Pagoda Hill – but failed to bomb and strafe west bank as requested.

To the people in the town, it was NOT a very impressive show.

29th April Sunday
The Indians brought us gallons of lovely milk. Jemadar Mya Thein, my Company Jemadar, returned and corroborated the story as above. Brought with him a few men.

NB. On returning the day before to Hklerhko we found Ohn Pe[29] and Wilson there – with some weak story of OP (Ohn Pe) having hurt his knee and being unable to join. "Where there is no will there is no way!"

Also, Ba Chit,[30] a Major whom the 14th Army had said was heading for Papun to help us in the attack – he had not been heard or seen!

At 3 p.m. we set off for Bawbaw leaving Darlington and his men behind at Hklerhko. At Bawbaw (maps, page 242, caption 9) we killed 2 pigs and fed the men – then rested.

30th April Monday

Early start at 3 a.m. Arriving at Nankhukhi at 7.30 a.m. Rested. More men re-joined us. At Hklerhko, Aaron had allowed a Karen elder to put some herbs on his wound. When I examined it, it had gone green. I again plugged it with M&B 693 and hoped for the best!

Jemadar Thadin still missing with 2 of my NCO's and about 5 men.

Rested until 3 p.m. then set off for the Rest House at Tahulaw. Arrived there at 6 p.m.

Their news was interesting – the ground strip was built. They had been maintaining an ambush party on the Bilin as ordered by Ronnie since the 27th. They had had considerable trouble with Shans moving down the road in bullock carts. They had to stop them – in one case the woman driving one cart drove right through and went over the mines blowing them up – her baby was killed, and she lost her hand.

1st May Tuesday

Aaron arrived during the night. In the morning Ronnie briefed me for my new area – south of Papun between the Bilin and the Kadaingti roads to Nankhukhi and Kwethe (SE of Nankhukhi, map caption 13, page 246, ref. 618/045) in the south. Enclosed are my tasks.

I reorganised my Platoon, as my No.1 Section Commander, Tun Shein, had to be made a Havildar in charge of A Section. I have now organised a Bren in each Section and in my Platoon, I have 5 Brens - one spare for luck!

In the afternoon I moved off with my men and about 50 porters. Arrived at Nankhukhi and organised my plan forthwith. Arranged for the Headman of Kwethe to come and contact me re. the arming of guerrillas between Kwethe and Mahtaw,[31] which comes into Darlington's area.

I also sent off a runner to tell Darlington to report to me with 50 of his men, leaving behind an intelligence system.

2nd May Wednesday

Received message from Darlington in the morning to say that the Japanese are preparing to evacuate Papun – they had transferred all their goods from the east bank to the west bank where they were building huts to store their supplies and also trenches to defend themselves – leaving the east bank – but building horizontal trenches on the west bank. Apparently in the rains the river washes away the bridges. They have also collected 18 bullock carts ready to move off.

I called in the Headman, whom I have appointed a Havildar and demanded 50 of his men for the afternoon. At 4.00 p.m. I set off to the ambush position taking all my men and 50 Home Guard. We got into position after a long and difficult walk through thick jungle and along slippery tracks.

From the ambush position you could look back down onto the road quite well in places. I placed out 5 Brens and all my men.

When night came it started pouring down with rain and kept it up all night. It was a hellish night.

3rd May Thursday

I decided to halve the ambush (squad) and arrange a relief system. So, I took away with me 2 Sections and half the Nankhukhi Home Guard leaving behind C Te in charge of 3 Brens, 2 sections and 25 Home Guards. Apparently, as I learnt at 11 a.m., at about 7 o'clock 200 Japanese, armed with rifles, came up from the south on the way up to Papun. C Te was evidently scared and did not fire upon them. This I take the grimmest possible outlook on – he could have fired upon them and then got the hell out of it, which is all one expects of any ambush. I am reducing him from the rank of Havildar to private – in disgrace. I must set an example and avoid a recurrence of this. On arriving back at Nankhukhi, tired, wet, weary, and feeling thoroughly run down, I found Darlington and his 50 men. We set to and formed a plan to cover the intelligence side and the harassing of the roads, which is as follows: to maintain permanent ambushes of varying sizes on the Bilin Road.

We have spies in Papun, Kyunbin Sakan, Nankhukhi, and Kuseik and on the road at Yakhekhi.

In the afternoon Arthur Ta Pi came to me – corroborating the information from Papun. He had also been in contact with Major Ba Chit, who is apparently north of Papun.

Sent Harry off with relief party for ambush. Also, with some Hawkins grenades to mine the road.

Arthur Ta Bi is the township officer of Papun and a great personality in the area.

The monsoons have quite definitely started – it is raining all day and all night long drenching everything.

My men are going down like fleas with malaria!

4th May Friday

Monsoons still on. News on the wireless is excellent; war in Europe seems to be nearly over! A letter came by runner from Ronnie at his HQ in Mewaing – from 14th Army HQ giving the tactical position. Brought all my men back from the ambush leaving 20 of Darlington's men and 10 of Nankhukhi Home Guard there.

The Bilin River is now getting very difficult to cross indeed, almost neck high and as Karens are scared stiff of water, it is getting increasingly difficult to get runners to go over to HQ at Mewaing.

5th May Saturday A DAY TO REMEMBER!

At 10 a.m., I was inspecting the men's arms and carbines when a runner from my ambush came to say that the mines had blown up a Japanese cart and that about 120 Japanese were coming down the road from Papun – the ambush (squad) had got scared and not fired on them!

I got all my men together and 30 Home Guard and rushed to a position about 2 miles south of Nankhukhi. I laid out 5 Brens, 4 Sections of mobiles and 30 Home Guard in line.

An excellent spot – looking down onto a long stretch of road – with reasonable camouflage but no cover at all – just thin bamboo clumps.

At 12 a.m. C Te, who had been watching on the road, came smiling and reported that the Japanese were coming. Sure enough 4 scouts passed about 300 yards ahead of the main Guard. Then came the rear Guard – it was a dream – they were all in a bunch, thickly all over the road – they were tired and weary, carrying heavy loads and were well armed.

My position was in the centre of my Platoon. I sighted my carbine at a Japanese – when the main Guard was well in front of us, I fired – my man dropped. There was an ear-splitting crescendo as the 5 Brens roared into action and 45 carbines and 30 rifles all spat their death sting.

We kept this up for 5 minutes – then we came under heavy fire from the scouts ahead who had trained a Bren on our position. I gave the order to withdraw – the day was ours – some 60 Japanese had been killed by my Platoon alone. The Home Guard, I afterwards learnt, killed a further 10 or more.

On top of the hill the bullets were flying haphazardly – suddenly Harry said one of the men was wounded – it was one of my Bren men. He had a nasty gash in his head just on the left side above the ear about ¼ inch deep and 3 inches long. I put a field dressing on and left him with C. Te.

We cut through almost impenetrable jungle – having no guides – but by using our judgement, we eventually reached Nankhukhi by 2 p.m. All the men had returned except two who were reported still missing believed to be wounded. I set to and dressed the head wound – it was a long and sickening affair – the hair had clogged into the wound – I am getting to be quite a doctor now, and know what to do.

At 4.30 p.m. I set off down again with my Platoon and about 15 scared Home Guard. But my scouts ahead were fired upon by the Japanese, so I called it off – we were only going to count the dead. Either the Japanese are burying their dead or something is going on. One thing is certain, and that is that the Japanese are waiting till dark before moving off down the road.

On the way back, it started to pour down in absolute torrential rain. We were drenched through and through.

Poor old Kya; the second time today he has had to strip and clean my carbine. It appears that whilst we were engaging the main Guard, Darlington and his men were kept busy with the Japanese rear Guard who tried to move round our north flank - he killed about 12 of them.

Unfortunately, the scouts ahead – whom I had not allowed for – were able to do some effective shooting, but not until we had dealt our crucial blow. It was incredible, all one had to do was fire into the midst of them, one could not possibly miss them. I am glad my first shot dropped a Japanese – after that Harry, C Te and myself kept firing at a bunch of Japanese on the other side of the road in a ditch. We killed at least 8 between us – the Brens must have accounted for at least 10 men each.

The other party returned from the northern ambush in the evening and said the bullock cart - the only one the Japanese had to carry their loads - had been completely wrecked – well placed Harry.

In the evening, I also discovered to my horror that the Bren Sections had left 30 Bren magazines behind!

At 8.30 p.m. I sent off C Te, Maw Gay with 4 chosen men and 20 Home Guard, to go and see what they could find out and return with any weapons they could pick up. Soon afterwards one of the missing wounded men came in – a bullet had gone right through his big toe and three other toes, making a hell of a mess of them. It was very difficult to dress them as there was a lot of dirt in them – he walked for some time in his bare feet before covering his wound. However, once again with my tongue in my cheek, I set to and did the job.

Now I am anxiously awaiting the return of my patrol to find out what they have seen.

I am going to give the men a rest tomorrow and work up a plan for felling trees and booby-trapping the jungle on either side. Also, I must blow the bridge at Tagundaing and destroy all bridges south of Kwethe to Kadaingti. I am longing now to get at the remaining Japanese in Papun. By God I am! At 12 o'clock my patrol, having seen nothing but a lot of blood, returned.

6th May Sunday

We went down early, me, Harry, C Te and a Section to the ambush position. There we found a gruesome sight. 4 graves – obviously 2 of them were Officers; a fire where they had burnt their dead – many telltale bones lay around.

On the opposite side of the road in one place they had left 6 dead all in a bunch merely covered over with leaves; then strewn around all over the place their dead were left. In some places, they had been carried right away into the jungle; the places where they had been dragged were quite obvious.

In the afternoon, I had to send C Te off to Major Burne as an interpreter for him.

I received 40 rifles, ammunition and rations etc., from Ronnie, also his congratulations on our show yesterday.

In the evening, I made plans to destroy all the bridges up the Bilin Road to Papun – the Tagundaing bridge.

This morning I sent off a Headman from the Kwethe area to destroy all the bridges from Kwethe to Kadaingti.

I sent off Po Kaing – ATP's clerk, to Papun – to get information on the Japanese there.

(Then) made arrangements to turn 3 Sections of Darlington's men into regular mobiles and equip them with carbines and Brens.

I am asking for a drop on the DZ near here as I am in need of lots of equipment.

7th May Monday

Headman of Kwethe came to see me. I armed 15 more Home Guard for him, which gives him a total of 31 Home Guard. I sent him off on the 8th (May) to Pawleha where Burne is taking a drop for both of us on the 9th.

I sent Darlington's men up the road felling trees. Nankhukhi men are felling trees across the road in this area.

In the morning, I received a message from one of Darlington's men that the Japanese were moving out of Papun. I moved all the men down to the same ambush place – we stayed there till 5.30 p.m. It was ghastly – the smell from the dead was unutterably horrible. However, it was a false rumour.

I sent off my two wounded to Mewaing to be cared for.

8th May Tuesday

War ended in Europe – **God! To be at home now**.

Many stores came in from Mewaing; rifles, a Bren, ammunition, food, carbine ammo, Stens. I sent word off asking urgently for medical levy sets and Tommy guns. Ronnie sent message to the effect that he has mentioned me for a decoration after the Papun show – as if I would ever get so much as thanked for anything I might do or have done, other than by Ronnie himself.

9th May Wednesday

Recc'ed new ambush position north of Nankhukhi – laid trip wire and grenades connected (up) with cordtex[32] on opposite side of road.

In the evening had trees felled and made a roadblock at a place where road was high ground on our side of it – put more trip wires with grenades and cordtex – ideal spot for a night ambush – just chuck No. 36 grenades and gammons into them as they reach the block.

Po Kaing came back with information from Papun – 200 to 300 Japanese still there – all living on west bank. There are no actual signs of them moving yet.

My guerrillas are ambushing them just south of Papun on the Bilin Road, then parties raid them from the west bank – parties also come down from the east side, shooting across the river at them causing them to retaliate by firing all day long in panic.

The Lysander came in to Mewaing and brought an Officer from HQ 14th Army, to discuss the situation. Apparently, all Japanese communications have been broken in Burma and parties of Japanese are wandering about here and there all over the place. The Army Commander sent his congratulations to Ronnie and myself (me) for the Papun show.

They brought a copy of SEAC[33] and the Jungle Times. It has made me feel suddenly very empty and homesick with the end of the War in Europe. God! What I would give to be in England now that peace is there. How can anyone realise the hell of this life – always surrounded by jungle – eating rice three times a day. Nothing to read – absolutely no distraction whatsoever, sweating and feeling heady all day long. With bedbugs, fleas, and mosquitoes at night. Alone - the only white man in the region. When, at what point, am I going to go mad – soon, I hope!

Even the Japanese are not moving (maybe famous last words!).

I would go crazy with joy if only they would drop me my mail.

10th May Thursday

Message from Calcutta reads: "Please congratulate Captain Trofimov. Splendid work x our 38 x". Rather nice of them, I think.

I sent the Headman of Kwethe off with orders to bring all his men up to a position just south of Kuseik – to recce' good ambush positions on the east and west banks and liaise with my spies south of Papun. It is difficult to know which way the Japanese will go out of Papun. They may try the Bilin Road or they may try going down the Kadaingti Road as far as Winpa[34] (NE of Kuseik) then follow down the track on the east bank of the Yunzalin.

Harry recc'ed the road for a good ambush position – there are none at all near here.

Letter from Ronnie saying he is moving his HQ down to Mebawkhi[35] about a 3-day trip south from here.

11th May Friday

Letter from Wili Paw to effect that he has only 20 Home Guard with which to block the Papun – Bwado[36] track, armed only with Chinese rifles. He reports a further 100 Japanese arrived in Papun from the north and that the Japanese are mining the east bank.

Ti Pawkoo he reports ambushed on the 4th May: Eight Japanese – killing 5, capturing 2 pistols and 100 Japanese yens. I have asked him for a pistol – as I have not seen Japanese pistols yet. Sent off 7 men, whom I armed – Home Guard from Winpa – to join Kwethe men and to transport 19 rifles to Wili Paw.

An ex-Burma Rifles – more recently Head Constable of Police Papun – came to join the Home Guard but I made him join my mobiles – have appointed him a Section Commander and given him 10 men – this gives me 5 Sections, each armed with a Bren.

News from Cuthbert – 300 Japanese in Lagunbyo[37] digging in – threatening surrounding villages for rice.

Ronnie thinks the Japanese will make 3 main Garrisons and supply places – Papun, Lagunbyo (maps, page 141, caption 18) and Lower Natkyi.[38] If such were the case, I am going to let the devils in Papun have right and left.

Pagoda started to wear a collar – beginning to show signs of recognition when I call his name out.

Feeling unbearably bored and homesick – I am fed up with this bloody life!

12th May Saturday

Quiet, uneventful day. Played some basketball with improvised coconut ball. Life is getting more boring every minute.

13th May Sunday

News in afternoon from Burne – he is moving down to operate in Lagunbyo area and south of it, leaving the road open between Lagunbyo and here. Saw Daniel Pan at Htibawlaw is to be our link. This means I am completely isolated from my kind – not another white man for miles. I am fighting the greatest struggle to keep quite sane. God! I loathe Burma and the life here.

14th May Monday

Quiet day. News coming up about Japanese concentrations in Lagunbyo, also Japanese dispositions in Papun. Japanese attacked Ghurkha quarters presumably for supplies.

15th May Tuesday

Removed all the stores to Urekhi[39] – where I have a dump hidden in the jungle. I also ordered the villagers to build supplies of rice and salt at Urekhi.

Papun upon my request was bombed and strafed by 6 aircraft. They destroyed nearly all the houses on the east and west banks. The attack took place at midday.

Report came in that 30 Japanese were moving up to Kyauktaung and would probably move up to Papun in the night. I rushed an ambush party with No. 36 grenades down to the road.

16th May Wednesday

Took all my men down to ambush position – by 11.30 a.m. nothing had come through so I decided to go back to my HQ to find out what I could. On the way, I met a sentry who said the 30 Japanese were coming up the road. I returned and waited.

A further message came from Daniel Pan at Kyauktaung saying 100 or more, well-armed Japanese, were moving up to Kyauktaung from Lagunbyo and would be moving through my area at night. The 30 Japanese moved in to Nankhuhta and stayed there until dark – my spies were watching them.

At 5.30 p.m. I left the ambush and returned to HQ. Harry followed up after dark – leaving 30 men behind with grenades.

On my return a runner from the Kuseik side said that the Japanese were leaving Papun for Kuszik (Note: assumed to mean Kuseik). A further runner came to say the Japanese were moving down the Bilin Road from Papun and were only 3 miles away. What a party – Japanese moving up the road and down the road. The question is what will happen when they meet? Those coming down will inform those coming up of conditions in Papun. And I think the whole bloody bunch will go back.

Stayed up all night making plans, interviewing Arthur Ta Bi[40] and Darlington. Made arrangements for everyone to be on the alert – in case the Japanese came to take reprisals for my last ambush. They know I'm in the area so they may come and burn this village. I have had all stores moved into the jungle and sentries laid out all along the track to the road.

17th May Thursday

My ambush squad of 30 Home Guard South of Kyunbin Sakan (west of Papun) fired on a party of 52 Japanese and threw grenades at about 3 p.m. on the 16th yesterday. Casualties unknown – but one of Home Guard spies was caught by the Japanese. Further reports coming in about Japanese movements down the road. But they are not sticking to the road – rendered difficult by countless trees lay(ing) across it and all bridges destroyed. Sometimes they walk along jungle tracks. Hence my ambush party last night never saw a single Japanese.

Now changing my tactics with these developments. I am now sending small parties consisting of one Bren and 6 carbines and 2 Nankhukhi Home Guard to act as guides. They go north and south of here far way. Shoot up the Japanese then get out and return here. In this way, I am bound to get some of either party of Japanese.

My dispositions are now:

- 41 Kwethe Home Guard, ambushing in Kuseik area
- 30 Darlington HG and a Bren, ambushing in Kuseik area
- 20-30 Darlington HG, north of Kyunbin Sakan (west of Papun)
- 30 Darlington HG, south of Kyunbin Sakan
- 10 Darlington HG, acting as spies in Papun
- 50 Darlington HG, kept at HQ for ambush & defence
- 30 Nankhukhi HG, acting as guides to ambush parties
- 41 Nankhukhi HG, acting as runners, spies, sentries
- 251 – 261 in **Total**

Mobile Levies, effecting 5 ambushes along the road – remainder resting in camp.

Reports continued to come in that Japanese are moving down the road.

Results

One ambush party that went just north of here fired on 20 Japanese who rested on the road just in front of them. They were heading down the road from Papun – just as they were getting up to move – they fired killing 15 and wounding five.

The other ambushes were unable to fire on the Japanese because they were walking in the jungle and were unable to shoot at them

Some of the Home Guard though fired on the Japanese on the Kuseik side and killed 5 with many more wounded.

Another of my Home Guard ambushes just north of Kyunbin Sakan (south-west of Papun) fired on a party of Japanese and killed 10.

Furthermore, one of my Hawkins mines blew up – but no reports as yet.

Total score (count) for the 17th – 30 Japanese known definitely killed, and 5 wounded.

Situation became very strange. Japanese appeared to have met at Nankhukhi about 1½ miles from here – they are all along the road in the village and in the jungle around the village. Some fired mortar shells in every direction – others killed the buffalo in the paddy fields. Then settled down to a feast – because at night Wataw returning with the elephant from Urekhi said he saw many fires in the paddy fields.

To take precautions I had double sentries all around the village – spies watching north and south of Nankhukhi to see which way they might decide to go. Reports continued to come in until late at night that parties of Japanese were moving up the road – to Nankhuhta and others that Japanese, over 2,000 in number, had moved down. They appear also to be clearing all the roadblocks and rebuilding the bridges.

At 1.00 a.m. a report came in to say a bus has arrived in Nankhuhta. Reports came in that 3-400 Japanese concentrating in area south of Papun from Metharoot[41] down to Kuseik.

On west bank (Papun) – south of Pagoda – Southwest of Bilin Road, reports of 3-400 Japanese in bamboo jungle. A B2[42] arrived from Ronnie.

18th May Friday

Sent two ambush parties off one right north and one south of Yakhekhi.[43] Remaining men sent to a place in jungle ATP said was a good place to go should the Japanese come up after me. I went up later in morning but found the place was too far away and it was a dreadful place.

Maw Gay's ambush returned – having killed 16 Japanese. They were ambushing south of Yakhekhi.

During the morning Japanese came up to my most outward sentry post and fired on them – I ordered all equipment to be put in the dump just near the village – I then sent up for the men – all the Nankhukhi Home Guard deserted me and left their posts. I urged the Headman of Nankhukhi to get as many of his men back as possible. By degrees they came back from their hiding places in the jungle. News came through that the Japanese were in Thahokhi[44] village, destroying the place.

Harry tried the B2 but heard nothing in the morning Sked. The Japanese are now in their thousands in this area – it will be getting too hot to stay here soon!

19th May Saturday

In the morning sent all the men with their equipment and ATP into the jungle to build a house, where I proposed to put my HQ and wireless. Everything on the alert – we had a few Nankhukhi Home Guard out on their sentry posts down the track to the road. Apart from myself there was only Harry and Darlington, Kya and Poking (my new cook).

At about 10:30 hrs a sentry rushed back to say a Japanese had been seen on the edge of the Paddy field – below the road. All the Home Guard again deserted sentry posts – we managed however to get them back into position. About ½ an hour later a shot rang out quite close by – we got our equipment on – Kya and Poking left with Pagoda for the dump. I forgot, little Morris was there too. Only Harry, Darlington and I remained in the village – we could not find a single Home Guard around the place so Harry and myself (I) went down to check on the sentries and find out the cause of the shot. We reached the lower village where the first sentry post was – nobody there. Harry was just a few yards in front of me – we went slowly down the track. Suddenly we ran slap bang into the Japanese. Harry fired and killed the first Japanese – the others took cover. That was our salvation. We both turned and ran like hell – calling Darlington on the way and made for the little store in the jungle. There, fortunately, were some Home Guard. We loaded them with my sacks and the medical supplies, and then cut through the jungle and joined ATP and his party. We then heard sounds of shooting coming up from our north side. We proceeded slowly up to our Tanya(hta)[45] retreat – the one I had thought bloody.

Once there we were sorting ourselves out – when a runner arrived by luck from Burne, with a message from Ronnie telling me to be careful and if it got too hot to go down to P_____ (town name not revealed due to sensitivity), the food dump.. I couldn't agree more! This area is now a closed chapter to my group. (Note: Trofimov began to think of getting his men away in small groups towards Critchley's location). I told the runner I would reward him if he would take another message back for me – but he disappeared in the night. Our only hope lies in the wireless. Report came in that the Japanese are in Urekhi – now they are on all sides – also at Hklerhko. (*Note: Trofimov's interview in the Imperial War Museum makes clear that he was firmly of the opinion that the Japanese had embarked on an operation to capture or kill him and as many as possible of his guerrilla force. He was advised that he had a price on his head*).[46]

20th May Sunday

Tried the wireless out – heard Base QSA 5 (signal strength code) but they did not hear us. Sent Wattaw off with 25 men to Urekhi to bring over some food stores. As soon as he arrives, I will move off – to Mawkhi – one of my men knows the way. We will have to be careful crossing the Nankhukhi – Bawbaw track. All morning nearby sounds of shooting coming from the village below – it is quite nerve racking. Last night a big explosion was heard – it may be one of my mines.

We now have to hope that my ambush party will be warned by the Yakhekhi people – and that he will make his way here by a different route – the shooting will give him a warning if he does head for Nankhukhi though. Now we must wait for Wattaw to return.

Today I will have been here exactly 3 months – 3 long months – so far it has not been too bad – but now with the rains, which come down in a drenching deluge every hour or so, and with the Japanese occupying every village – life is not too pleasant. However, "c'est la guerre"!

At 1.30 p.m. Wattaw arrived with the stores – but he could not find the 500 silver rupees we had put there for safety. So, I have sent a runner to warn the villagers to bring forth the money quickly. I will move tomorrow at dawn – one of my men knows the way and may God remain with us. All our nerves are tense – every time somebody shouts or a bamboo breaks, we all start – a rest and a change of atmosphere will do us all good!

Aung Win[47] and the missing ambush party re-joined us at the Tanya(hta) thank God! He saw two Japanese pass – thought the main body would follow, but none did. However, he laid his mines and the explosion we heard was indeed a motor bus, he went down the following day and saw where the car had been pushed off the road – one badly wounded man lay on the roadside crying and shrieking in agony.

Results then for this area are:

- 1 bus
- 1 bullock cart
- 77 Japanese killed by mobiles
- 6 known badly wounded by mobiles
- 15 known killed by Home Guard but two ambushes and almost daily jitter raids on Papun and Kuseik side – results not known.

21st May Monday

Set off from Tanya(hta) for Mawkhi – en route for Pawleha the dump. A dreadful trip up and down, the first part through the jungle with no track. On arrival, quite a pleasant little spot - rather out of the way – we were all drenched. On arrival two messages came in – also found medical supplies and explosives here. Also, a rumour that 1000 British troops are in Papun – this turned out to be a ridiculous story. Woolf gave his position as Polohta[48] and Burne's as Mekyonkyaung.[49] Ronnie is at Lakyokawthi[50] and Daniel Pan near Dehta. Now I can get in touch with each direct if necessary. Woolf and Burne have nabbed two Japanese vehicles.

A runner came with a message from Palatoo to say many Japanese at Mewaing, so we will have to organise another landing strip and DZ.

It is grand to rest and have a good cup of tea – after the excitement of the last few days. A letter is reported to be coming from the north for me – I am intrigued and will hang on a day or so to get it. Sent off a long letter to Ronnie explaining the whole situation to him. Should reach him soon.

22nd May Tuesday
Early start – arrived in Pawleha at 1 p.m. Pleasant spot in the valley – large flat paddy fields. Arranged for rice and food to be brought in – the people here are keen and want to fight. Sent off Ba Chit, whom we found here on our arrival, to look for a good hideout. Arranged an intelligence screen around me to warn me if any Japanese appeared down the track. We killed two pigs and had a good feast.

23rd May Wednesday
Sent off ATP to build a house for us in the jungle. Food came in – of every description. In the afternoon – one of my sentries fired a round by mistake – the whole village became a seething rush of people, picking up belongings and leaving. I had an awful job getting all my things out. When I eventually got a man to go and see what it was, they found it was my miserable sentry. Nevertheless, after Nankhukhi episode we take notice of these shots.

A letter arrived at 6 p.m. from Ronnie with orders to report with my men to him. Army has sent a long message to the effect that they are not going to be able to keep us supplied by air – they are making a dump at Toungoo with a few Dakotas there to take advantage of any spell of fine weather to make a sortie – they will only supply us with food and ammunition. Army says that they do not anticipate eliminating the Japanese from the Karen Mountains till the end of June or early July. They want the bulk of mobiles to become static and remainder to act as bodyguards to our HQ – they will try and supply such bodies with food but make no promises. They won't withdraw officers and troops as it might bring reprisals on to the locals.

God damn it another month or so of this filthy rain, mud, leeches and sleeping in filthy native huts!

I think this will be my last operation of this kind.

I made arrangements for our move – to be the day after tomorrow – calling in 5 elephants for transport of stores.

Mr. Churchill resigned today – what a changed place England will be when I eventually return.[51]

24th May Thursday

First thing in the morning I got a report in that some Japanese are now at Lenaw[52] right on the route Ronnie has told me to come. I must now take another route, which means going back into the bloody mountains – the ridge is about 2,000ft high. Sent off early in the morning most of my luggage – then began to feel restless – so decided to go off myself with my men and leave Wattaw behind to bring on the elephants. I left Darlington behind and ATP who is anxious to go and find out about his things. I gave to each 50 RS. I dismissed the new NCO who joined me at Nankhukhi and let him go home.

Arrived at Htitabluhta[53] about 3 p.m. and decided to spend night there and start the climbing – at the moment as I am writing this, I am feeling perfectly bloody – never in my life before have I felt so homesick and so lonely – my enthusiasm now that the rains have come has completely gone. I have to force myself to take any interest in anything these days. To be home with somebody to talk to of my own standing – Oh Hell!

25th May Friday

Set off early – for Mekyonoya across the hills – a very stiff walk it was indeed – but we arrived quite early there and over a good cup of tea, I felt refreshed.

The elephants with all the stores from Pawleha had arrived during the night and were now following up just behind. We arrived at Lakyo-kawthi[54] at 3 p.m. to find Ronnie comfortably established and Cuthbert Burne there too. They all admired Pagoda very much – noticing a great difference in him.

The plan was there and then unfolded – we were to make our dumps in this area and in the Southern Hills - then slowly move south into the lower hills, recc'ed the place and when the situation clarifies, operate against the Japanese on these plain tracks leading eastwards from the Bilin Road to the Kadaingti Road. But for the time being hold our fire and delude if possible, the NIPS.[55] It was nice seeing all the chaps again.

26th May Saturday

Spent a wonderfully lazy day in perfect happiness – my kit spread out all over the show. It is grand thing to sit in a river and let the cool water rush by the tired and nerve strained body – the men are enjoying it immensely. The village itself is not a good one – but the setting is very pleasant – a cool shady valley flanked by low hills. One hill to our east has our wireless and all its equipment on it – a regular little settlement with a magnificent view of the southern hills across the plains. We waited hoping to see the drop – as an Officer is coming in today. But we did not see it.

Captain OHN Pe is here looking after the "Q" side. Captain Woolf is still at Polohta doing a purely intelligence role.

Ronnie is now looking much fitter. There was a drop a few days ago which Ford took – who is further south – quite a useful drop. Drops are going to be scarce now – and if the Japanese close in on us, we may have to cut out the drops altogether or start night drops again. We shall see.

In the afternoon, I did a Sked with Van Kyte (Kett) testing out the BII, which worked perfectly – both got each other QSA. 5 (signal code strength).

In the evening Tony St. John arrived from India. He had been in Burma before – a young Lieutenant of 22 years old. Rather fat and pleasant – he brought in Ronnie's camera – bless him and some mail but still none for me. But a copy of Rupert Brooke from the 14th Army. I had asked Ronnie to mention it to Kaulback[56] he and (John) Hanbury-Tracey (Officer at ME 25) went on the trek together and afterwards wrote this book. He had written to Calcutta – had the book procured for me – and Tony brought it in. But God damn it, still no mail!

27th May Sunday

Another gorgeous lazy day. Find Tony is quite a pleasant chap to get on with – he wants to get fixed up with me for any subsequent operations.
Grand reading over all the old favourite poems. I am enjoying life. Pagoda and I had our photos taken.[57]

At 5 p.m. an Indian, who we suspect may be a spy, came into the camp area. I have tied him up and put him in Maw Gay's Section for custody until we can check up his story. I hope he is genuine – I loathe cold-blooded killing.

(Maj.) Cuthbert Burne set off south and will join up with us at Kyowaing[58] – Ronnie's party is moving off early and I will bring up the rear.

28th May Monday

Ronnie's party moved off early – followed by the stores on the elephants. Captain Ohn Pe, then my Platoon. We had a pleasant lazy walk down in the heat of the day.

In the village where we changed our porters, we had eggs and tea with a Christian family. The daughter had been raped by a Chinaman or someone 2 years ago, so now says the mother "it does not matter". I felt tempted to stay.

We passed on the way the Landing Strip – an excellent field with low ground on all sides – it has just been completed.

Arriving in Kyowaing we put up in Po Tin's large house. Po Tin is possibly the richest Karen – his house is huge and had such amenities as beds, chairs, tables, lavatories and water tanks; bullock carts, ponies etc.; four English speaking sons, one daughter and one niece, the latter I rather scared by following her onto the balcony. Here, I met (Capt.) Dennis Ford, (Capt.) Phil Williams and (Maj.) Burne – in fact, the whole party.

It was grand to rest on a camp bed. Po Tin provided a pillow and plates for our food.

29th May Tuesday

Conference on what is to be put in all the dumps. And drawing of clothes for immediate use. Then I had some handkerchiefs made by the daughter. For lunch, I had roast chicken, mangoes, and milk (fresh). Before lunch one of Po Tin's relatives operated on my finger and cut open the nail – puss oozed out and then withdrew the splinter that had been there for over a month.

A Lysander came in during the morning – St. John took a photo of my Platoon all together, Morris and Pagoda complete. Then proceeded to go up to the Lysander strip.

Message came in from Calcutta saying: "regret serious error regarding Trofimov's mail, in future will send it through Ash." They have obviously been sending it to Hyena. But why, whoever has been receiving it – has not reported the matter. I cannot think – at least I can. So now I may get some mail in.

Yesterday, I had a bath in the tub – it was heavenly!

3.30 p.m. I was talking to the daughter and sons of the house. I should say at this point that his sons are fine looking boys, very well educated. The daughter is a lady – she speaks no English but her manners, her dress, her deference to us is lovely to watch. Extraordinary that she had reached 30 years of age and still unmarried.

Anyhow to resume – at 3.30 p.m. Ronnie called me – (to say) a spy, a Burman, had come into the camp. I was to execute him – I selected Maw Gay's Section, we took him out into the woods and tied him to a tree. Then I explained to my boys why we had to kill him and that the reason so many of us were shooting was that nobody would know who had killed him. I lined them up – we all aimed – fired – they got nervous and kept on firing – eventually they stopped firing. We buried him with the cartridges.

Pagoda is fast growing into a fat and strong dog – some people think he is a cross between a high breed Japanese dog and a Shan dog – I hope so.

The daughter is making me a silk shirt – from one of the white nylon parachutes.

Rupert Brooke is giving me intense enjoyment – I feel I can recapture the former atmosphere: "and laughter learnt from friends; and gentleness, in hearts of peace, under an English heaven."[59]

30th May Wednesday

Lazy day – absolutely grand, relaxing, and doing nothing in comparatively comfortable surroundings. The family are quite charming – the daughter is making me a set of pyjamas out of white silk parachutes. My men are all enjoying themselves very much – the rest is doing them all the good in the world.

We had the Platoon photographed in the morning and in the morning, St. John went up to see the Lysander in, so he sent off the film. Ronnie sent off a wire to Ash telling them he wanted to send me off on leave and that, if they agreed, would they send Lysander in soonest.

31st May Thursday

Went off with the Platoon early in the morning to the aerodrome and reorganised Havildar Wilson's[60] layout. Spent the rest of the day just lazing around.

Ronnie went off in the evening to shoot Sambar (deer) on an elephant – he was unsuccessful.

Reply from Ash re my leave: "Definitely agree. Lysander coming on 2nd." Immediately I became inundated with letters and lists of personal requirements.

1st June Friday

Went off to DZ – plane came in at 11 p.m. about 200ft and dropped 3 bags of salt – all the parachutes came out – so he came around again at about 150ft and dropped containers and everything free – all the 4 containers with compo tins in were smashed – we had to issue the stuff out there and then.

Returned in absolutely ghastly heat.

2nd June Saturday

It had rained absolutely all night. In the morning, the sky was still grey and drizzly. I doubted that the Lysander would come to evacuate me. However, my men went up and I set off for the strip on an elephant. Williams was there too. The ground was actually hard enough for it to come in – it did at about 10 p.m. Once it had landed it turned and got stuck in the mud and it was one hell of a job to get the thing out.

Pagoda was terrified throughout the trip. We went to the Mewaing strip, circled around three times but saw nothing so came on to Rangoon, where I was met and taken straight to 136 HQ, where I found Major King, Major Kaulback and a Major Harrington. Everyone was very friendly and helpful. They fixed me up with the dentist and I was dealt with that afternoon. They promised to fix my denture the next day at 4 p.m., which they actually did.

I spent the rest of the day discussing the situation – I was scheduled to leave for Calcutta on the 4th.

3rd June Sunday

Forgot to mention found a whole batch of letters waiting for me from Yvonne and Marie and Joan Dixon. Yvonne's last letter was one saying she thought there could be nothing more between us after having seen the relationship that exists between Tommy and Marie.[61] 'Quelle Guerre!'

Went round to Army HQ and was interrogated by … (unreadable) and gave him the complete picture. Was introduced to BGS the new one, Brigadier Armstrong. He was perfectly charming – said "enjoy your leave – yours is a 24-hour job and you deserve it." I thought that was very nicely put.

In the afternoon, I managed to get a complete belt of American equipment for Ronnie and myself. So, that is something achieved at any rate.

Heard in the evening, plane was cancelled until the 6th. Took a jeep out for the first time in my life – and found it quite an interesting experience. Lucas arrived – evacuated by Lysander to discuss situation re his position.

4th June Monday

Went up to the aerodrome and sat around in the hopes that a plane would come along, and I could hitch to Calcutta. None did. Craster[62] stayed in the hope of getting a plane to take him near to Calcutta. It looks as if I shall have to wait till the 6th. Damn it!

Had a long chat with Lucas re his new policy. BGS stated any party that was in such close proximity to the Japanese troops that they might be nullified if they continued with offensive action during these rains was to lie low until the time was ripe for action.

[1] BFO – Beat Frequency Oscillator used to create an audio signal from morse telegraphy in order to make it audible.

[2] Burma Country Section.

[3] PT physical training.

[4] Lokhi – 18° 6' 0" North, 97° 7' 0" East.

[5] Kyaukkyi – 18.3282° North, 96.7735° East.

[6] Shwe Ma – the Karen cook. Reference to a Shwe Mya in the Platoon Lists – in 'B' Platoon.

[7] IO Intelligence Officer Captain Ivan Justin Woolf – served Merchant Navy 1942-44. Joined SOE 1944 and saw service in France before transferring to the Far East. March 1945 parachuted into Burma as part of Operation Character (Mongoose) *see* https://soeinburma.com/the-men-of-soe-burma/ (accessed 16th February 2022)

[8] Signals Officer Lieutenant. Van Kett – Anglo-Burman radio operator deployed 3rd April 1945 on Operation Character (Mongoose) *see* https://soeinburma.com/the-men-of-soe-burma/ (accessed 16th February 2022)

[9] Lt. Colonel Hugh Warton Howell – Joined the army in 1940 (King George V's Own Lancers) and SOE in 1944. Put in command of Operation Character (Hyena). – *See* TNA: HS 9/752/5 for his SOE personnel file.

[10] Kadaingti – 17° 37' 0" N, 97° 32' 0" E.

[11] Captain John Philip Williams, British Army 1939-43 (Welsh Guards or Welsh Regiment) – Served with Operation Character (1/5/45). *See* TNA: HS 9/1598/1 for his SOE personnel file.

[12] Major Cuthbert Burne – dropped into Burma as part of Operation Character (Mongoose) on 9th April 1945, *see* https://soeinburma.com/the-men-of-soe-burma/ (accessed 16th February 1945). *See also* TNA: HS 9/239/3

[13] Metkyihta – 17° 56' 0" N, 97° 15' 0" E.

[14] Khauchi – 18° 3' 0" N, 97° 3' 0" E.

[15] Leklede – 17° 57' 51" N, 97° 10' 2" E

[16] Nankhukhi – 17° 55' 0" N, 97° 22' 0" E

[17] Dubaw – 17° 55' 0" N, 97° 13' 0" E

[18] Sergeant Robert Glyn Loosmore (1923-2007), Croix de Guerre and Military Medal, served Royal Armoured Corps, SOE Jed W/T operator parachuted into the Haute-Vienne, 11 July 1944. Effectively became team leader when the two officers of his group were injured on landing. Subsequently assigned to Mongoose Blue. *See* TNA: WO 373/98/801for the citation for his MC and HS 9/939/2 for his SOE personnel file. RG Loosmore interview, Imperial War Museum, 16th March 1998. Catalogue Number 17949, https://www.iwm.org.uk/collections/item/object/80019746 (accessed 8th January 2022).

19 ATP – assumed to mean initials from representative of the 14th Army with instruction.

20 Yunzalin River, a tributary of the Salween River.

21 Pyinmana – 19° 44' 17" N 96° 12' 26" E.

22 Citation for Maj. Turrall's DSO in 1945 reads: 'This officer, who, at the age of 54, commanded the original 'blind' parachute jump of Force 136 personnel to Pyagawpo on 25th February 1945, organised the reception of operations Otter and Ferret a few nights later in spite of Japanese forces having arrived in the area from PAPUN. He also organised and trained several hundred Levies who eventually became the hard core of Operation Hyena. On 15th April 1945, he personally led the successful attack on Kyaukkyi which resulted in enemy supplies, spare arms and a W/T set being destroyed. Later he operated in the area East of Kyaukkyi and with his Levies killed over 500 Japanese and gave intelligence for air strikes and artillery which resulted in 924 estimated enemy casualties. For his outstanding powers of leadership and great gallantry shown on numerous occasions I recommend very strongly that this officer be awarded the Distinguished Service Order.' https://www.tracesofwar.com/persons/72470/Turrall-Rupert-Guy.htm (accessed 16th February 2022).

23 Havildar Saw Wilson Thet – Burma Army Service Corps 1942, later joined Force 136 and was deployed to Character (Mongoose) April 1945.

24 'Compo' or Composite Rations.

25 Tahulaw – 17° 52' 10" N 97° 17' 36" E.

26 Kaukpok – 18° 6' 0" N, 97° 30' 0" E.

27 AEW [AAE] Trofimov interview, reel 5, Imperial War Museum, 24th April 1992. Catalogue Number 11760, https://www.iwm.org.uk/collections/item/object/80011503 (accessed 12th October 2021).

28 The salām, (meaning peace') has become a religious salutation for Muslims worldwide when greeting each other, though its use as a greeting pre-dates Islam.

29 Captain Saw Ohn Pe Joined SOE in April 1945 and was assigned to Character (Mongoose) as part of Critchley's team.

30 Major Ba Chit – With SOE since 1942, joining SIS in late 1944, on 9th April 1945 he parachuted into support Character (Hyena).

31 Mahtaw – 17° 54' 0" N., 97° 25' 0" E.

32 Cordtex – type of detonating cord.

33 SEAC – South East Area Command.

34 Winpa – 17° 5' 0" N, 97° 20' 0" E.

35 Mebawkhi – 17° 37' 0" N, 97° 27' 0" E.

36 Bwado – 17° 58' 0" N, 97° 36' 0" E.

37 Lagunbyo – 17° 43' 0" N, 97° 18' 0" E.

38 Lower Natkyi – 17° 27' 0" N, 97° 15' 0" E.

39 Urekhi – 17°58'0" N, 97°22'60" E.

40 Arthur Ta Bi – included on Expenses Sheet for Captain A Trofimov's Platoon – Trofimov Archive.

41 Metharoot – 18° 2' 0" N, 97° 26' 0" E.

42 Type 3 MkII.B2 – British WWII clandestine radio set.

43 Yakhekhi – 17° 52' 0" N, 97° 22' 0" E.

44 Thahokhi – 17° 57' 0" N, 97° 22' 0" E.

45 Tanyahta – 17° 56' 0" N, 97° 21' 0" E.

46 AEW [AAE] Trofimov interview, reel 5, Imperial War Museum, 24th April 1992. Catalogue Number 11760, https://www.iwm.org.uk/collections/item/object/80011503 (accessed 12th October 2021).

47 Aug Winn – included in B Platoon Lists – Trofimov Archive.

48 Polohta – 17° 43' 0" N, 97° 20' 0" E.

49 Mekyonkyaung – 17° 38' 26" N, 97° 18' 18" E.

50 Lakyokawthi – 17° 36' 0" North, 97° 25' 0" E.

51 In the aftermath of the defeat of Germany the Labour Party declined Churchill's offer to continue the Coalition Government thereby initiating a need for a general election. In the ensuing election the Labour Party won 393 seats to the Conservative Party's 189.

52 Lenaw – 17° 38' 0" N, 97° 29' 0" E.

53 Htitabluhta – 17° 21' 0" N, 97° 54' 0" E.

54 Lakyokawthi – 17° 36' 0" N, 97° 25' 0" E.

55 Short for Nippon. Japanese name for Japan.

56 John Hanbury-Tracy, *Black River of Tibet* (London: The Travel Book Club, 1938), by Ronald Kaulback, *Salween: The Black River of Tibet* (London, Fredrick Muller, 1938).

57 Amongst Trofimov's photograph collection is one of him and Pagoda which is presumably the result of this moment.

58 Kyowaing – 17° 27' 0" North, 97° 25' 0" East.

59 Rupert Brooke – *The Soldier* (1915).

60 Havildar Saw Wilson Thet – Burma Army Service Corps 1942, later joined Force 136 and was deployed to Character (Mongoose) April 1945.

[61] Marie Trofimov (nee Woodcock, 1901-1982) – Capt. Trofimov's mother in England, who had married Edgar Morton in 1919, giving birth to AAE Morton in 1921. Edgar and Marie Morton went their separate ways sometime thereafter with Marie marrying MV Trofimov (1884-1948) in 1925. At some point later MV Trofimov and Marie went their separate ways, with Marie very much leading her own life. Yvonne had been AAE Trofimov's girlfriend in England.

[62] Captain Oswin Edmund Craster (1916-2006) – Served with Oxfordshire and Buckinghamshire Light Infantry 1939-43, joined SOE 1943, Jedburgh 1944, Force 136 1945. OE Craster interview, reels 1-4, Imperial War Museum, 6th July 1992. Catalogue Number 12612, https://www.iwm.org.uk/collections/item/object/80012344 (accessed 23rd January 2022).

Diary III

2nd June Saturday (*overlaps with Diary II and there appears to be some confusion over Dates/Days*)

Set off in the morning on an elephant for the landing strip. Harry took all 'B' Platoon up earlier on. It had been raining all the previous day and night and I was frankly worried as to the state of the ground. On arrival, there the clouds began to clear. At 10 a.m. the Lysander appeared and landed. Phil Williams was with me on the ground at the time and we both agreed to share the Court Martial if the plane could not take off again. Of course, the plane would have to go and get bogged up – it took hundreds of Karens to push the thing out!

However, we embarked – Pagoda and self – having told the pilot to go to Mewaing to drop Milner his mail – It was fascinating flying over the countryside with millions of Japanese all around below us. We reached Mewaing – flying over at about 100ft – 2 or 3 times, not a sign of anything. Pilot said over the intercom "*don't like the look of this place*", so we set off for Rangoon. Pagoda terrified of all the noise and buried his head between my chest and arm, inside my shirt.

Arrived Rangoon at about 11.30 a.m. Met by Guy Aubrey, who took me straight down to the office in his jeep. There we met Major King, Major Ronnie Kaulbeck and Major Harrington. Was informed no planes leaving for Calcutta till the 4th.

That afternoon (I) went to dentist and got my tooth repaired immediately and my denture they promised for the following day. Returned to the mess – a pleasant little villa on the edge of Lake Victoria.

Here I met Captain Craster, who had just been overrun and was awaiting a trip up to Calcutta. We talked idly for hours.

3rd June Sunday

The next day was spent in interviews with Maj. King – the Officer who does the actual information for army in liaison with Force 136. I was introduced to the Brigadier General Staff Armstrong – a charming individual who had some very considerate words to say. I managed to wangle some American equipment out of the Americans – complete belt equipment.

I presented our situation in the field to Maj. King pointing out that if they wanted us to continue with offensive action, they must be prepared to have us out of action within a month. We are surrounded by garrison static troops, who patrol and picket both the Bilin and Kadaingti roads – it is quite impossible to effect an ambush on either road.

At Kamamaung[1] there are 3,000 permanently. At Lagunbyo another 1,300 – at every important place there is about 2-300 picketed troops.

I met Lucas up there plus beard – his situation is critical – he is absolutely surrounded – the BGS gave him the following directives that any troops who by continuing with offensive action would get themselves cut up hopelessly and any further usefulness nullified. Such troops were to "lei quiet" *(lay quiet)* and adopt a purely intelligence role and await such time as army began to move across the Sittang. This rather indicated that King had not consulted anyone "au sujet" *(on the subject)* of our situation.

In the evening, I drove a jeep up to the dentist – and collected my denture.

4th June Monday

The ferry plane was cancelled so Craster and I went up and sat on the aerodrome in the hope of jumping a plane. At 12 p.m. I gave up – Craster remained and as luck would have it a plane came in half an hour later bound for Calcutta.

5th June Tuesday
Went up to the aerodrome at about 1.30 p.m. got a seat on the mail train for Calcutta. Arriving in Calcutta at 6.30 p.m.

Went to the office where I sent for Leslie Young who arrived and took me on to the mess close by at 207. Here I met Lt. Colonel 'Bing' Crosby[2] – Ben Hunter out on 28 days their area not being overrun as yet.

Also, met Matthew Hodgart[3] – the Major in charge of Character Operations – a sincere hard-working conscientious person – whom I liked immediately.

6th June Wednesday
Arranged through Alan Lockhart to stay at George Gemmel's home at 41 Ironside Road, Ballygunge, Calcutta. I moved in there during the morning – a lovely house with plenty of fans and large cool rooms. My room had a balcony room as my bedroom, then a large room, and a bathroom right at the end.

The heat in Calcutta was absolutely unbearable – I need two baths a day and a complete change of clothing. Every time you move you get soaked in perspiration. At lunch, I took a girl out – and that evening took her to the 300 club, where we danced and dined very pleasantly.

7th June Thursday
Interviewed "Q" Ops[4] – rubbed them up the right way – they got interested in what I had to say about free drops – types of containers that were unsuitable etc. Anyhow they drew up a long list of requirements for us and said they would try and get me a camera. I then interviewed the medical people – and drew up a list of stuff from them to take with me. I had a long conference with (Maj.) Hodgart – put him in the picture again.

That lunchtime I met the same girl and took her out for lunch. First, we gate crashed the Saturday Club where we had a bathe. Then rushed down to the Great Eastern Hotel for lunch.

George Gemmel, with whom I am staying – is a small jolly person – full of fun and drink – absolutely no affectation about him – "you do just as you wish here" – "drink and eat what you want." His wife Helen was away in the hills and I rather gather George was making hay while the sun shines!

William Phillyos – 'Phil' – a Major was another guest lodger – awaiting the boat back to England pending his discharge – a charming genial fellow – always ready to laugh at anything. That evening I went to the 300 Club – tipped Martin the headwaiter this time I was with an unattractive but amusing partner.

8th June Friday

Was in the office at about 11 a.m. – suddenly in walked a gorgeous girl – I turned (a)round to Matthew and said "By Jove that's a smashing girl" – the nicest girl I have seen here as yet.

I walked out met Hanbury Tracey – suddenly she passed me – I dived for her and asked her to come and have lunch with me. She said she would – we were to be a party – but at 12.30 a.m. the party thank God did not materialise – we went together to the Great Eastern Hotel and had lunch. Her name was Brenda …,[5] who's 24 years old with blonde mousy hair, two of the loveliest brown eyes, a woodcock nose, a lovely chin, and a lovely figure. Altogether I was capsized immediately. I fell like a log and told her so.

She was to go to the dentist that afternoon, but we cancelled it and instead went and bought food for a picnic party she was going to that night. We ate watermelons in the market then tea at Flury's. Then a brilliant idea – we went out to Tollygunge and bathed at 7 p.m. She was upset because of the party – wanted to stay with me. We arranged to meet again outside her mess at 11 p.m. – she said she would "get there by hook or by crook".

I left her and spent the evening at George's just around the corner from the mess.

At 11 p.m. sharp she was there. We went around to the park and lay happily in each other's arms. I possessed her that night – it was glorious; we are so ideally suited to one another.

I knew then I had fallen in love with her. It was at this point she told me she had been married and had lost her husband with whom she was madly in love, in Normandy in September – she had been married 3 years, had a daughter of 2 (who) lived with her mother-in-law.

9th June Saturday

Feeling gloriously happy. Had lunch with Brenda. It was then I asked her if she was the girl Sgt John had said he was going to marry. She laughed; said she knew him – he had pestered the very life out of her. So, that settled that. We went to the 300 Club that evening and finished up in each other's arms.

God! I know now what it is to love again.

NB. I forgot to mention that in Rangoon they had all my mail – it had been dropped to Lt. Colonel Howell[6] – this greatly delayed – one[7] of the letters from Yvonne – her last – stated she had been to a party at the flat and had stayed the night with one of the other people in the block – in the morning had taken tea into mother and found her evidently with Tommy – she deplores such a state of affairs and says she will discontinue to write – I was frankly amused at the little hypocrite!

So now I have carte blanche to do as I choose!

10th June Sunday

We both met at 8.30 a.m. and went out to Tollygunge with George Gemmel and some friends. He really is a smashing fellow – full of friendliness and kind-hearted. I like him immensely.

After breakfast, we went and sat by a little lake – then we went and bathed together. Oh! It was such fun – after the bathing we lay outside on the lawn together.

At 12.30 p.m., we returned to George's home and waited for them to return for lunch.

After lunch, everyone went to bed, so we followed suit – we went and lay on my bed together – naked in each other's arms – the naughtiness of it gave it just that little extra zest. Then I bathed her, and she bathed me – it was such heaven.

She went and changed – then we foregathered at the house and all went off – to the flicks where we saw *"Suspect"*, which was rather good – with Charles Laughton. We returned had dinner, then the rest of the party dissolved – Brenda and I remained on the couch – the lights turned off – the fans caressing our naked bodies – once again we forgot all else in the land of complete oblivion.

We have discovered that we both love each other – what heaven. We are both very alike. We both carry around a Rupert Brooke – we both adore dogs – Brenda adores Pagoda – who is very fond of her – she used to keep kennels before the war.

We like riding in taxis sitting right upon the canopy – neither of us gives a damn about anyone or anything.

11th June Monday

Back to work for Brenda – we met for lunch and arranged to go to the 300 Club. We have eyes only for each other – we have given so much to each other – that we are inextricably a part of one another. God! I love her. I think together we could have immense fun.

We lunched together and that evening met at the 300 Club – afterwards we lay on the lawn – I brought down a blanket and a sheet – Pagoda was intrigued.

12th June Tuesday

We had arranged to spend the afternoon off together. We had lunch then did some shopping – all afternoon I was feeling flat because I had booked a seat on the plane for Rangoon for the following day. At 4 p.m. we rang up and found that I was not going – thrilled to bits. There and then we decided to go out to Tollygunge and bathe. We did – we stayed on the lawn afterwards. Brenda's closeness sending me almost crazy with desire. She has a wonderful womanly body. She is the best companion I have ever had – as the French would say she is "*Sympathique jusqu'au bout des doigts*" (sympathetic to the fingertips).

At about 7.30 p.m. we were both ravenous – we decided to go to a Chinese restaurant. We did. We ate so much we felt sick and could hardly leave the place.

We went back to the house and relaxed there, and then we decided to go quite mad. Ritchie Gardner (Lt. Col) my BCS boss was back and staying in the same house – he made one or two rather caustic remarks in his rather dry Scotch humour. Both of us (Brenda and I) went down to a low dive called the Porta Rico Club – where we danced till late. Then returned and lay in each other's arms in the park.

13th June Wednesday

Had lunch together – then Phil, Diane, Brenda and I went to the 300 Club, where various people tried to get off – unsuccessfully – with Brenda.

Phil tactfully took Diane home and left Brenda and myself on the divan at the house.

14th June Thursday

Met for lunch – acquired from "Q" ops. A Kodak 35 mm camera, a beauty!

We had lunch at some quiet place – then Brenda was supposed to be going to the dentist – we went there as a gesture – then took the taxi on to Tollygunge – where we waited till 4 p.m. Rang up – once again **not** leaving on the following day. Happily, we bathed – then went to some wretched restaurant – then we had decided to act on impulse – we went to see *Arsenic and Old Lace* at the Elite cinema. We had to sit in the 'Gods' and consequently got bitten to death. We then went back to the house where I suddenly began to get ghastly pains in my stomach and started violent diarrhoea. I tried to see Brenda home, but I felt too ill. That night I had to wake up the whole household, I lay writhing on my bed in agony. George put me to sleep.

15th June Friday
Doctor came and gave me 14-sulphur guanidine straight off and then 7 every 4 hours – quite a dose!

Brenda came to house for lunch. In the evening, she came and sat and talked with me. I went (a)round to their mess and had a light dinner. I was sad I was to leave her the following day. We spent that last night together in each other's arms – it was perfect.

16th June Saturday
At 3.30 a.m., the car came – I called round for Brenda – we went off to the aerodrome – we were sweating it out, whether we would get Pagoda on or not. We had lunch on the aerodrome – they said they would put all my kit on as someone was missing. I arrived together with Pagoda at Rangoon at lunchtime. Met Freddie Milner and Hugo Hood.

17th June Sunday
I left Rangoon in a Lysander at 8 o'clock and arrived at Kyowaing (maps, page 258, caption 27) at about 9 o'clock. Ronnie was there together with 'Giraffe' and 'Cow' parties who being evacuated.[8]
Ronnie stayed in the field and caught the 3rd aircraft out and went to Rangoon. He is not looking well – and has a dreadful cold.

Sent message off via Woolf to Cuthbert at HQ asking him to send on Kya with all my things.

18th June Monday
Rained all day – not feeling well – lousy diarrhoea again. Kya didn't arrive. Ford here also.

19th June Tuesday
Feeling really ill – Dennis Ford[9] went up and brought Ronnie in all right.

During the afternoon, to my relief Kya arrived – looking very fit and very well.

In the evening Ronnie enfolded his plan – which was what I had anticipated; that Ronnie, myself, would go across to Milner – leaving Dennis behind here, who would adopt a purely intelligence role. We might still be able to (a)effect a spot of offensive action on two tracks.

20th June Wednesday
Had a lousy night. Dosed myself with sulphur guanidine in the morning. Took it very easy all day long.

21st June Thursday
Set off in the morning with minimum of luggage – all surplus luggage going to the strip to be ferried across.

We went light to Lakyokawthi,[10] where we met up with Ronnie who had gone on with an elephant. He is very ill with this chest cold of his.

Woolf walked up with me – poor chap is feeling disgruntled with his role of operator to the Colonel. It is rather pleasant to rattle on in French with him – he used to be in SOE (Jed) and went to France as an agent.

22nd June Friday
I had an early start for Lakyoko (most likely Lakyokawthi) arriving there within one hour.

I passed a very poisonous snake – which struck at Kya but thank god it missed him.

Message came through in the evening from Ronnie to effect that HQ had been out of touch with Milner for 2 days, so we will not be able to move across until we hear something definite.

In the meantime, I am spending the time getting clothing and food distributed out to the men. Woolf is still with me.

23rd June Saturday

Jemadar Thadin's Platoon joined us in the afternoon. A very quiet day. No incidents whatsoever.

24th June Sunday

HQ is still out of touch with Milner. HQ were not able to evacuate from Htilawthihta[11] as the pilot said the strip was too short.

So, (Maj.) Cuthbert Burne and party are now on their way down to Kyowaing from where they will be ferried as early as possible to Milner's side.

25th June Monday

Early start – left Lakyoko (Lakyokawthi) with my Platoon, Woolf and the wireless.

Dreadful march – in one place we went down a rocky mountainside riverbed – dreadfully slippery.

We reached Polohta[12] at 3 p.m. tired, wet and very hungry.

Since last night I have had a very bad throat. Ronnie joined us later in the evening.

Woolf did the evening Sked – message from Army saying that Milner has tipped all his batteries into a river and had therefore not been able to come up on the air.

26th June Tuesday

Preparing to move tomorrow. Major Burne's Platoon plus Indians arrived in the evening.

St. John has been making a complete fool of himself telling everybody he intends to marry Brenda – also airing himself telling everyone what a jolly fine fellow he is. Ronnie dislikes him.

27th June Wednesday

Early start – we went plodding on in the rain. All three of us feeling ill. Ronnie, Woolf and me. Arrived at Htinade[13] where we had lunch. Then we crossed the Bilin Road '*en masse*'. One of Milner's Jemadars with two sections had met us at Htinade to lead us down and across river. We reached the Bilin River at about 3 p.m. Hoping to see 10 rafts, there were 3 long, narrow, precarious bamboo rafts. It took till 5 p.m. to get my Platoon across.

I then set off on a hellish walk, in pitch black night to Walaw,[14] which I reached at 9 p.m. The Platoon did not come in together. Poor Ronnie and Woolf did not turn up until midnight – tired, wet, and hungry.

And, the 12th Army has gone into winter training quarters.

28th June Thursday

Set off for Mewaing – arriving on the aerodrome just as the plane took off. It had been bogged up since the day before. This means it will have to have a bamboo runway made.

St. John was there. I treated him coldly – so did Ronnie. St. John got worried and asked Woolf what was the matter. I then took my Platoon and Woolf up to Shweh(ti). The Colonel left with Burne's platoon and the Indians for Methako (Metakho).[15] Ronnie gave me a new area and Woolf to keep me company. A very good set up indeed.

29th June Friday

Set off to HQ for my orders. Reached the Mewaing river and found the rafts could not cross as the river had risen and the current was too strong. Tried to swim – impossible.

Returned to camp feeling very ill.

Discharged 15 men who were medically unfit and who had had enough. Several more wanted their discharge – but I had to be firm.

I can quite see their point of view. They joined thinking it was only for a few months. They trained and fought well, and then suddenly the 14th Army announced it was not going to cross the Sittang until after the monsoons. A blow for them and us.

During these rains, the Karens go down like flies with malaria and dysentery.

30th June Saturday

Set off for Metakho after having verified that I could cross the Mewaing. Reached the river and found Ted Bourne was ferrying a platoon across with St. John to go and make the strip.

Reached the camp – very well organised. Hospital, stables, stores, etc. All men employed on building further quarters. The men look smart too.

Ronnie gave me my orders. I am to proceed to an area just east of Mekahta[16] and to organise an intelligence screen. Get to know the main track, Schwegyin-Mekhata. Find good spots on which to ambush the Japanese as they come through.

Returned to camp in the evening. Harry came and asked for his discharge. He has been drinking – so had Gte, the new Havildar Major – and the two new Havildars.

Apparently, they had been discussing the situation relative to promotion. Certain privates had been made Jemadars, whilst latecomers of fairly high NCO ranks in ex-Burma Rifles were supposed to say 'Sir' to them. A very delicate situation. No amount of reasoning would make him see sense.

I solved the situation on the following morning by saying that I would put the matter up to the Colonel and leave it at that. Harry, slightly soberer, agreed.

In the afternoon, I sent for St. John. I told him the whole situation re: Brenda and self. He seemed dreadfully upset. Said he thought he was engaged to her. St. John strikes me as being very young and immature for his 21 years. I had reason to tell him off good and proper about some of his remarks to Woolf about the better smartness of Bourne's men to mine – the fool! I cannot understand how a mere child could imagine that a mature woman could wish to marry him. But women are strange creatures. There is no accounting for their idiosyncrasies. She may be trying to have a good time with the man – '*sur place*'. This I simply could not believe – she could not have acted the emotion that she put into those 7 days. She could not have given so much of herself to me for a mere flirtation. My own interpretation of the situation is that St. John with his pathetic youthfulness, his naïve manner – had had a smile and a kiss and imagined the world was his.

1st July Sunday

Early start – 4 elephants to carry stores and NCO's kit. All the NCO's were hopelessly drunk. It was difficult at first, but by the time we reached Plawkhi[17] we had the situation solved for us. The Colonel sent a wire telling me to make Harry a Jemadar. I did. Harry hesitated, but I gave him no time in which to think.

2nd July Monday

The worst walk I have ever done. Heartless, exhausting, slogging, one mountain after another. There are times on these mountain marches when I lose all my *'sang-froid'* and long for death as a release from all this ghastly toiling and sweating.

When we eventually did reach Metklekhi[18] it was pleasant to find a friendly welcome from a priest who placed his church at our disposal.

I think I shall make this my rear HQ and make a store near here. A good place for wireless too.

A Pungyi is a useful man to have – his connections cover and in this instance, several of the villagers of my area.

3rd July Tuesday

Stayed in bed all day with a lousy cold – head and chest absolutely made up.

Started the men onto building a hospital. The men started drilling. I am out to make first-class soldiers out of them.

This place is a healthy spot – right up on the top of a mountain, with a good parade ground; a clean newly-built Pungyi Kyaung (church). I had a partition made to give Woolf and myself some privacy.

4th July Wednesday

Hospital finished – moved sick men in. Message came in from Ronnie telling us to hold back and stuff ourselves with K.

Because Lucas had apparently got worried about my conducting offensive action in this area, he thinks with the present dispositions of the Japanese that should I start something, positions will become untenable.

Japanese dispositions at present are:

Bilin One battalion
Danyungon One battalion
Mepok 500 Japanese
Melaung 500 Japanese
Wingalon 1000 Japanese
Winkadeik 1000 Japanese
Natkyi Large force
Winamuang 300 Japanese
Kinmunsakan 1000 Japanese
Shwegyin Surrounded to the north and east.

57,000 Japanese still in Burma – of which 12,000 are still west of the Mandalay – Rangoon line. And, we have a **VICTORY PARADE!**

5th July Thursday
Weather is dreadful – rains all day long and every day. Thank God – for the time being at any rate – that we have a good roof over our heads.

6th July Friday
Yet another message telling me not to take any offensive action.

Woolf's finger very bad – septic.

Apart from the incessant rain it is bloody cold here now.

7th July Saturday
We have now read all our reading material – sitting here with nothing to do. Rain pouring down all day long outside.

I have set about making our quarters as comfortable as possible. We each have a bed, a couple of tables, and deck chairs.

Food is a problem. There are no vegetables and very few chickens so one has to rely on Compo almost entirely.

8th July Sunday
My cold is definitely improving. Sent off a message asking whether Ronnie wants me to be completely quiet pro tem.

Store in jungle now built.

Pagoda very ill – all day long.

9th July Monday
Morning Sked – telling us to lie back very quiet. Also, message saying our baggage is on its way up. I hope there is a steam generator with it as we have broken the hand generator. Mail too – God! What a heavenly thought.

Woolf is going off on leave as soon as Ronnie gets another Officer. What he means by this I really cannot imagine. I hope I am not being saddled with an Officer who is not to my liking. I should have to make him so dreadfully uncomfortable. We shall see.

Moved all my stores to the dump – endeavouring to make myself as comfortable as possible for whatever length of time I am to be here.

10th July Tuesday

Baggage arrived in the morning with loads of books, mail, compo, 6 loaves of bread, steam generator, etc.

Much of mail was from Yvonne and Joan Dixon – backdated stuff. I did not bother to read them. But, from Brenda, there were some heavenly letters, books, and magazines.

Re: St. John – she told me to put an end to any false impressions that might have been created. And consider the matter closed henceforth. Brenda has completely won my heart. Her beautiful letters, one thing for certain it is good for his morale! written so nicely – warm and alive. She is in love with me. Oh, God! – *The heaven of it all.*

A message came in to send Woolf down to Mewaing – plane coming in on the 13th to take him to Rangoon. We set about writing loads of letters – and I compiled a long list of my requirements.

I have asked Brenda to arrange our leave and when I next see her to wear my ring.

I gave a tin of compo to Harry. Training is going on in full swing. The men seem to like it. They are keeping fit and looking much smarter these days.

11th July Wednesday

Woolf left in the morning. Started men onto transferring to a better place in the jungle.

Found myself feeling rather flat now that I am on my own again. No rush of letters to get on with.

That evening a soldier, who had brought up some medicine – for throats – and two bottles of rum, said two Burmese (reputed to be Japanese spies) were in the next village at Mepawkhi (Meponkhi).[19]

I sent Jemadar off with a section to bring them both in. He brought them back at 4 a.m. and tied them up.

12th July Thursday

Questioned prisoners – only one turned out to be a Burman. Eventually satisfied myself they were innocent but decided to detain the Burman whilst I sent the other one off to Clarke at Mekadikhi.[20] However, this was not necessary as at lunchtime Lucas, with his two sergeants, Shepherd and Usher all appeared.

That afternoon Shepherd, with some help, drank two of my bottles of rum. His behaviour was intolerable. I will certainly treat the whole party coolly on future occasions. There appears to be absolutely **no**, repeat **no**, control over his subordinates. I was glad to rid myself of them the following day.

13th July Friday

Lucas' party set off early. I settled down to another quiet day. The situation as I see it is as follows:

There have been no Japanese on these tracks for over 2 months. If, and when they do come, the tracks are difficult to move on. One would not be able to put in a reasonable ambush.

So, at the very most, one might kill a few Japanese, and what would have been achieved? Nothing of any strategical value, and valuable lives would have been risked unnecessarily.

So, it resolves into the following:

1. To stay here quietly continuing with the training programme and await such time as it is opportune to move, or
2. Move back into the valley and operate in villagers along the Bilin Road.

This latter I consider highly dangerous in view of the large numbers of troops in the area off the road. There are 3000 Japanese reported to be in Papun – they have come down from Mawchi, and another 2-3000 Japanese with 300 elephants are expected soon.

To summarise:

Guerrilla warfare – to have any strategical value has to be effected in conjunction with an army advance. The army at present is at a standstill – apart from isolated skirmishes and the slow progress on the Mawchi Road.

The Karens in the south – between Bilin Road and the Sittang – have been killed; their villagers burnt down to the ground as a reprisal for Lucas' activities in this area.

Surely, army should have realised all this would occur – why then permit all this if they are not prepared to advance. The poor Karens are paying heavily for their loyalty to the British.

14th July Saturday

Nothing of any significance all day. In the evening, I got myself into a disgusting frame of mind – dark evil spirits were at work inside me!

15th July Sunday

Awoke late – rather disgusted with my mental state of the previous night.

A message came through on the morning Sked: I am to operate on the Shanywa-Meyitha-Mekahta track, which comes from Shwegyin. Secondary mission is to operate on the Wingalon-Mekahta track. Also, I am responsible for intelligence from Shwegyin to Kunzeik (on the Sittang River south of Shwegyin).

This all left me extraordinarily flat. The idea of operating – or should I say – attempting to in these rains gives me a headache.

I am receiving a man who apparently knows the whole area.

10 p.m. I have read a book this evening – completely. I am feeling tired and mosquito bitten. I cannot describe my feelings tonight. Here I am sitting alone – alone except for the natives around me in the village. Surrounded by jungle-covered mountains. Every few minutes the rains come over the mountain tops and engulf the whole place in a haze.

It is a dark, stark night outside. Not a single fellow creature in relentless miles of jungle mountains. And yet, I do not feel in any way lonely – except that I long for Brenda. No. I find that it is sharpening my wits. I know, poor fool that I am, how little I am in this world of millions. It seems hard to believe that as I am sitting here now, millions are enjoying themselves the world over. In that, I do feel alone because I doubt if tonight anyone has had time to give me a thought.

16th July Monday

Training, as usual, in the morning. In the afternoon took the men on a spot of *'unarmed combat'* – to promote that offensive spirit.

17th July Tuesday

Started arrangements for the plan to move to new area. Sent off Mg Mu's section to build a dump.

18th July Wednesday

In the morning Saw Sankey[21] came en route for Lucas' HQ – brought mail from Colonel.

At lunchtime Capt. Bissett, a relief W/T operator arrived – en route for Major Lucas' party – to change with Loosmore.

An amusing character – Scotch – full of dry humour. He brought 12 fresh loaves of bread with him and letters from the Colonel, from Brenda, Marie, and Nora Collins.

Apparently, the airstrip is an excellent affair – built with 4,000 bamboos, it is 400 ft. x 50 ft. and liable to remain an all-weather strip. This means that now we will get mail regularly and more food. The Colonel is sending me: tinned tomatoes, steak and kidney, cocoa, coffee, milk, fruit, porridge, and bacon. We are to feed ourselves well during these rains – thank God!

I must say it was grand to have toast, butter, and jam for tea.

In the afternoon Saw Htoo – Havildar of 44 Home Guard in my new area – arrived, bringing supplies with him. I discussed the plan with him and arranged to move to his village shortly and establish my HQ there. I am sending him off in order to prepare the village for us.

I wrote off letter to Colonel and several more letters to Brenda.

19th July Thursday

Sent Saw Htoo[22] off early with mobiles as escort. All carrying heavy loads for the dump at Meyitkhi.[23] Sent Havildar Jagha with them to take over the place – till I pass through and collect them all. Sent Capt. Bissett off with escort to Mekadikhi (*south of Mekatha*).

In the evening, had a dinner party to celebrate 15th anniversary with Harry and Gte. We had gin cocktails – snaffled from Bissett's flask; steak and kidney, potatoes, onions in butter, beans in tomato sauce (Gibbs); followed by grapefruit and fresh bananas. An excellent repast. Unable to sleep after it. Still awake at 2 a.m. – so had a cocoa. Due to complete lack of exercise.

Harry is still treating me for these ulcers under my arm.

20th July Friday

Weather turned really bad again. I spent the day – now reading – now seeped in introspective self-analysis. If it were not for the possibility to become oblivious to earthly realities and lose oneself in that absorbingly interesting pastime of introspective analysis – a process of getting to know the various aspects of one's character, and then after studying each and every part, then fitting the pattern together and finding it possible then, and then only, to understand something of the whole.

Lt. Moore arrived in a pretty bad state in the evening. He was Royal Navy SOE, a youth of 21 with a terrific beard. He was pale and thin; his voice was weak and sad – as if he has lost all his will to be a man. He has a mastoid in his ear. I must get him off the strip – earliest.

(Message through on Sked to say that Ronnie was sending me up some rice on an elephant).

21st July Saturday
Moore unfit to move, spent day in bed.

Message through to expect Lucas soon – provide him with 3 elephants.

I sent message back – no elephants and few porters. He can (sort these) himself as far as I am concerned. As for his Sergeant Shepherd, he had better decide to behave himself.

My jungle ulcer trouble seems to be improving considerably.

22nd July Sunday
Sent Moore off – he is a little perkier after his rest.

In the afternoon Lucas arrived.

23rd July Monday
Lucas left with escort.

Despatched Tun Shein with orders to get cracking on the intelligence in the area. Also, to organise my new HQ.

24th July Tuesday
Clarke and Glyn Loosmore arrived – interesting conversation '*au sujet de*' (on the subject of) Lucas. Gleaned some interesting facts. He apparently is apt to grossly exaggerate situation in his messages, giving false figures.[24]

To my horror Pagoda started a fit – his jaw going at an incredible rate – saliva dribbling out – and all his muscles seemed to paralyse. It went on at intervals throughout the night.

25th July Wednesday
I am going crazy with anxiety over Pagoda. He threw a terrible fit in the morning, and when he calmed down, he lost his balance and walked as if he was drunk right off the balcony.

Clarke and Loosmore left in the morning. After they left my old faithful bodyguard turned up – the one I had given up as lost and left behind at Kyowaing.

In the afternoon Pagoda had two more seizures. I made up my mind there and then. Sent him off with our NCO. It was then I realised how much I loved him. I cried my heart out until exhaustion and grief lulled me to sleep. I think Ronnie may be able to help him. Certainly, a break away from these cold mountains may help him a lot.

Messages have been coming in to the effect that some 6,000 Japanese are making a break through out of the Pegu – Yomas,[25] across the Sittang near Kyaki and are expected to make for Shwegyin.

The rice situation is critical – also no washers for the steam generator. HQ keeps saying they are sending me up rice – but it does not seem to materialise.

26th July Thursday

Feeling a bit better – able to face the world again, empty as it is without Pagoda. I swear if he dies, I will kill a thousand Japanese.

Message through that from captured Japanese it is estimated that the Japanese will make for Shwegyin, then to Shanywa and thence to Wingale – Bilin and, Thaton, which means I must get cracking.

Message from Ronnie – God bless him – to say he will do his best for Pagoda.

Had to send to Meyitkhi for rice.

Letter from Tum Shein to say that Mrs. Saw Ohe Htoo has arrived and is ready to start work. Also, he gives the situation as follows:

> Japanese all the way up and down the river from Shwegyin to Kunzeik. They have large food dump at Kyongaung (or may mean Kyaungywa – on west bank of the Sittang River). No circulation allowed into Shwegyin – or around area.

Karens fear that with repeated bombing Japanese will come up into the hills.

27th July Friday

Sent off elephant with steam generator with escort and HM (Havildar Maj.) James to go to Tatukhi[26] in order to recc'e good spot for wireless also – build a camp, miles from nowhere, in case of an emergency. Propose to move tomorrow.

Maw Gay returned from Plawkhi with news that supplies had not reached Plawkhi yet. This is rather a blow:

1. We have been out of rubber washers for generator for over a fortnight.
2. I have no sugar left at all.

28th July Saturday

Early start. Weather fine for once – quite a pleasant walk once we got into the Madama Cloe valley.[27] I took some photos of the men crossing this river.

Arrived in Meyitkhi and went up to the temporary camp that had been built for us. It was a nightmare. Every imaginable type of biting insect; rain poured through the improvised roof.

Messages came through. Another captured Japanese disclosed operational order – to attack and hold Shwegyin and allow 28th Army and 54 Division to escape through.

Milner, who has moved to Thauthekhi[28] area, reports 2,000 Japanese at Mezaungwa[29] were attacked by Home Guard. 36 Japanese killed – 5 HG killed.

Also, messages to say Woolf and Bourne returning 30th.

Three elephants of rice coming via Northern track.

29th July Sunday

Early start. There followed the bloodiest march across one mountain after another. No proper track. Eventually reached Tatukhi – found HM James had had everything made ready for me. A bed, a table and screen made.

It appears mush warmer down in this valley. Thank God!

Message from Wattaw to say that some rice and stores had reached Meyitkhi – a lot remains at Walaw. I suppose I shall receive it someday. Mrs. Saw Ohe Htoo is coming on the 30th.

Rather a friendly village. Saw Htoo was here to meet me. He has his patrols already out in the Shanywa and Wingalon areas.

I am sending off HM James to Meyitkhi to arrange about the stores and rice dumps, and intercept supplies coming from Mewaing.

Jemadar Harry I am sending off to recce a likely DZ as Ronnie is trying to get me a Dakota drop.

The village will be able to supply me for not more than a fortnight.

30th July Monday

Started men onto clearing an old Tanya – in a valley right upon a range of mountains.

Word arrived from Ronnie to the effect that Ivan Woolf is returning on the 31st and leaving straight away.

31st July Tuesday

Milner sent message – he is back in his old hunting grounds – holding up 2,500 Japanese from crossing over the Shwegyin River near Mezaungwa. Sent section off to meet Ivan.

Mrs. Saw Dhe Too – my new nurse – arrived. Not favourably impressed.

Sent off long letter to Colonel about set up.

Htipado warns me that Japanese from Mezaungwa may try to cross to Wingale – Bilin – Thaton.

1st August Wednesday

Ivan arrived morning with useful stores. Delighted with set up I have here. Full of news. He is looking very fit.

Hugo Hood to replace Cuthbert Burne as 2nd in Command.

31st (July) – heard that Pagoda had been shot for rabies in Rangoon. Woolf tells me Pagoda was left chained up in Cronin's room at Rangoon. Next morning slipped his chain – threw a fit and a BOR suspecting rabies, shot him. God help Clarke when I see him.

Ivan was dreadfully cut up because he had not mentioned it earlier to him and he might have been able to do something about it.

Apparently, several of the firm's FANY's now in Rangoon. Diane – Brenda's friend, met Ivan – told him Brenda adores me and is prepared to marry me anytime I want to!

St. John out with hellish temp. Poor chap. Lha Twe[30] arrived soon after Ivan – with more stores and letters and a parcel of books from Brenda. She is a darling.

Still no signs of stores sent by Ronnie on 29th, or of the stores sent on the 24th.

2nd August Thursday

Got men onto building camp away from village to move into, should Japanese come through here.

Out of wireless contact since 31st as batteries completely flat – and still no sign of washers for steam generator.

Tun Shein arrived with information, and a bullock for the men.

Japanese generally have blocked all tracks leading eastwards to here, from Shwegyin right down to Kunzeik. But the Japanese at Mezaungwa may try to come down through here.

Tun Shein reports several spies – one in particular at Shanywa.

3rd August Friday
Sent Tun Shein and a Havildar off to deal with Shanywa spy.

Went off with Ivan to DZ. Excellent place. Saw Htoo has made a (damn) fine job of it. Ready for use at any time.

In the evening, urgent message from Milner:

> He has been holding up 2500 Japanese on the other side of Shwegyin River – he has expended 30,000 rounds and yelling for ammo drop.

His line is too long – he wants me to come and help him consolidate the line. This we are going to do. Within a few minutes I had runners going off all over the shop – for ammo. – to Milner, telling him we are coming.

To Ronnie – to Havildar Major.

I am leaving tomorrow with 'B' Platoon and 20 Home Guard commanded by Saw Htoo.

3rd August Friday (*Note: partial repeat of above entry – notes from separate sheets in Diary*)
Word came in from Milner saying that he was holding 2500 Japanese up on the Shwegyin river – preventing them from crossing, but his line is too long, and his ammunition is running out – could we go and help him.

I was out of communications with HQ so decided to move next morning.

4th August Saturday
Set off with 'B' Platoon, Saw Htoo and 11 Home Guard and Ivan Woolf. We walked through to 'Bolo C' – heavy going.

Received a letter from Colonel telling me that he had recommended me for promotion.

5th August Sunday
Early start. Walked through to Thauthekhi – met Mya Schwe Schwyi on the way – a charming and well-educated Karen – but a very scared man.

At Thauthekhi discovered Thaung Tu – doctor's son – he had taken a drop!

Ammunition and rice are being supplied to keep us going. Thank God!

6th August Monday
Went through to Mesikhi and then left my Platoon there with Woolf. Took one section up to Milner's camp – another 3 hours' journey – a dreadful walk in these monsoons.

Milner and Bourne in good spirits. They have 3 Japanese prisoners. We discussed the plan. The set-up is that the Japanese are trying to cross at Sinbyu-ain-auk, Mezaungwa, Tikeda, Tanipa,[31] Kyauktaga and at Yebezu.

Milner informed me the Colonel was on the way down to join us.

Milner said he could hold Sinbyu-ain-auk to Tikeda; and Bourne from Tikeda to Kyauktaga; me from Kyauktaga to Yebezu, and I also have to watch our left flank, their southern limit, the Padet Chaung.[32]

I put Woolf in charge of this area with Saw Htoo and the Home Guard.

7th August Tuesday
Set off back to camp at Mesikhi and moved my men to Kyauktaga. There split 'B' Platoon into two halves – Havildar Ja Gain to be responsible of northern half of line, Kyauktaga and Yebezu,[33] and the other Havildar for the southern half.

8th August Wednesday
Went down and checked each position. Some of them of very good. I made them entrench with good rain cover – their sleeping quarters right back. They did quite a lot of shooting during the course of the day. But it is over 150 ft. range – we killed one Japanese during the daytime and wounded another.

Then we set about making plans. I am to concentrate on finding out if the Japanese are crossing the Shwegyin River south of our line and heading for Shanywa[34] or coming up to outflank us. In the former instance, I am to double back to Shanywa and crack at them again.

More interesting news: Americans dropped latest invention – an Atomic bomb – on Japan, equivalent to 5 tons.[35] Americans have called upon Japanese to surrender. God! I hope they do.

Whilst walking around in the swamp something bit me in the ankle. It was bloody painful. My foot swelled up hopelessly.

10th August Friday
Set off to Tanipa. I met the Colonel there. He pounced up and congratulated me. "Let me be the first to congratulate you, Trof. You can

wear that always and be proud of it." It was a message from the 12th Army:

'Trofimov awarded Military Cross'.

'B' Platoon killed one Japanese today.
Total score (death toll count) now 100.

11th August Saturday
Another one Japanese killed

12th August Sunday
Japanese tried to cross en masse just south of Kyauktaga. We got 25 of them.

13th August Monday
Japanese made two attempts to cross – in two different places. My men came under LMG (Light Machine Gun) fire. Total of 41 Japanese killed.

News is red hot. Surrender terms being negotiated. Russia has now attacked Japan and are advancing into Manchuria and Korea.

Another atomic bomb dropped.[36]

Met the Colonel. He had with him an F/O Snelling – a Japanese interpreter who took a good deal of feeding. I stayed down in the line – to see that he was OK whilst he shouted across at the Japanese to try and make them surrender.

14th August Tuesday
Japanese made another attempt to cross. We got 35 of them. I had sent up to Milner and Bourne for reinforcements as I was worried about the Home Guard line south of Yebezu. These were immediately put into position and helped a lot. I got 3 x 2-inch mortars, 1 Bren and 2 sections.

Spent rest of that day making plans for final 'pay off'. General idea is Milner and I to take our men to Shwegyin and have final pay off there.

15th August Wednesday
Japanese surrendered at 05.30 hrs IST. Not that it affects us very much – we still have to carry on. During the night, a further 25 Japanese were killed trying to cross. I sent Snelling back that morning with the Japanese prisoner.

16th August Thursday
One Japanese killed – up a tree. This brings our total up to 230.
    We sent to see Ted Bourne for lunch. Made a break.

17th August Friday
Little firing. Order came in from Army that we are to round (up) ALL Japanese in Mongoose Area. Recc'ed DZ's and sites for PoW camps.

    Many Japanese very likely not to surrender and as such they are to be treated as outlaws. This is a dangerous and difficult and lengthy job. The show now being over, we have had our share, let some other (bugger) come in on it. A nice job for Army of occupation.

    Ronnie disagrees whole-heartedly with this idea. Off to Rangoon to talk to Army about it.

    Sent for all my kit for my HQ.

    Ronnie is now pleading our cause in Rangoon. If he fails, we are likely to have to round up some 25,000 Japanese in the whole of our area.

    Killed 10 more Japanese who came down the river on 4 rafts.

    Total (death toll) now 240.

18th August Saturday
Japanese started making attempts opposite Tanipa, Ted Bourne's HQ. They made a very desperate attempt, but he withheld them with 2 and 3-inch mortars and plenty of LMG.

19th, 20th and 21st August Sunday to Tuesday
Japanese made repeated attempts to cross opposite Tanipa. Ted ran short of 3 and 2-inch mortar bombs. I had to share out my reserve with them.

    My kit arrived from Tatukhi – I am beginning to clear that place.

22nd, 23rd, 24th and 25th August Wednesday to Saturday
Japanese made attempts all over the place. Message came through that it is unlikely that Japanese HQ Burma will know of Japanese surrender on 22nd. And, that Japanese in our area will **not** know until the 30th.

26th August Sunday
Japanese HQ Moulmein reports that all main bodies south of the line Shwegyin – Papun, have been informed of the surrender. Japanese Commander.

But still the Japanese opposite the Shwegyin River are attempting to cross. Either they are unaware of the surrender or they are determined to become outlaws.

Japanese Commander now in Shwegyin with Ghurkha troops to help contact enemy still trying to cross this river.

27th August Monday

No signs of Japanese opposite our position, but they still make attempts to cross further north. One party of 20 Japanese did actually succeed in getting across – so Milner had to detail off a strong patrol to try and round them off.

Apparently, Captain Yadav[37] came into Bolo,[38] our present airstrip. He is ADC. to the Army Commander. I shall be interested to learn why he has come in.

Colonel is going to be out for some time. His eye has gone bad again. However, he flew in a L1 (Stinson L-1 Vigilant) with 4 L5's (Stinson L-5 Sentinel) and evacuated 3 wounded. He told (Maj.) Milner that he thinks it will all be over in 2 weeks. God! I hope so.

28th August Tuesday

Just another day – nothing exciting.

(Saw) Harry, incidentally, presented me his gold signet ring on the 26th. It is from gold taken from Mewaing river.

I have recommended for decorations:

Jemadar Harry. NK Maw Gay, NK Ag Win and Havildar Saw Aaron.
For honours: Arthur Tabe

And sent the list on to Mewaing.

29th August Wednesday

Milner and ADC to General Officer in Chief 12th Army Capt. Yadav, an Indian Prince. A grand fellow speaks English perfectly. Fred Milner brought bottle of gin from Colonel. Excellent!

30th August Thursday

Major Milner left in the morning. I started to get to know ADC 'Kim' Yadav in earnest. He is an authority on (affairs of the heart) – taught me many things I did not know!

31st August Friday
Received message from Colonel Critchley in Rangoon: To go to the strip at Bolo and meet him there. I literally tore up there.

Arrived early at Bolo – nice large open place. I set to and designed a tower control. Colonel did not come in.

1st September Saturday
Colonel came in with 2 x L5's. I took many photos. He was looking very fit. Said I could finish when I wanted. I arranged to pack up as soon as it was safe to withdraw my boys.

But I arranged to move my HQ to Bolo where at least I can busy myself on the strip, and then be ready to pay off my boys quickly.

2nd September Sunday
Went to Museko.[39] Made necessary arrangements for transferring HQ. Returned to Bolo. Have now established a very nice little house in the Shan quarters – very clean and quite comfortable.

3rd September Monday
Had a busy day on the strip. 4 Dakota drops: 1 compo, 3 rice.

Major Milner has now to feed the whole area with rice.

Mad rush to get the strip ready for receiving a Lysander. One end has to be covered with bamboo matting to strengthen.[40]

Ted Bourne came up. Had a party in the evening. Harry got very drunk. I had to carry him to bed.

4th September Tuesday
Spent morning repairing damage done to strip by previous day's drops.

Clarke arrived in the afternoon to explain about Pagoda.

4th–8th September Tuesday to Saturday
Evacuated Clarke who had been putting on a sick act for some days.

On 7th, Major Milner went to Rangoon – returned with Major Garesby, who gave me details to enable me to contact Japanese delegation on opposite bank of Shwegyin Chaung.

9th September Sunday
Set off to Yebezu. At 4 p.m. contacted Japanese Officer, Lt. Iuchi. I had to cross to his side as he was scared of coming over to us. I took him up to Tanipa where we spent the night with Ted Bourne.[41]

10th September Monday

Sent Lt. Iuchi off up west bank to contact Japanese at Mezaungwa,[29] and tell them to report to Shwegyin. Pushed up to Bolo – went down river to Mezaungwa with Milner. Met Ivan Woolf. Japanese did not turn up for 2 o'clock RV so we went across to see Japanese corpses in a village just the other side of the river.[42]

Made contact that evening with Iuchi. He had failed to meet any Japanese.

11th September Tuesday

Two Lysanders arrived at Bolo strip in the morning with Hugo Hood and a party of Japanese. One Major, an absolute brute of a fellow. One 2nd Lt. and one Corporal.

They went to contact Japanese and inform them of Surrender along the Kyaukkyi – Shwegyin. We called Iuchi up to Bolo to act as interpreter as he speaks English slightly.

(No further diary entries for the 12th to the 26th then last entry is shown as:)

27th September
Left field.

---

[1] Kamamaung – 17° 20' 49" N, 97° 39' 24" E.

[2] Colonel Michael George Marsh Crosby (1911-1993) – Commissioned Gordon Highlanders 1940, joined SOE 1941, Jedburgh (Team Graham) 1944, Force 136 1945.

[3] Major Matthew Hodgart (1916-1996) – Commissioned into the Argyle and Sutherland Highlanders in 1940, he served as an instructor with SOE in the UK in 1941-1942, before deploying to the Mediterranean, Italy and the Adriatic in 1943, eventually joining Force 136 in December 1944.

[4] 'Q' Ops – Quartermaster (Operations).

[5] Full name has been kept back in the interests of privacy.

[6] Lt. Colonel Hugh Warton Howell – Joined the army in 1940 (King George V's Own Lancers) and SOE in 1944. Put in command of Operation Character (Hyena). – *See* TNA: HS 9/752/5 for his SOE personnel file.

[7] Language tempered but indicates his frustration and anger over not receiving his mail during his first 4 months in the field.

[8] Giraffe and Cow – other areas within Operation Character zones.

[9] Major Dennis Ford – Joined Army 1938 receiving an emergency commission in 1940. Served France, Crete and Burma before joining SOE in 1943. Sent to Ceylon as an instructor in 1944 and later deployed to Burma as part of Operation Character (Mongoose, commanding *Red* area). *See* TNA: HS 9/526/5 for his SOE personnel file.

[10] Lakyokawthi – 17° 36' 0" N, 97° 25' 0" E.

[11] Htilawthihta – 17° 43' 0" N, 97° 27' 0" E.

[12] Polohta – 17° 42' 43N, 97° 20' 19E.

[13] Htinade – 17° 46' 60" N, 97° 21' 0" E.

[14] Walaw – 17° 48' 0" N, 97° 17' 0" E.

[15] Metakho – 17° 55' 0" N, 97° 17' 0" E.

[16] Mekahta - 17° 35' 0" N, 97° 11' 0" E.

[17] Plawkhi – 17° 47' 54" N, 97° 15' 12" E.

[18] Metklekhi – 17° 43' 60" N, 97° 10' 60" E.

[19] Meponkhi – 17° 45' 0" N, 97° 12' 0" E.

[20] Mekadikhi – 17°40' 0" N, 97° 7' 60" E.

[21] Captain Saw Sankey, commissioned into the Burma Rifles 1941, Joined SOE 1945 and was deployed with Operation Character (Mongoose) – *See* HS 9/1303/6 for his SOE personnel file.

[22] Jemadar Saw Tha Htoo – Joined SOE 1943, Served with Operation Character (Otter).

[23] Meyitkhi – 17° 46' 0" N, 97° 8' 0" E.

[24] On the subject of Major Lucas the interested reader should consult his redacted National Archives file HS9/947/5 which allude to a number of allegations against him.

[25] Pegu Yomas, a range of hills between the Irrawady and the Sittang River which originates within the range.

[26] Tatukhi – 17° 49' 0" N., 97° 5' 0" E.

[27] Madama Cloe Valley – near Htiphado – 17° 45' 0" N, 97° 13' 0" E.

[28] Thauthekhi – 18° 1' 0" N, 97° 1' 0" E.

[29] Mezaungwa – 18° 2' 0" N, 96° 57' 0" E.

[30] Lha Twe – recorded in the Platoon lists of names – for final pay for period May-September 1945, Trofimov Archive.

[31] Tanipa – 17° 59' 0" N, 96° 56' 0" E.

[32] Padet Chaung is a tributary of the Sittang River.

[33] Yebezu – 17° 57' 0" N, 96° 56' 0" E.

[34] Shanwya – due west of map ref 15 Tatukhi - 17° 49' 0" N, 97° 5' 0" E.

[35] *See* A Tin Trunk, A Diary and A Journey into Our Father's Past for mention of Critchley's messages to Trofimov about the Japanese surrender following the atomic bombing of Hiroshima (6th August) and Nagasaki (9th August).

[36] On 9th August 1945, a second atom bomb is dropped on Japan by the United States, at Nagasaki, resulting finally in Japan's surrender.

[37] Captain Yadav – Hukam Singh Yadav, Royal Regiment of Indian Artillery, serving from May 1945 as ADC to General Sir Montagu Stopford, Commander-in-Chief British 12th Army.

[38] Bolo-auk – 18° 3' 0" N, 96° 58' 60" E.

[39] Museko – 17° 59' 0" N, 96° 58' 0" E.

[40] Bamboo matting for airstrip.

[41] Major Harold Edward Bourne was born in Aldershot on 19 December 1909, Bourne joined the army at 18 years of age, serving with the Coldstream Guards. He was in the Sudan in 1932, Egypt in 1933, and was with the BEF in France from 1939 to 3 June 1940. Employed by SOE from 21 September 1943, Bourne was recruited to be an instructor.

In 1944, Captain Bourne went to the Far East as a Jedburgh. He served on Operation Character from March 1945 for which he was awarded the MC.

The Karen affectionately called him 'Pa Ma Dai' which translates as 'Mr Tentmaker', because wherever they went, Major Bourne asked them to make bamboo shelters for the troops.

[42] In one of Trofimov's photos badly decomposed bodies of Japanese troops are evident.

A Most Irregular War: SOE Burma, Major Trofimov's Diary 1944–45

Album Part I
Original Mountings

OPERATION CHARACTER.

MONGOOSE AREA.

Cruiser Newcastle. Reporting to Calcutta for our briefings.

Trofimov's photos as he mounted them.

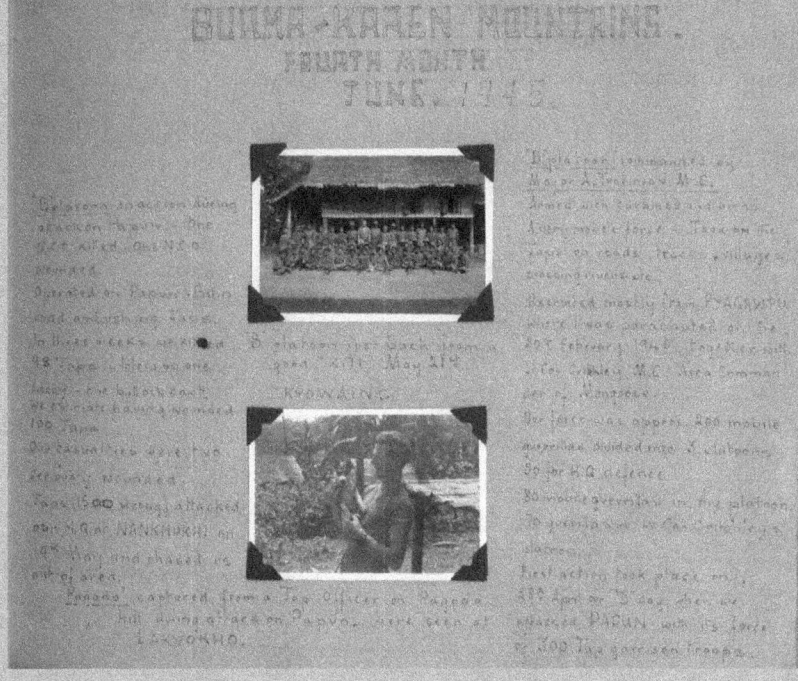

Album Part II
Training in Ceylon

Capt. Trofimov sailed to India on the troopship Otranto together with several other 'Jeds,' in October/November 1944 arriving in Bombay and then travelled across India by train and then by boat to Ceylon and the jungle training camp at Horana.

He records: 'We were put through an all too brief jungle training course which did not prepare for the conditions in the Karen mountains such as the voracious insect life.'

11th February 1945 – 'We left Horana for Trinco and then by sea on the cruiser *Newcastle* arriving in Calcutta on the 12th to 15th with Peacock Force. We proceeded to a camp at Jessau on the 16th February. Major Critchley and several others were there.'

Note: The penultimate photograph in this Album shows Major Critchley with his orderlies and although this relates to Album V In the Bush, it is shown here as Critchley features throughout the diaries as Capt. Trofimov's commander of Operation Character, Mongoose Area.

HMS *Newcastle*, Reporting to Calcutta for our briefing.

Ben Toto, Ceylon.

Tea party Ben Toto, Ceylon.

Orderlies Horana camp.

Horana camp.

Christmas day 1944, Captain Blaithwaite, Major Hood and Captain Trofimov.

P/O Arthur Braen.

Lt. Col. Critchely (Ronnie) with his two orderlies 'Kanini' and 'Shwema' visiting the line

Capt. Harry Despagné.

A MOST IRREGULAR WAR: SOE BURMA, MAJOR TROFIMOV'S DIARY 1944–45

Album Part III
People

SOE including some 'Jeds', Karens, Burma Rifles as well as new recruits, together with an American pilot of one of the Lysander aircraft.

Morris with Major Trofimov.

Lt. Van Kett (centre) our wireless and signals officer, dropped to us on 3 April. Seen here with two wireless operators proceeding to new HQ at Dubaw.

Shway Ma (right), Lt. Col. Critchley's orderly – joined us at Pawludo. Very attached to his master – a little rogue – always making us laugh. Seen here during a halt making tea.

Pagoda captured from a Japanese Officer on Pagoda Hill during an attack on Papun – seen here at Laksyokho.

And Top right: 'Lt. Col. Critchley on Kyowaing strip evacuating party of British Officers to Rangoon. They had been kept on the run by the Japanese and after six weeks had had enough.

Sgt. Gubbins (left), pilot of my plane.

As all my men were in the line I had to recruit and quickly train fresh men for camp sentries, runner etc.

Self and Harry plus a Japanese prisoner who swam across and was captured.

B Platoon 'Back After a Good Kill' 21 May 1945 Kyowaing, Burma.

Saw Harry – my platoon Jemadar – one of my best and most loyal friends. He had been a Havildar (Sgt.) in the Burma Rifles Commandos – he was left behind in the retreat from Burma in 1941. He joined forces with Hsi Tai and Arran and their party. Harry joined my party on the 27th February 1945 and became my right-hand man, helped me train my men and subsequently distinguished himself in the Papun battle and throughout the campaign. I have cited him for a decoration.

Major Lucas, a Mongoose Outstation Commander, with his two Sgts. Shepherd and Lister – they went in for beards and longyis! Major Lucas derailed a train carrying several hundred Japanese at Kyaikto. Seen here passing through my training camp at Metklekhi en route for the Mewaing air strip to be evacuated to Rangoon.

At my HQ Metalekhi – "One of the trials of guerrilla work is the periodic phases of inactivity waiting for the enemy to move out. Such phases are lonely ones. Here, I am looking out over a panorama of high jungle clad mountains – pagoda, my little dog was very ill – I sent him to Rangoon for treatment – but he was killed by a BOR who thought he had rabies. This left me alone – except for memories of my recent leave and my hopes for the future.

Dangar Bahardu – an Indian – who joined me in Papun district and followed me everywhere. He was the only Indian in my platoons.

Fun and games with a snake – not the one sticking out his tongue!

Captain Ted Bourne with Zoobrig, his faithful Indian orderly.

Jemadar Saw Harry, my Karen 2nd I/C BGM.

Centre page back margin.

Mobile guerrillas of Major Trofimov's force. These men were the pick of the fighters and took part in the last offensive on the Shwegyin Chaung.

A Most Irregular War: SOE Burma, Major Trofimov's Diary 1944–45

Album Part IV
Life among the Karens

Many of the photographs in this section were taken after the surrender in September 1945 at the final camp at Bolo. They include Karen and some Shan womenfolk who supported the local recruits throughout this campaign and shows their local costumes together with Maj. Trofimov who joins in wearing a traditional longyi (a skirt two meters in length and eighty centimetres wide). It includes a group picture taken at the camp at Metklekhi in July with the Pungyi priest and villagers as well as some Karen style huts built off the ground to help deter insects and other animals. There are also photos of some elephants used to transport stores and equipment to the various camps and from DZs to hidden dumps in the jungle.

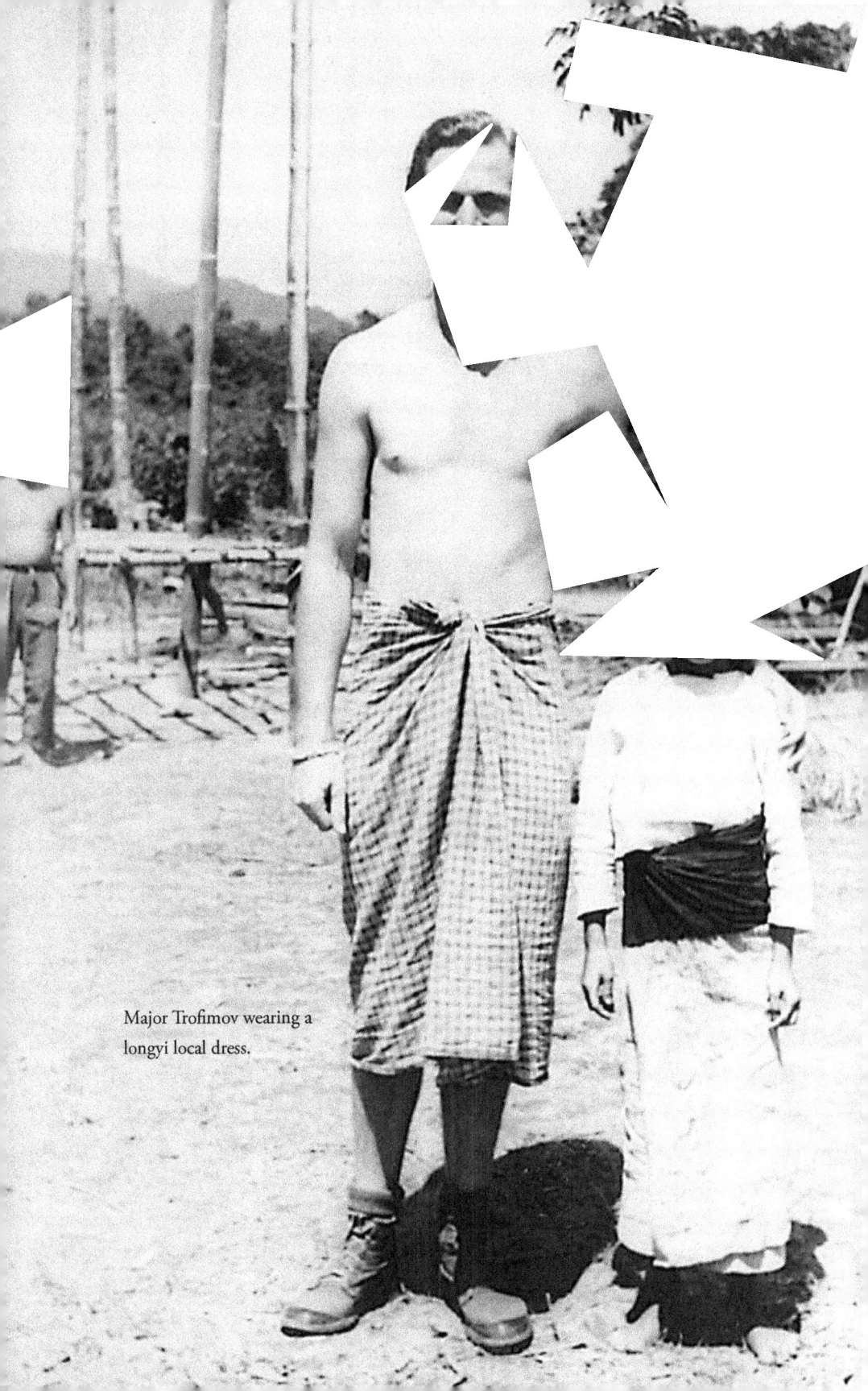

Major Trofimov wearing a longyi local dress.

The Karens and Major Trofimov (also below left) – after the surrender – 'happier times'

Karen elder.

Elephants moving my wireless and food stores to my training camp at Metkdekhi.

Album Part V
In the Bush

The last part of the campaign with the defence of the east bank of the Sittang River and its tributary the Shwegyin Chaung throughout August 1945. 'The Japanese are trying to cross at Sinbyu-ain-auk, Mezaungwa, Tikeda, Tanipa, Kyauktaga and at Yebezu. Maj. Milner said he could hold Sinbyu-ain-auk to Tikeda; and Bourne from Tikeda to Kyauktaga; me from Kyauktaga to Yebezu, and I also have to watch our left flank, their southern limit, the Padet Chaung.'

And this is what they see from the Bren pits – opposite at the foot of the white tree lies a dead Japanese soldier. Over 1500 Japanese were killed by us – trying to cross the river – many hundreds more died from wounds through lack of medical supplies and food.

Two Bren gun pits on the east bank of the Shwegyin Chaung. These pits covered a line of approximately 25 miles. We used 3" and 2" mortars – about 30 brens and some 300 carbines and about 250 rifles to hold the Japanese. From the time of their first attempt on the 30th July to cross to long after the surrender – we held them from crossing the river.

Another Bren pit along the line.

The fords at Yebezu. The Japanese made several unsuccessful attempts to cross here.

Word had come through that the Japanese were attempting to cross the Sittang River on its northern tributaries – in an attempt to evacuate the Pegu Yoma mountains. Here we are seen moving up to Shanywa area to take them on crossing rivers and on the tracks.

One of my tours down the line – here is a little shelter just behind the riverbank. On extreme right is NAIK (Corporal) Mg MU, a loyal old soldier who was with me to the last.

One of the line HQ's at KYAUKTAGA. Myself with some of those mentioned below.

(L to R) Foreground my orderly KYA, Havildar KYA SAING, Jemadar Harry, Havildar SAW BYU – both these Havildars were ex-Burma Rifles Havildars.

On patrol in dense swamp jungle near the riverbank.

It looks easy but in these native boats a trip down a monsoon swollen river is no joke!

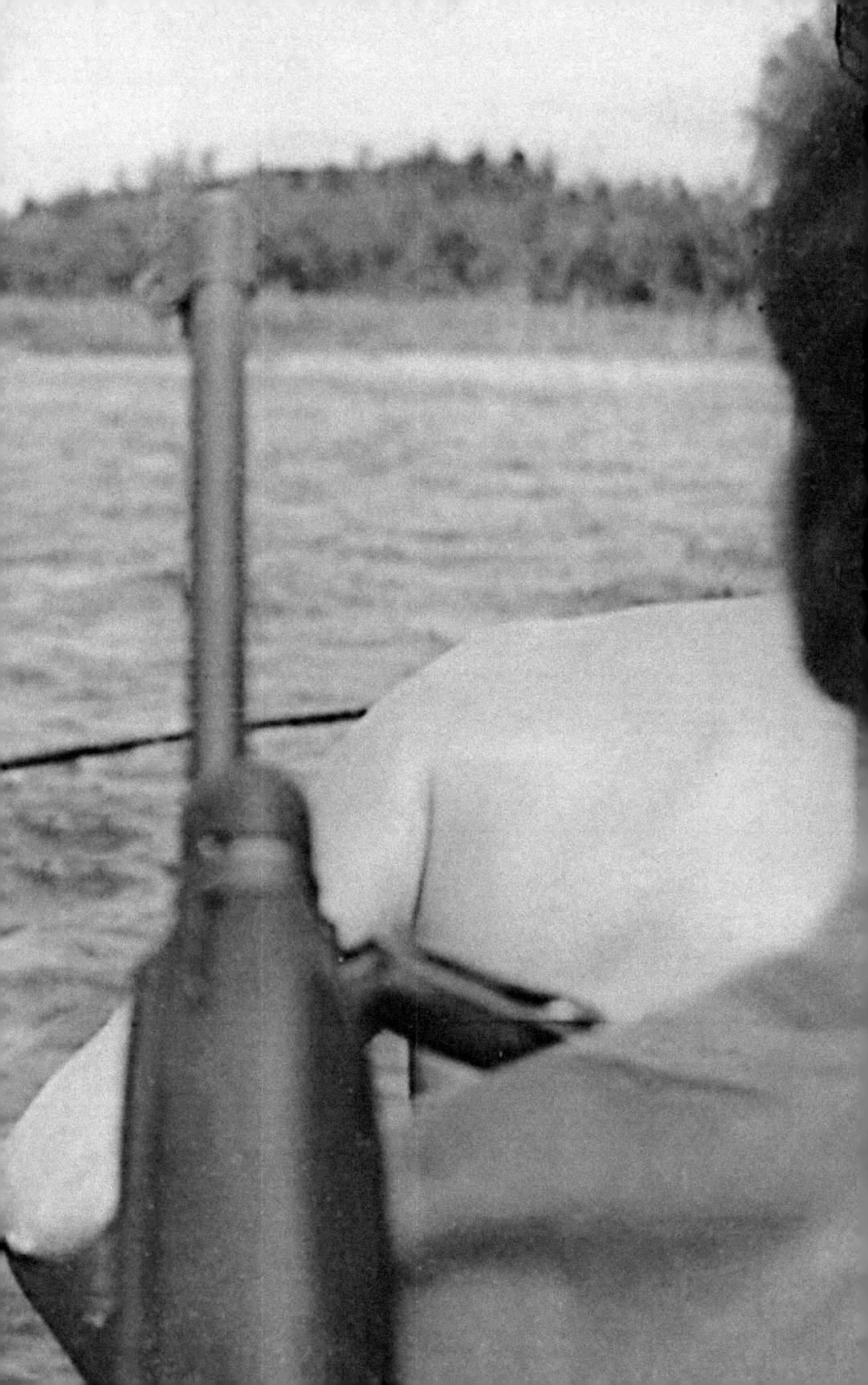

A Most Irregular War: SOE Burma, Major Trofimov's Diary 1944–45

Album Part VI
Resupply by Air

Photographs taken after the Japanese surrender during the final period in September 1945 at the temporary Bolo camp. Showing the makeshift bamboo airfield, supply drops by parachute from Dakota, and the B24-Liberator aircraft, the latter notable for its distinctive 'Davis Wing' tailfin, the B-24 used two vertical stabilizers at the rear helping to reduce aerodynamic drag whilst the bomb bays were open and being used specifically for these supply drops, to provide essential provisions for the troops as well as Japanese prisoners before cessation of operations in late September/October.

Dakota drop at Bolo camp.

Right Collecting the drop for the stores.

A Liberator lining up to drop.

Album Part VII
Air Operations

Mostly taken at the end of the war in Burma at the final camp at Bolo where a temporary bamboo airstrip was built so that Lysander and L5 Stinson Sentinel light aircraft used by SOE for clandestine operations of this kind could land to evacuate the wounded and Force 136 personnel. American pilots were mostly deployed in Burma to service Operation Character and other SOE manoeuvres but on this occasion, we feature here Squadron Leader George Turner along with two American pilots who all partook in the clean up of operations at Bolo airfield. Turner was a London policeman before and after the war and he features in the publication *The Moonlight War* by Terence O'Brien – *The Story of Clandestine Operations in South-East Asia, 1944-45*.

Below Squadron Leader Turner – who flew into us in occupied territory in a Lysander – evacuating our wounded, bringing us supplies – and some luxuries!

Bottom right Captain 'Ted' Bourne's platoons coming back from the line to BOLO air strip. These men sustained the hardest fighting on this last line. Ted, through his amazing courage held the Japanese night after night when they tried to cross opposite his positions. On one occasion, his ammunition was almost expended he fired his mortar bomb at point blank range and saved the hour!

Throughout the operation the RAF gave us air strikes – sometimes in support of an attack – or upon a very large concentration of Japanese – here here is a crater from one of the strikes we had during our last stand – in this strike 92 500lbs bombs were dropped – Furthermore, the RAF gave us the last air strike in Burma sometime after the surrender.

Above and below Bolo – Major FS Milner started an airstrip here to evacuate our wounded. Here are the platoons building houses for each section – the existing village not being large enough to accommodate all our men.

The Stinson L5 Sentinel was used primarily in India-Burma theatre by US forces.

Taking a nap.

The pilots of the L5s were Americans.

American Pilot, Major Trofimov, Captain Yadov ADC and F/O Snelling and another.

Squadron Leader Turner – who flew into us in occupied territory in a Lysander – evacuating our wounded, bringing us supplies – and some luxuries!

Above right Major Trofimov ("Trof"), Squadron Leader Turner and Major "Fred" Milner, Captain "Kim" Yadov ADC 12th Army.

Squadron Leader Turner supervising an elephant rider to pull logs etc.

Major Milner off to Rangoon.

Below Major Milner, Major Trofimov, and an American pilot and others taking a tea break by one of the Lysander aircraft.

Saw Morris and his wife plus Po Kyae being evacuated to Rangoon to represent the Karens in the discussions on future Government policy.

Saw Morris' wife on board the plane – Lysander.

Take off to Rangoon.

Major Milner (right) with pilot of the Lysander, Squadron Leader Turner.

A party of RAF personnel from the Lysander flight who flew in ... to see a few of the sights on the other side of the river (Japanese encampments and conditions).

Major Hugo Hood – who became Area Commander of Mongoose when Colonel Critchley left for England.

Evacuating troops.

His Tai being evacuated to Rangoon.

Captain Ivan Woolf my W/T and 2nd I/C being evacuated from field.

Captain Clarke – 2nd I/C to Major Lucas being evacuated with Maj. Milner on his left.

Album Part VIII
The Japanese Dead

A harrowing experience occurred as the diary entry for the 10th September 1945 records: 'Sent Lt. Iuchi (the Japanese prisoner who is assisting with communications) off up west bank (Shwegyin Chaung) to contact Japanese at Mezaungwa and tell them to report to Shwegyin'. Meanwhile Maj. 'Trofimov (recently promoted from Capt.) went down river to Mezaungwa with Maj. Milner. Met Capt. Ivan Woolf. Japanese did not turn up for 2 o'clock RV so we went across to see Japanese corpses in a village just the other side of the river.'

Landing on the west bank to investigate a camp full of dead Japanese near Mezaungwa 10th September 1945.

Skull with a bamboo pole in its mouth.

An emaciated and starving Japanese we found deserted by his comrades and left to die.

Album Part IX
Sports Day

The responsibility of maintaining order after the Japanese surrender and prior to release from service when the local Karens are being kept fit and occupied with a sports day full of activities close to the airstrip at Bolo.

Keeping the troops occu

Album Part X
Final Parade

Soon after the Sports day there was the final parade of all those involved in Operation Character, Area Mongoose, and some from Hyena too with principally Major Milner, Captain Ted Bourne and Capt. Trofimov's platoons of local Karens and some Shans participating in a march past and final salute.

Dakota drop during final parade.

The march past.

Album Part XI
Final Pay Day

PAY ROLL
CAPTAIN A. TROFIMOV'S PLATOON

RANK	NAME	VILLAGE	SERVICE	PREVIOUS PAY	FINAL PAY
JEM	HARRY	THATON	FEB – SEPT		500 Rs +240
HAV MAJ	JAMES	SHWE DAW	APRIL – "		300 +120
HAV.	KYA GAING	SHWE DAW	APRIL – "		225 + 90
"	SAW BYU	SHWE DAW	APRIL – "		225 + 90
NK	MAW GAY	HTI MU KI	FEB – "	35 Rs	228 + 76
"	Mg MU	KAW HAI	FEB – "	38 Rs	228 + 76
"	Ag WIN	LAR MU HTI	FEB – "	38 Rs	228 + 76
"	LHA TWE	MAW LU	MAY – "		152 + 76
"	WA TAW	DAPAW DAR	FEB – "	38 Rs	228 + 76
L/NK	GU HAI	LAI KAW DAR	MARCH – "		204 + 68
"	LHA HTOO	TAW FAW DAR	MARCH – "		204 + 68
"	Ag HTOO	WA LAW KLO	APRIL – "		170 + 68
"	TA HA	SAW MI TA	APRIL – "		170 + 68
"	KA MU	LAR E DAR	MARCH – "		204 + 68
RFM.	NH SHWE	SHWE TI	APRIL – "		150 + 60
"	TA ME SAY	LER WA KO DAR	APRIL – "		150 + 60
"	BA PYU	MAW THEY DAR	APRIL – "		150 + 60
"	TA NA MU	MAW THEY DAR	APRIL – "		150 + 60
"	Mg TOE	KYAUK TA LONE	APRIL – "		150 + 60
"	PU XBO	NGA NET PYA	APRIL – "		150 + 60
"	KYA KIN	NAN KHO HTA	APRIL – "		150 + 60
"	NYA PAW	KA NE LUR DAR	MARCH – "		180 + 60
"	KYAW HTOO	LAR WA KO DAR	APRIL – "		150 + 60
"	PLAW JI	SAW KLO DO	MAY – "		120 + 60
"	AYE Mg	SHWE HTI	APRIL – "		150 + 60
"	LINKYA MIN	WANE DAY	APRIL – "		150 + 60
"	MYA PO	ME THE KHO HTA	APRIL – "		150 + 60
"	PO HLA	KA LAW LAW	APRIL – "		150 " + 60
"	PA BA AH	BAW LU DAR	APRIL – "		150 " + 60
"	NARI HAI	KO PAR KI	APRIL – "		150 " + 60
"	MORRIS	SAY BAW LU	APRIL – "		150 " + 60
"	BA SAING	MA UNI	JULY – "		60 " + 60
"	SAW ME	HTI KO KI	MARCH – "	30 Rs	150 " + 60
SERGEANT? KLY	KYA YWET	SAW E DAR	FEBRUARY – "		240 " +160
"	JAN NYUNT	LAY KI	JULY – "		60 " + 60
"	TA LI	TA LAY KAW DAR	MARCH – "	30 Rs	150 " + 60
"	PA DOE	ME DA KO LAW	MARCH – "		150 " + 60
"	KYA HTOO	PO HAI HTA	JULY – "		60 " + 60
"	DA JI	NYA CHAW NAW HTA	JULY – "		60 " + 60
"	KYI Ag	PO HAI HTA	JULY – "		60 " + 60
"	BA SEIN	PO HAI HTA	JULY – "		60 " + 60
"	KYA PE	NYA CHAW WAW HTA	JULY – "		60 " + 60
"	THAN MA	" " "	JULY – "		60 " + 60
"	THA CHE	BA NALA KO	JULY – "		60 " + 60
"	THET PAH	KHO PLK KI	APRIL – "		150 " + 60

Major Trofimov checks off the fighters one by one and records their name, rank, father's village, and time of service with pay ... see Platoon lists – original pay roll as seen opposite left.

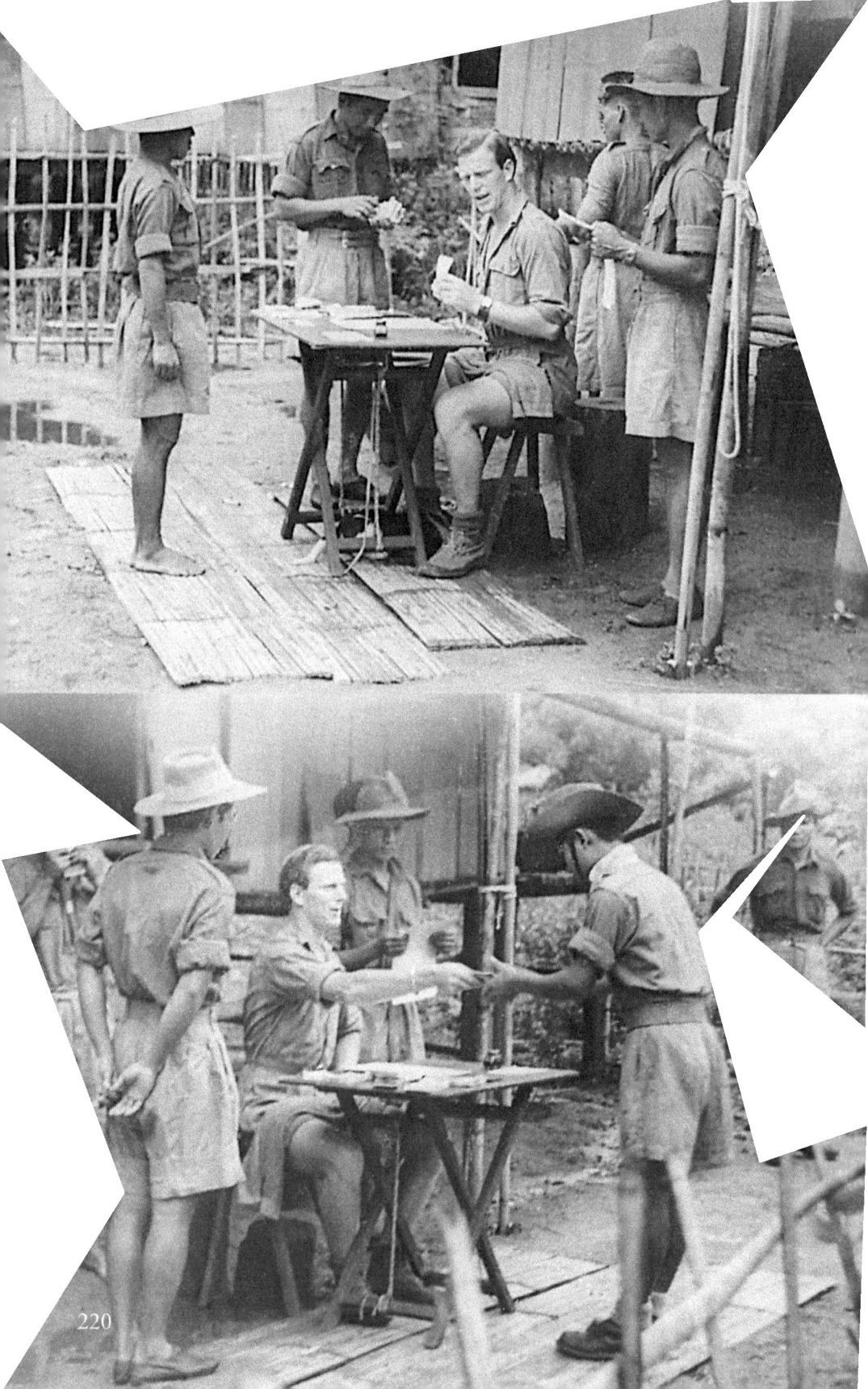

Album Part XII
Farewell

Although mostly taken at Rangoon and Calcutta with SOE Officers from the field (Maj. Milner, Maj. Trofimov, Capt. Ted Bourne and Sgt. Leney) as well as senior Officers in Rangoon and Calcutta, it also shows the farewell to the Karens along with their wives, mothers and sisters who came to bid farewell too.

Mothers and sisters of my guerrillas who came to give me a farewell.

Below Those who fought in the last bitter moment – (left to right) Sgt. Leney, Capt. Bourne, Maj. Trofimov and Maj. Milner.

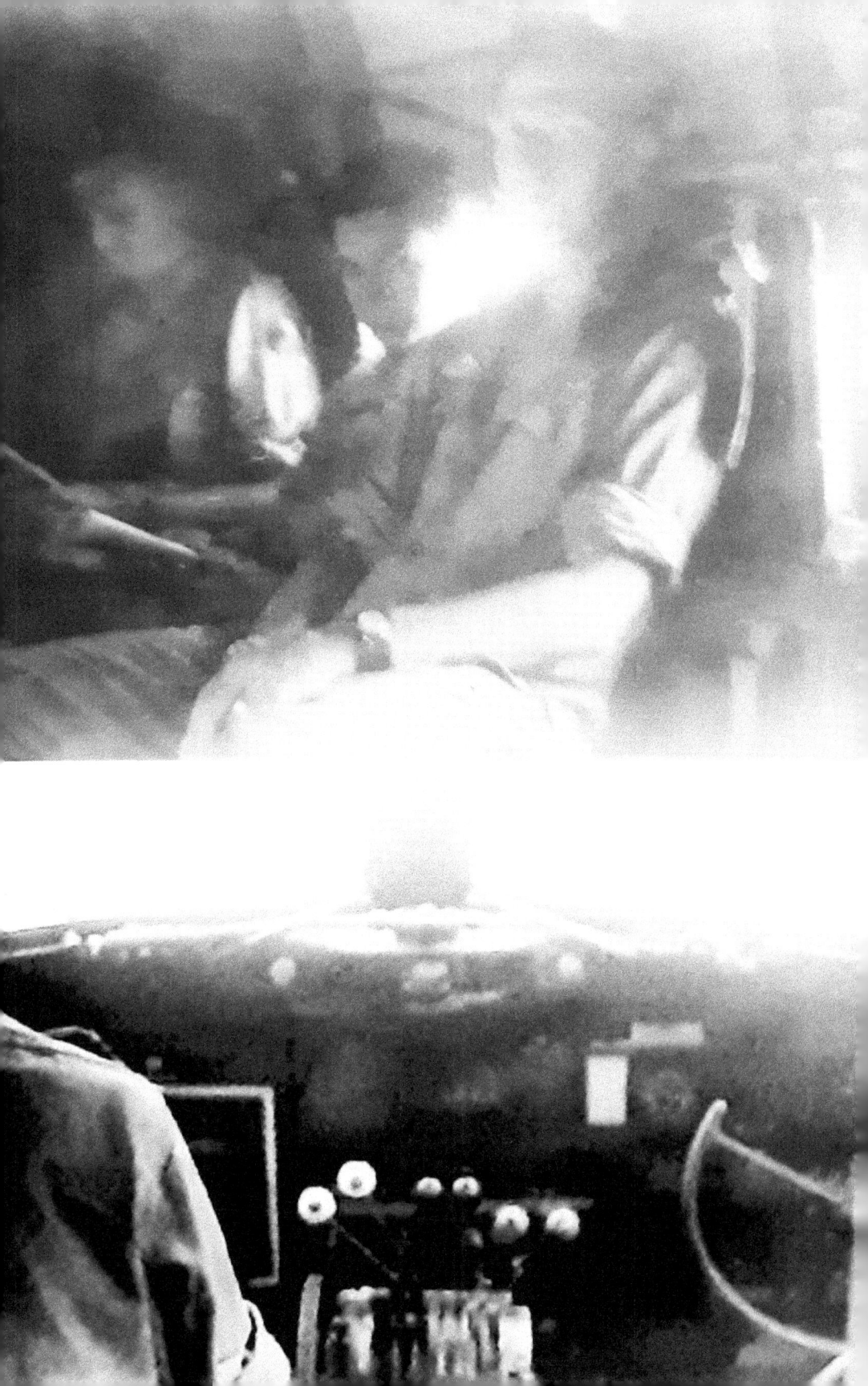

Relaxing in Calcutta.

Major Ted Bourne MC relaxing after the Japanese surrender!

Lt. Colonel Robin King – Operating Commander Force 136 in Rangoon.

Major Xan Fielding DSO.

Maps – Force 136 Operation Character

Images taken from the original sourced maps found in Major Trofimov's army 'Tin Trunk' comprising an OS paper map of Burma for the area of Operation Character, some larger scale OS maps to locate the smaller villages along the way as requested from Calcutta in some of his early diary entry radio messages;[1] and also the silk map[2] which he had with him when he parachuted into the Karen mountains.

His part of Operation Character[3] begins with where he is parachuted into the 'Hyena area' at Pyagawpu, near Pawlawdo on the 20th February 1945 and tracks his movements southwards to his camps at Lekawdo, east of Kaumudo (4000ft. mountain on 16th March), then to the area surrounding Mewaing with various camps, drop zones and stores referenced at Leklede, Metkyihta, Dubaw, Nankhukhi, and Tahulaw in the lead-up to the attack on Papun on the 28th April.

His post-war notes of his operations in Burma record his specific duties:

- 'My role was to organize DZs, recruiting, training and arming of local Karens, wireless and guerrilla warfare techniques including ambush and demolitions and to organise supplies for Peacock Force.'
- 'After organising parachute drops of arms and equipment for Peacock Force, Major Critchley and I set off with a handful of local Karens that we had enlisted and armed, to go south to recruit and organise a guerrilla army.'
- 'We established camp at Lekawdo and I commenced recruiting and training Karen volunteers. We had a series of drops of equipment, arms, food, clothing etc., and eventually we received several sub-area commanders, and I provided them with trained platoons (Karens and former Burma Rifles) and equipment.'

After attacking Papun, 'a garrison town with 300 Japanese troops', he moved his camp to Nankhukhi – his new area of guerrilla style operations for Mongoose 'Green' covering the area south of Papun between the Bilin and Kadaingti roads to Nankhukhi and Kwethe in the period from the 1st May up until the 20th May when he then proceeded south to meet up with his commanding Officer, Col. Ronnie Critchley who was then based at Lakyokawthi. A journey in which he traverses with his Platoon across the top of the Karen mountains via Mawkhi, Pawleha, Htitablutha and Mekyonoya and then further south to Kyowaing from where he departed on leave for Calcutta via Rangoon between the 2nd and the 5th June returning on the 16th June.

On arrival back in the field his orders were to move northwards from Kyowaing back to Lakyokawthi, Polohta, Htinade, Walaw, Mewaing and then eastwards to Schwehti, Metakho, Mekahta and where he established his new HQ in the mountains nearby at Methekhi on the 2nd July.

On the 3rd August he received orders from Major Milner to bring his Platoon to provide reinforcements to the defence of the east bank of the Sittang River from the retreating Japanese forces pushed back by the advancing British XIV army. After the Japanese surrender his final destination was at the Bolo camp before leaving the field on the 27th September 1945.

---

1 *See* diary entries for the 3rd, 7th and 21st March – requests for additional maps (1inch OS) and subsequently to a larger scale.

2 Original silk map can be viewed at Harrington Museum as the background to the cabinet display of Major Trofimov's SOE equipment which was gifted in the 1990s.

3 Major Trofimov records in his post war notes: 'Operation Character was estimated to last three months – in fact it lasted nearly a whole year' (7½ months in the field and subsequent administration roles in Calcutta).

A MOST IRREGULAR WAR: SOE BURMA, MAJOR TROFIMOV'S DIARY 1944-45

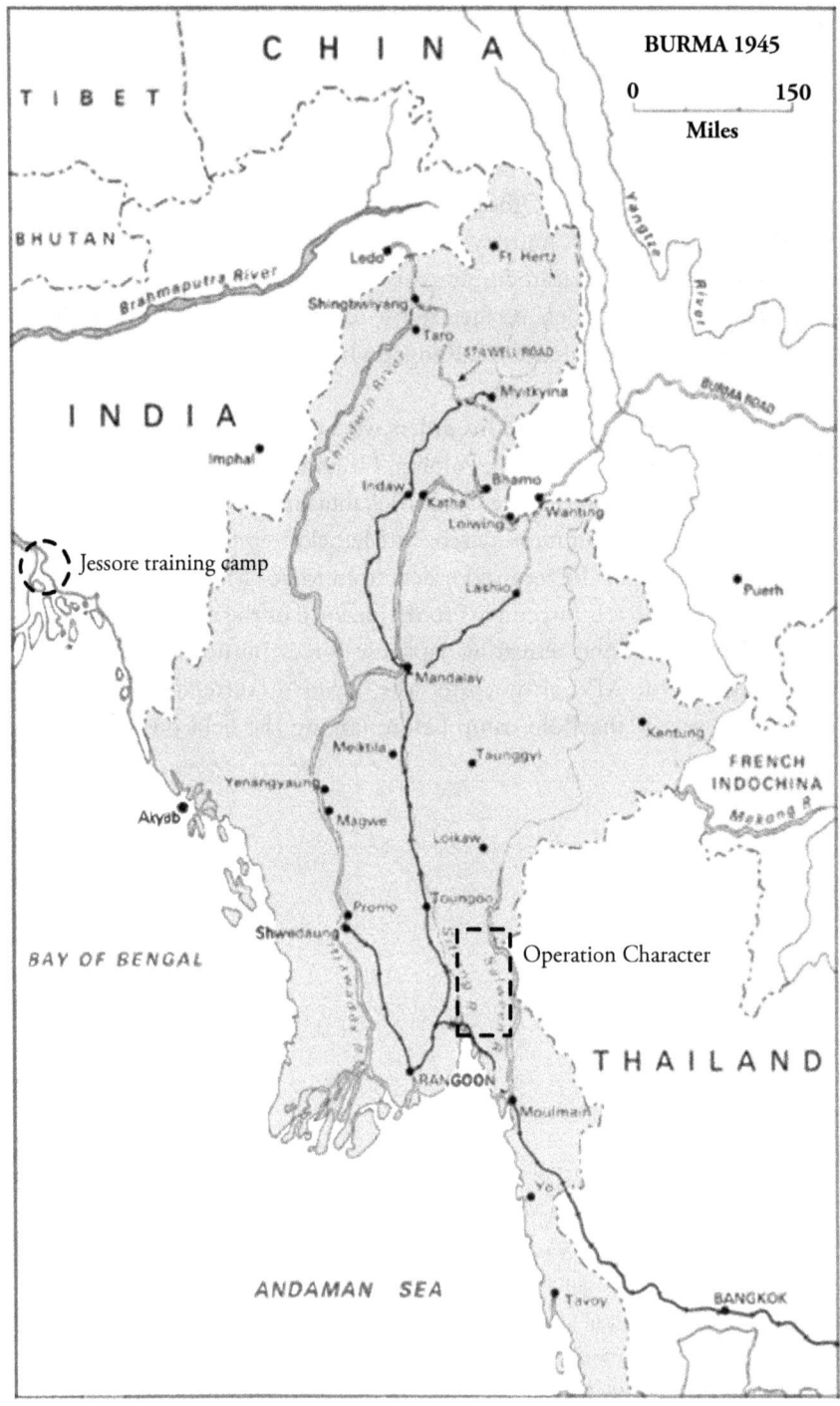

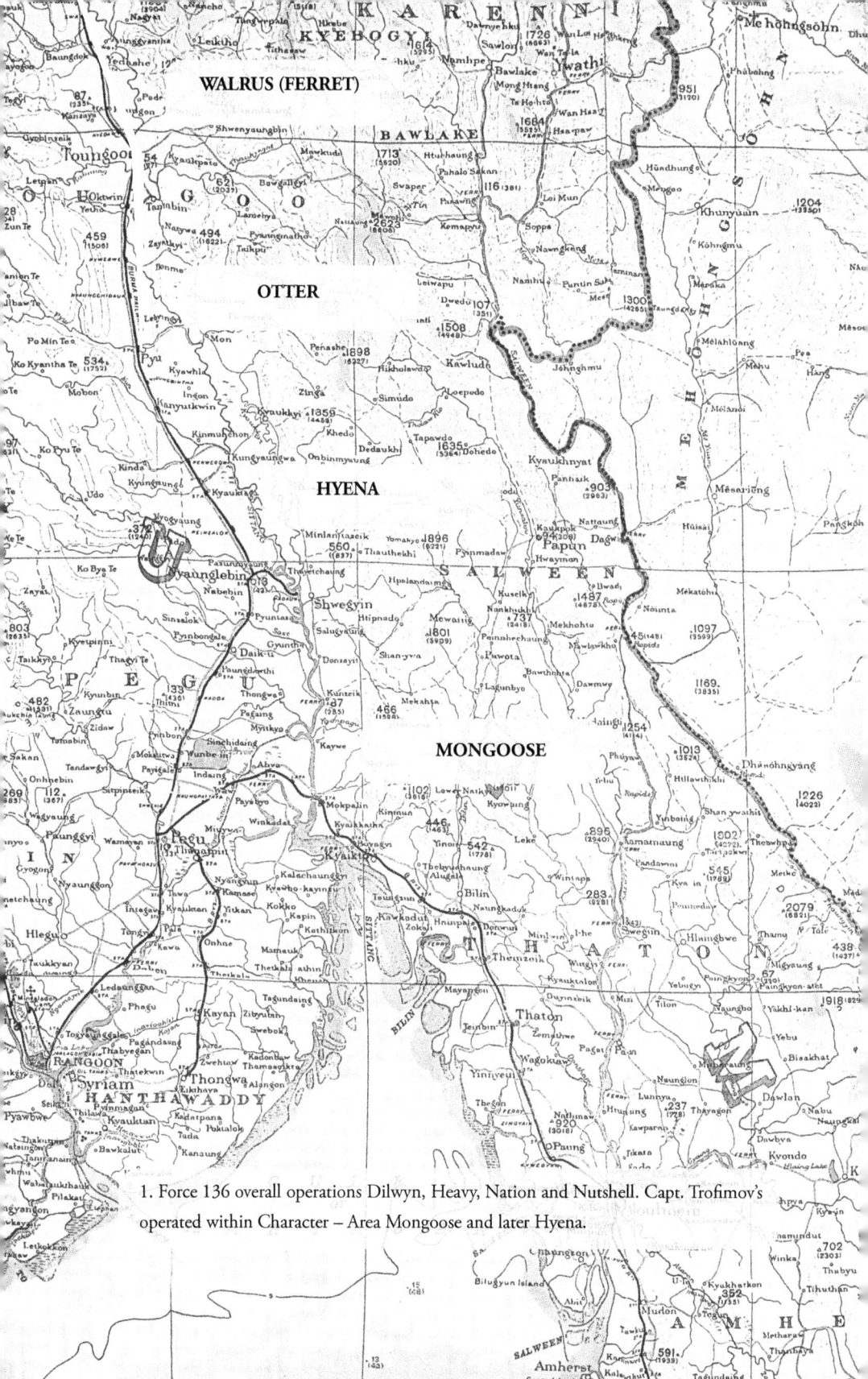

1. Force 136 overall operations Dilwyn, Heavy, Nation and Nutshell. Capt. Trofimov's operated within Character – Area Mongoose and later Hyena.

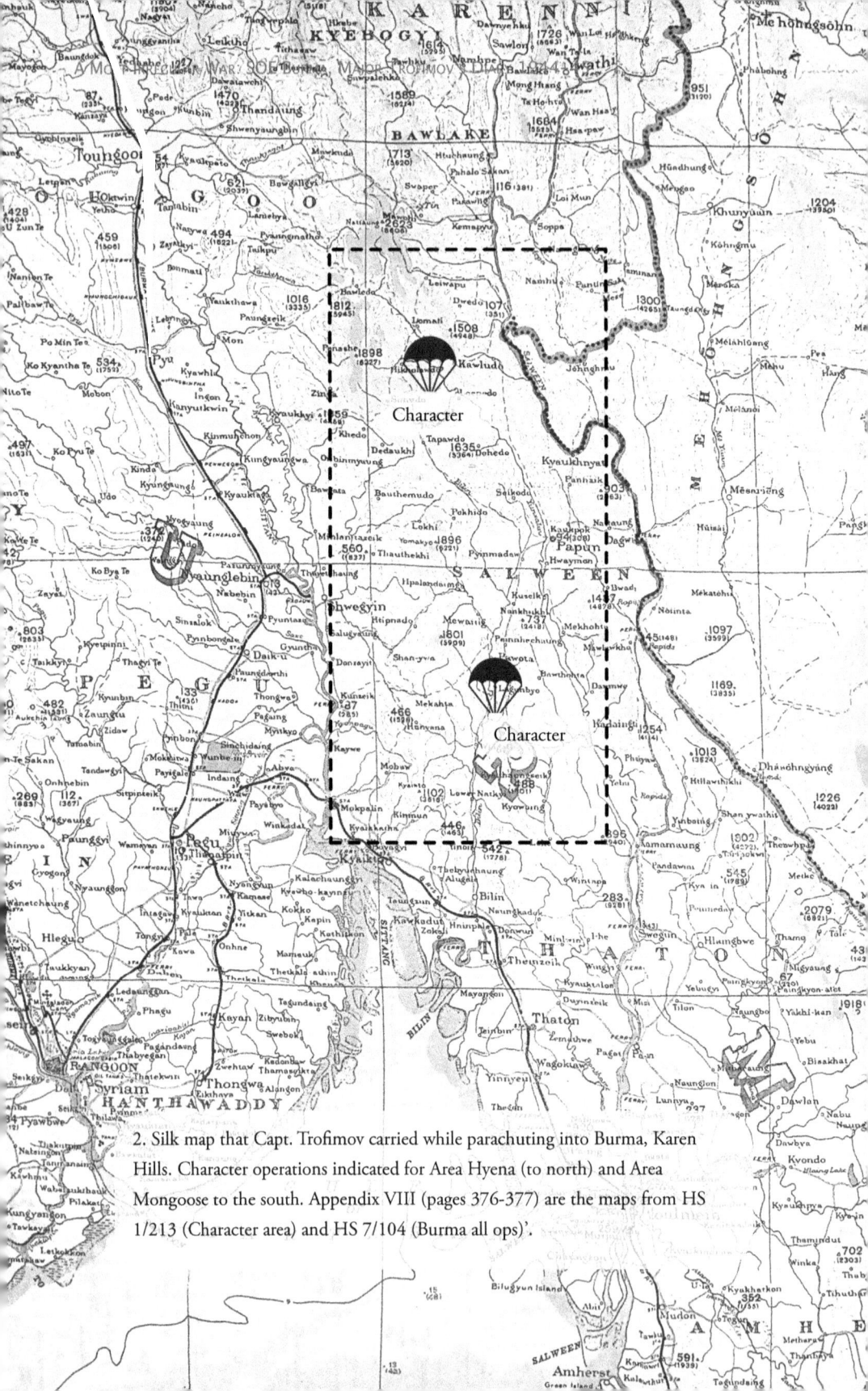

2. Silk map that Capt. Trofimov carried while parachuting into Burma, Karen Hills. Character operations indicated for Area Hyena (to north) and Area Mongoose to the south. Appendix VIII (pages 376-377) are the maps from HS 1/213 (Character area) and HS 7/104 (Burma all ops)'.

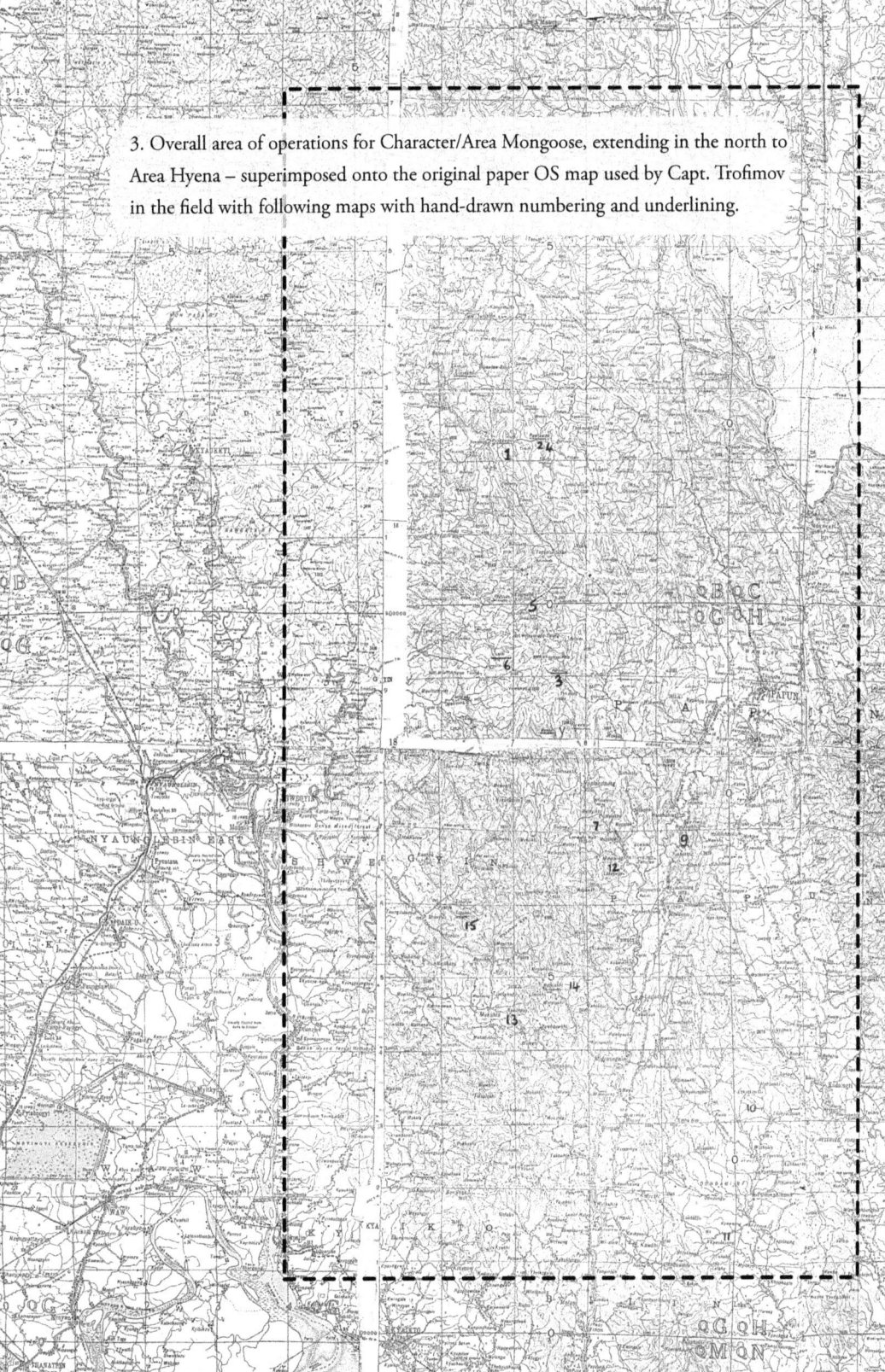

3. Overall area of operations for Character/Area Mongoose, extending in the north to Area Hyena – superimposed onto the original paper OS map used by Capt. Trofimov in the field with following maps with hand-drawn numbering and underlining.

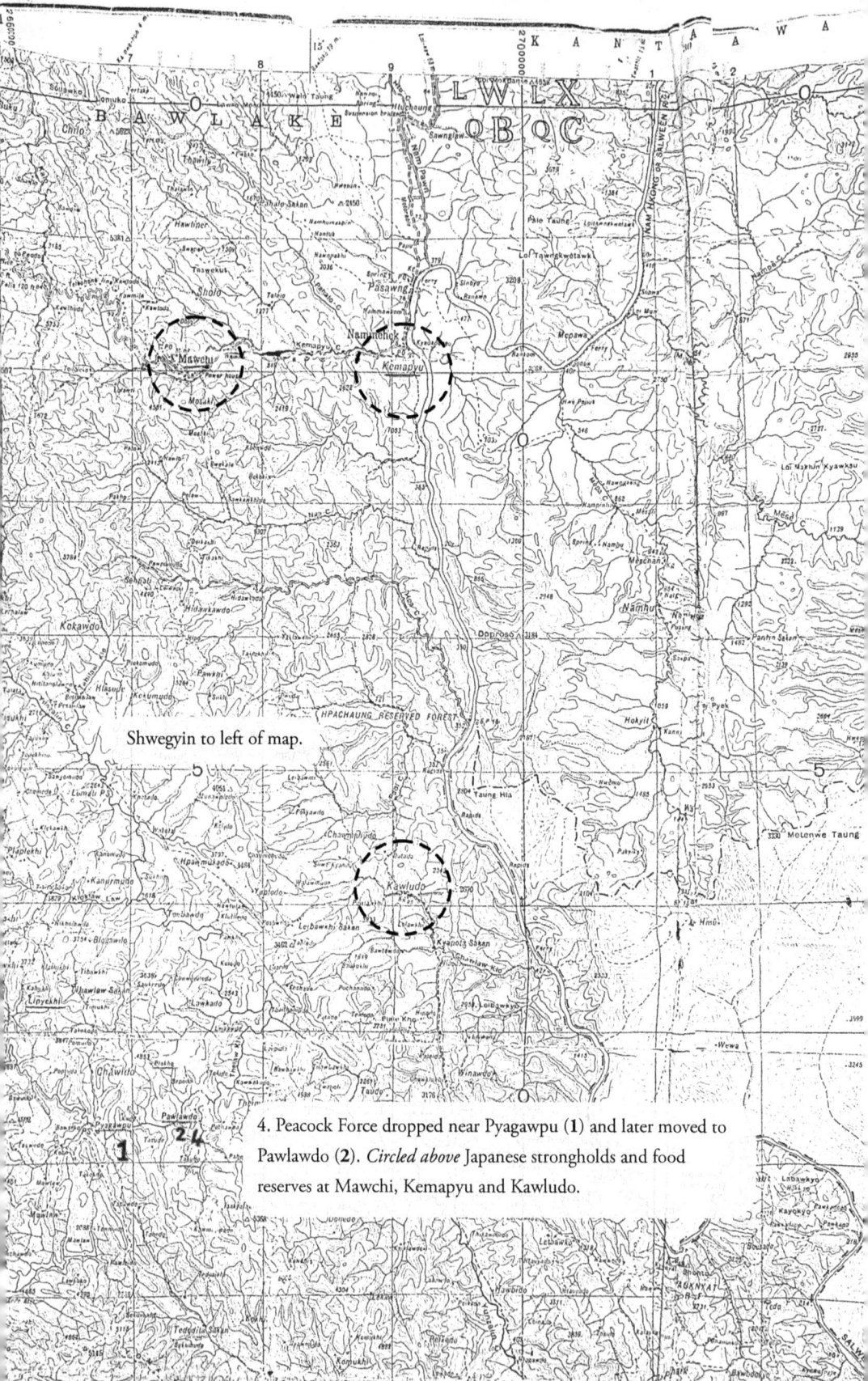

Shwegyin to left of map.

4. Peacock Force dropped near Pyagawpu (**1**) and later moved to Pawlawdo (**2**). *Circled above* Japanese strongholds and food reserves at Mawchi, Kemapyu and Kawludo.

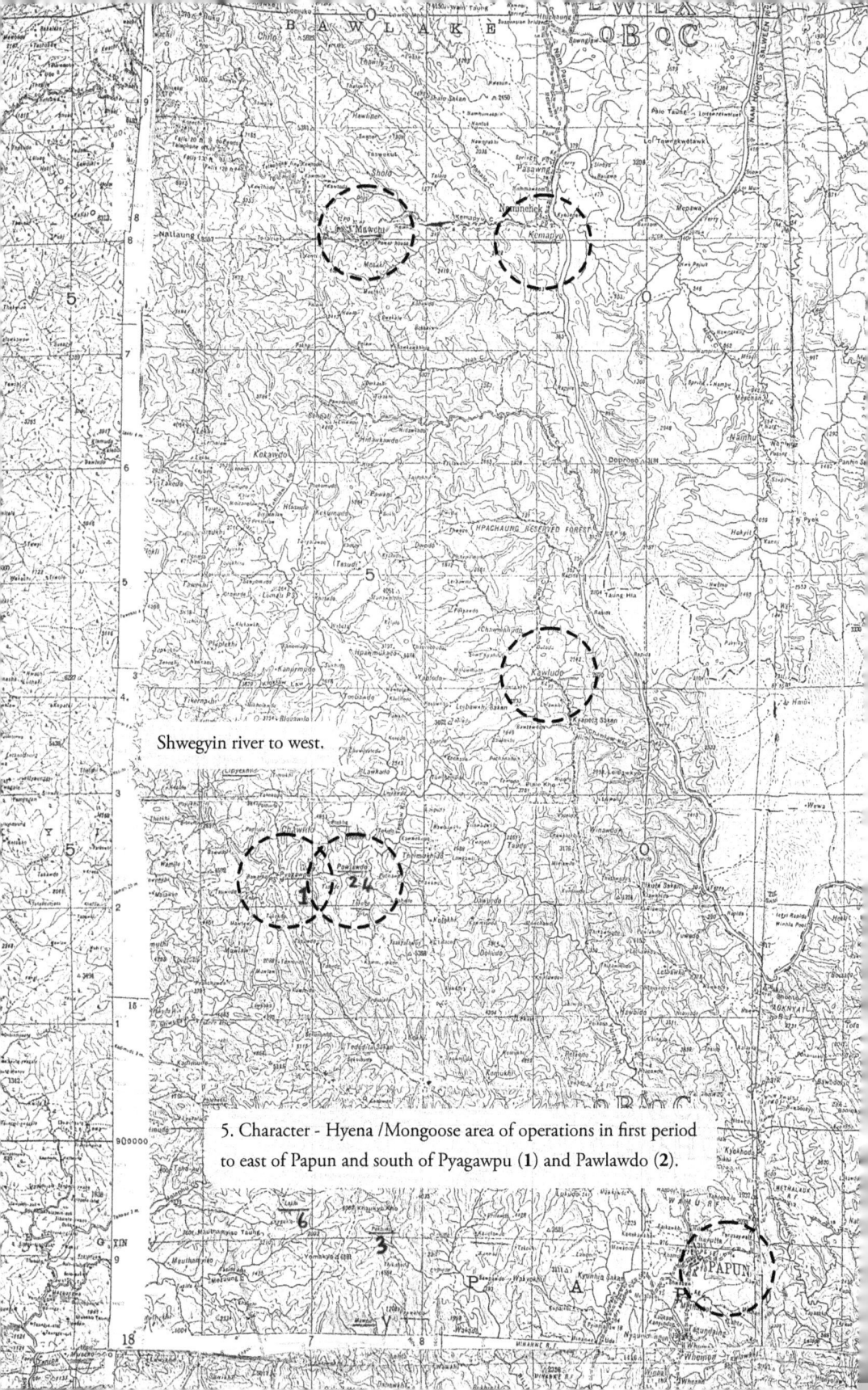

Shwegyin river to west.

5. Character - Hyena/Mongoose area of operations in first period to east of Papun and south of Pyagawpu (**1**) and Pawlawdo (**2**).

6. Kaumudo (**5**), Lokhi (**6**), Pokhido (**3**) and, Lekawdo (east of Kaumudo) – area south of original parachute drop at Pyagawpu (**1**) and 1st camp at Pawlawdo (**2**, **4**). Khauchi diary 8th April and then move off to Leklede shown on map to the south (map 7 opposite right).

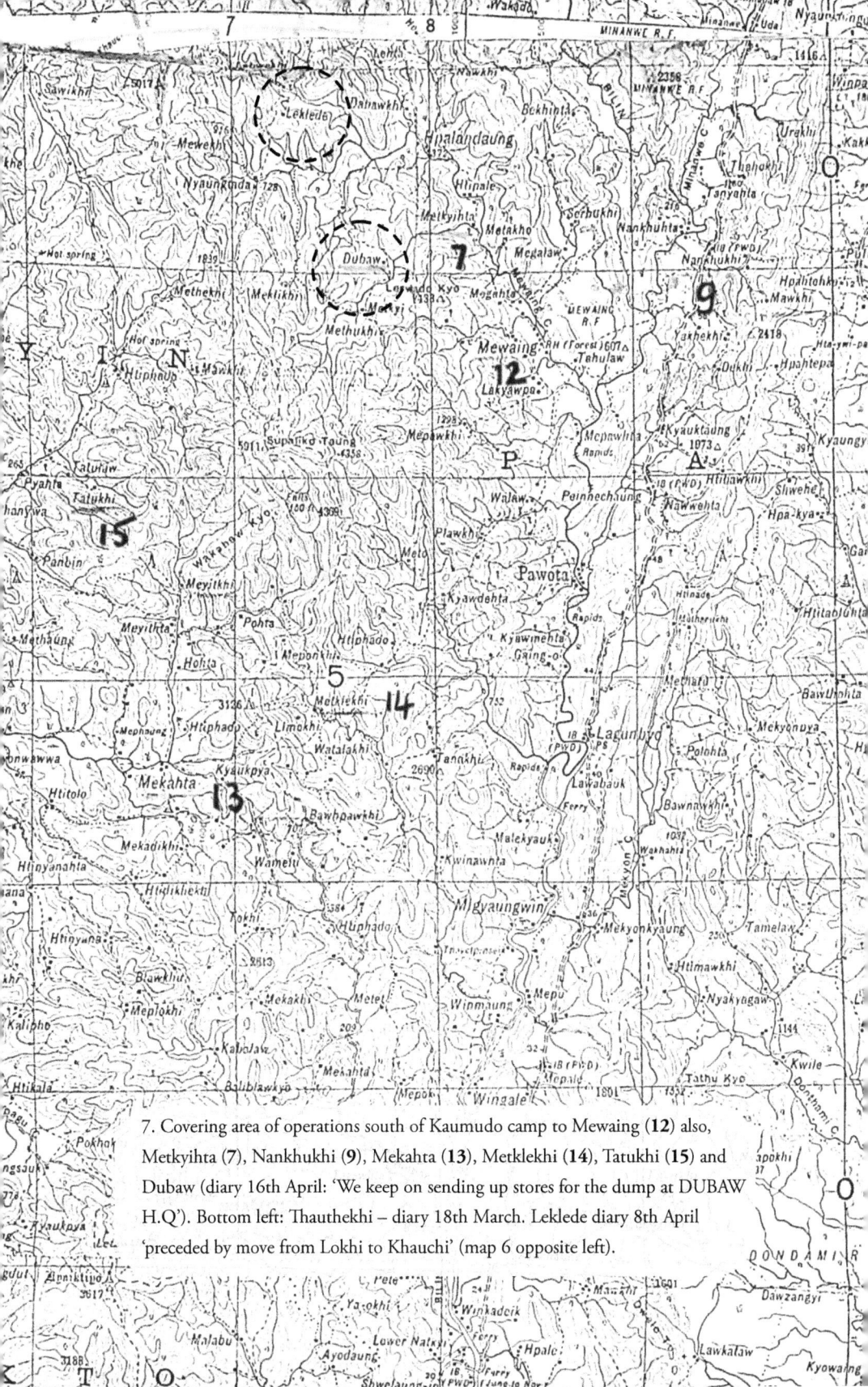

7. Covering area of operations south of Kaumudo camp to Mewaing (**12**) also, Metkyihta (**7**), Nankhukhi (**9**), Mekahta (**13**), Metklekhi (**14**), Tatukhi (**15**) and Dubaw (diary 16th April: 'We keep on sending up stores for the dump at DUBAW H.Q'). Bottom left: Thauthekhi – diary 18th March. Leklede diary 8th April 'preceded by move from Lokhi to Khauchi' (map 6 opposite left).

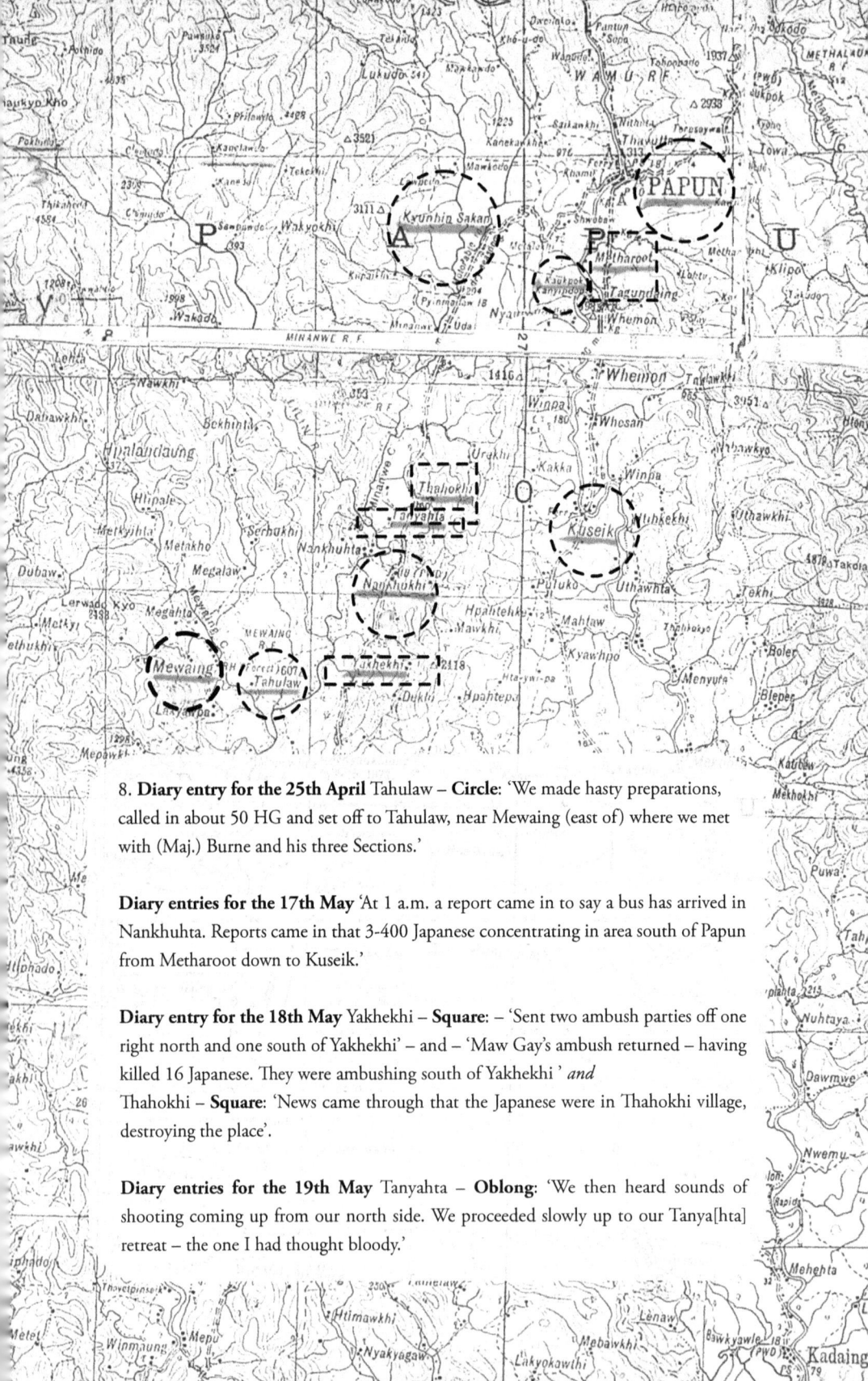

8. **Diary entry for the 25th April** Tahulaw – **Circle**: 'We made hasty preparations, called in about 50 HG and set off to Tahulaw, near Mewaing (east of) where we met with (Maj.) Burne and his three Sections.'

Diary entries for the 17th May 'At 1 a.m. a report came in to say a bus has arrived in Nankhuhta. Reports came in that 3-400 Japanese concentrating in area south of Papun from Metharoot down to Kuseik.'

Diary entry for the 18th May Yakhekhi – **Square**: – 'Sent two ambush parties off one right north and one south of Yakhekhi' – and – 'Maw Gay's ambush returned – having killed 16 Japanese. They were ambushing south of Yakhekhi' *and*
Thahokhi – **Square**: 'News came through that the Japanese were in Thahokhi village, destroying the place'.

Diary entries for the 19th May Tanyahta – **Oblong**: 'We then heard sounds of shooting coming up from our north side. We proceeded slowly up to our Tanya[hta] retreat – the one I had thought bloody.'

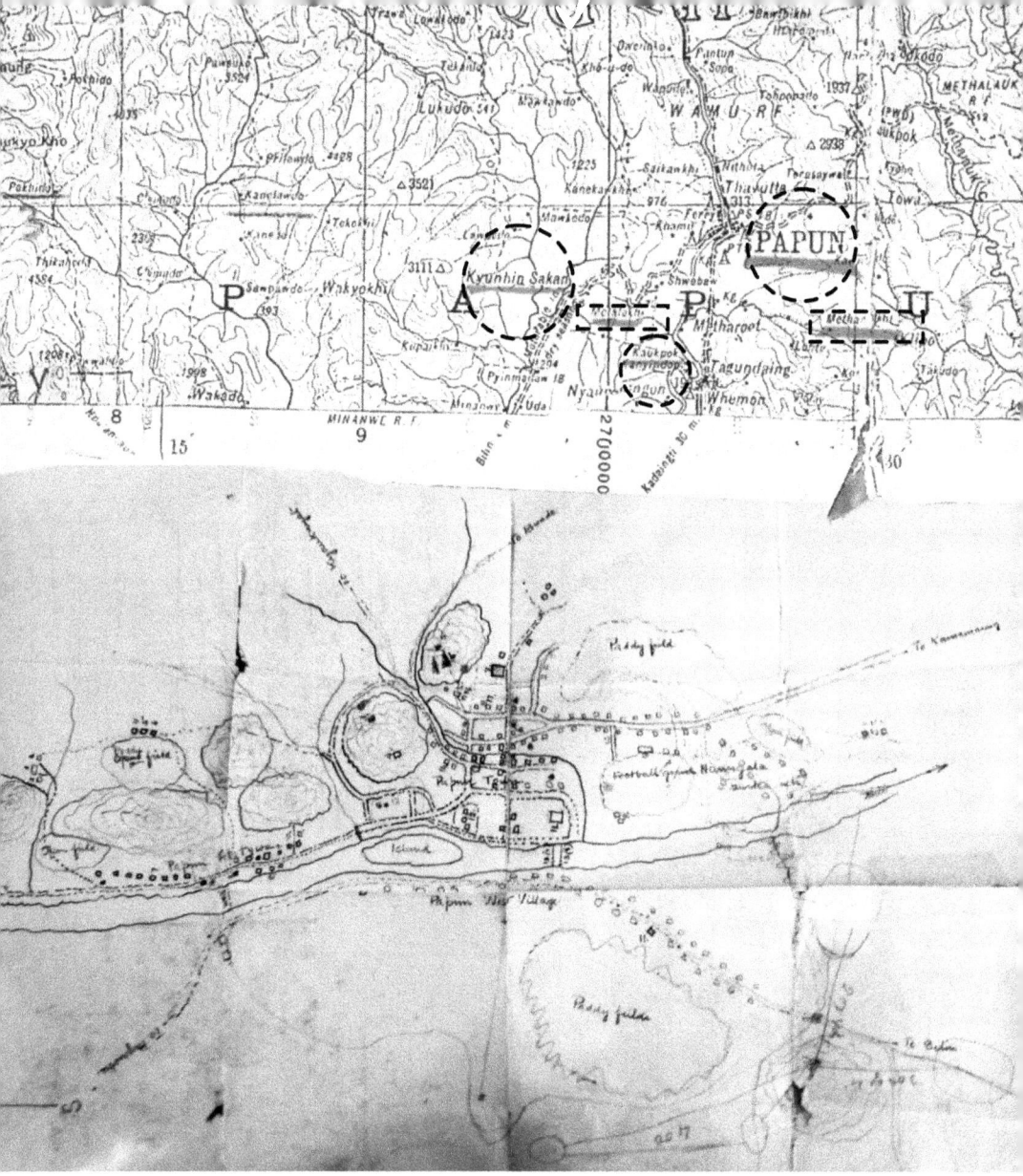

9. *Top right* Showing area south of Papun – Kaukpok Road. Also, area at Kyunbin Sakan where Japanese Garrison was concentrated to the west of Papun. Colonel Critchley approaching Papun from Kaukpok. **Oblong** Methalaukhi track to south-east of Papun. Alternatively, Metalekhi to the south-west of Papun.

10. *Bottom right* Hand drawn map of Papun.

The route taken from the south of Papun via Nankhukhi via BawBaw, Winpa through to Hklerhko – see diary entry for the 26th April (page 81).

MAPS – FORCE 136, OPERATION CHARACTER

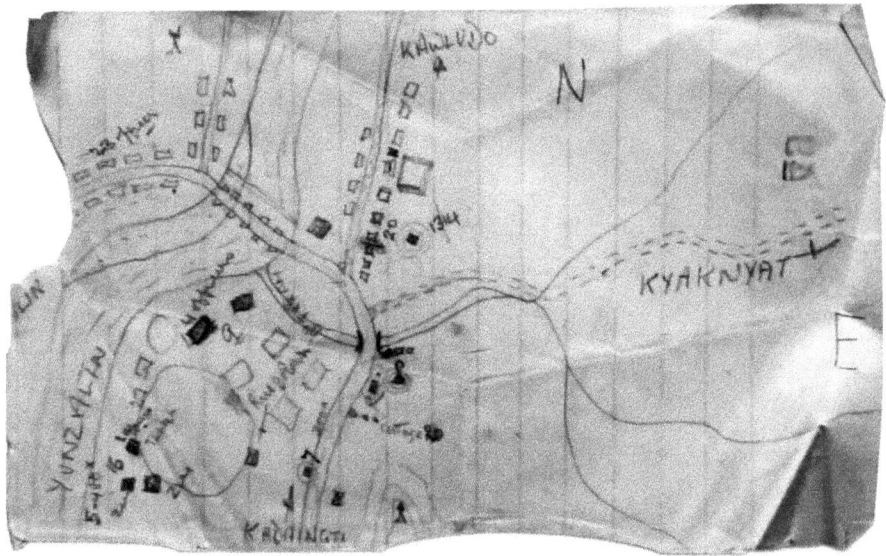

10. Hand-drawn map taken from Captain Trofimov's original diaries (2nd) showing intelligence gathering of the layout of the town of Papun for attack on 28th April 1945.

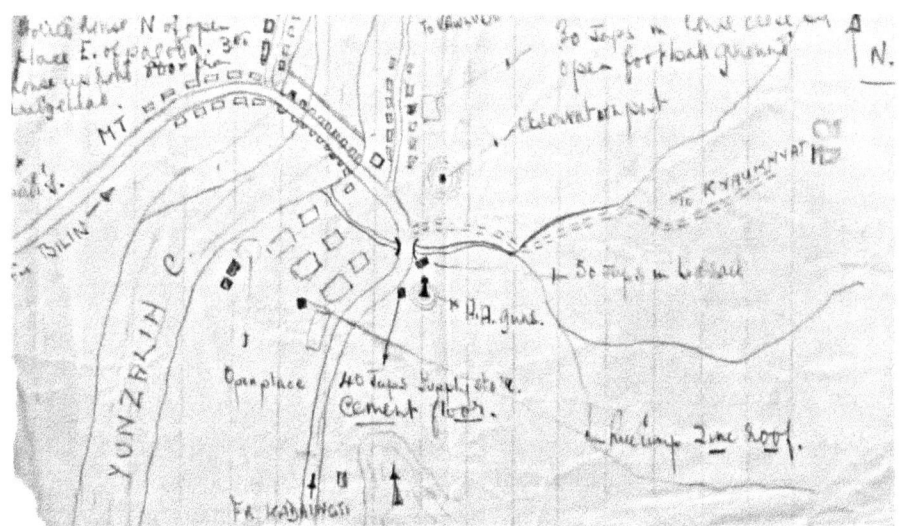

11. Additional hand-drawn map from original diary showing further intelligence gathering of Japanese positions within the town of Papun.

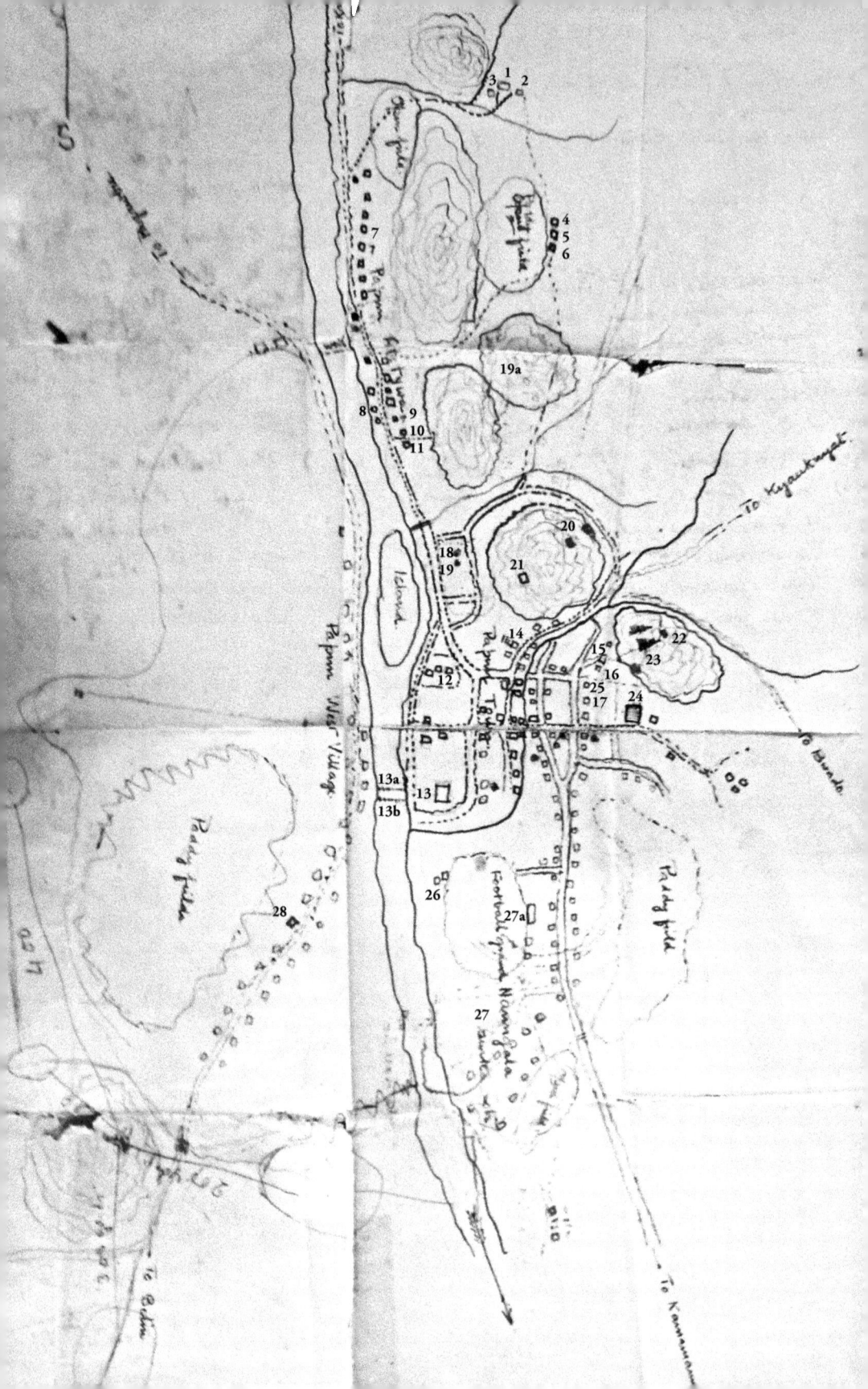

12. *Left* Hand drawn map of Papun (written on the rear of original paper map)

Original numbers in blue

1. Saw Mya Pauo's house (Pastor).
2. Thaung Byaw's house.
3. Saw Ba Sim's house.
4. 5. 6. 7. Karen houses.
8. Thaw Thi Koe's house (Chief Clerk, DC's office).
9. Saw Lim Byaw's house (Sub. Inspector of Excise).
10. Township Officer's house.
11. Church.
12. Police station.
13. DC's House.
13a. Bamboo bridge.
13b. Bridge for cart.
14. HQA's (Police) House.
15. Court House.
16. Nurse's House (Thraumu Dora).
17. Karen House.

Original numbers 1-11 in Red

18. 19. (1, 2) These are the 2 houses at Papun Atetrjwa village which the Japanese soldiers occupied.
19a. (2a) Rubber groves? Japanese soldiers dig trenches and lay in wait during daytime.
20. (3) The house the Japanese soldiers picketed.
21. (4) The Red (centre of original handwriting unreadable) during British time.
22. (5) Possible Japanese soldiers picketed here.
23. (6) 2 Pagoda.
24. (7) The big house where the Japanese soldiers and Officers are living.
25. (8) A Karen House which some Japanese soldiers are living.
26. (9) The 2 houses which JMP (Japanese Military Police) and MM Officers living quarters.
27. (10) Football shed with red corrugated iron sheet – Japanese store rice here.
27a. (10a) Nmgala Gurka Qtr. About 20 Japanese soldiers picketed here.
28. (11) The Headman UE Mg's House – some Japanese Army Officers and soldiers are living here.

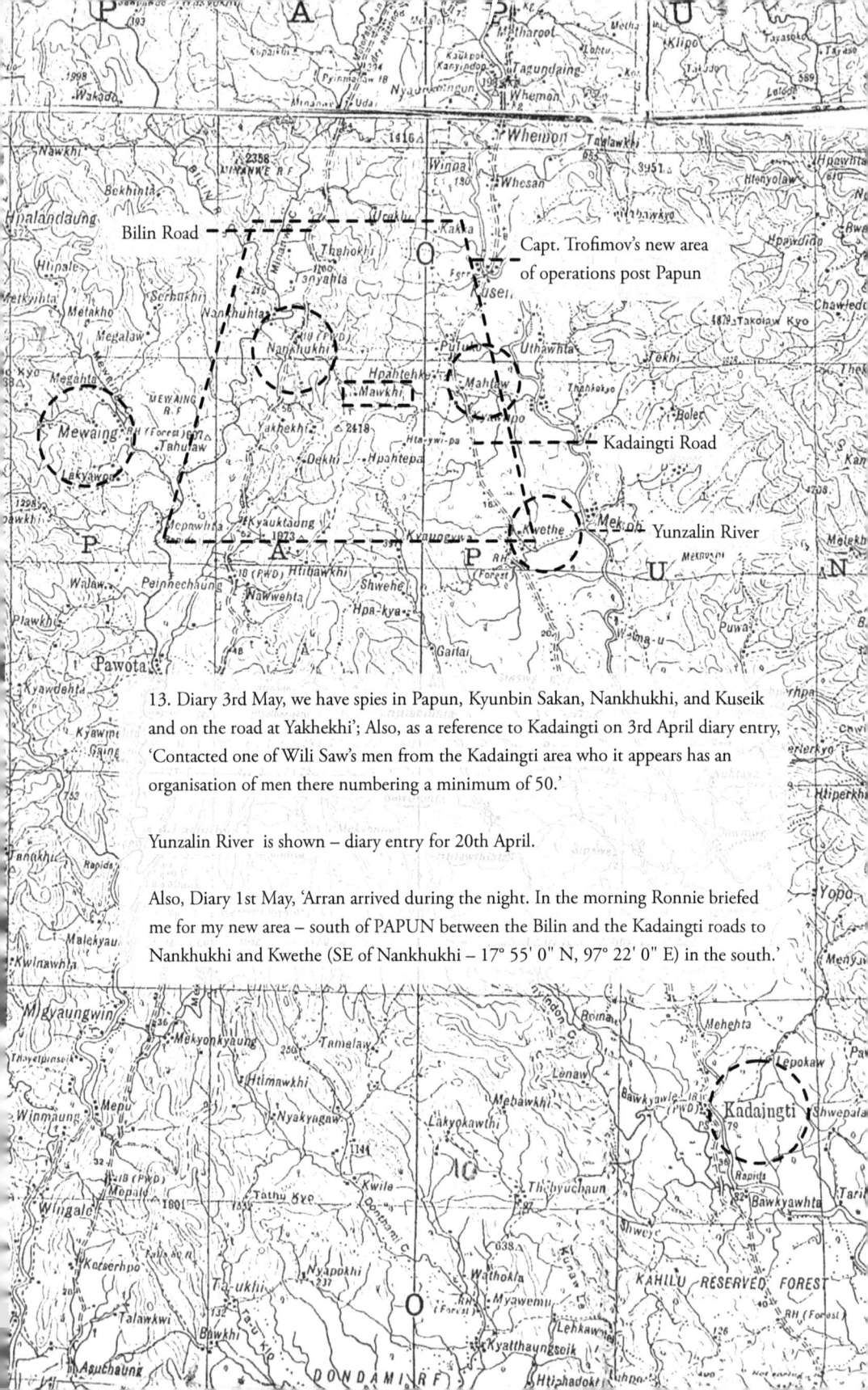

13. Diary 3rd May, we have spies in Papun, Kyunbin Sakan, Nankhukhi, and Kuseik and on the road at Yakhekhi'; Also, as a reference to Kadaingti on 3rd April diary entry, 'Contacted one of Wili Saw's men from the Kadaingti area who it appears has an organisation of men there numbering a minimum of 50.'

Yunzalin River is shown – diary entry for 20th April.

Also, Diary 1st May, 'Arran arrived during the night. In the morning Ronnie briefed me for my new area – south of PAPUN between the Bilin and the Kadaingti roads to Nankhukhi and Kwethe (SE of Nankhukhi – 17° 55' 0" N, 97° 22' 0" E) in the south.'

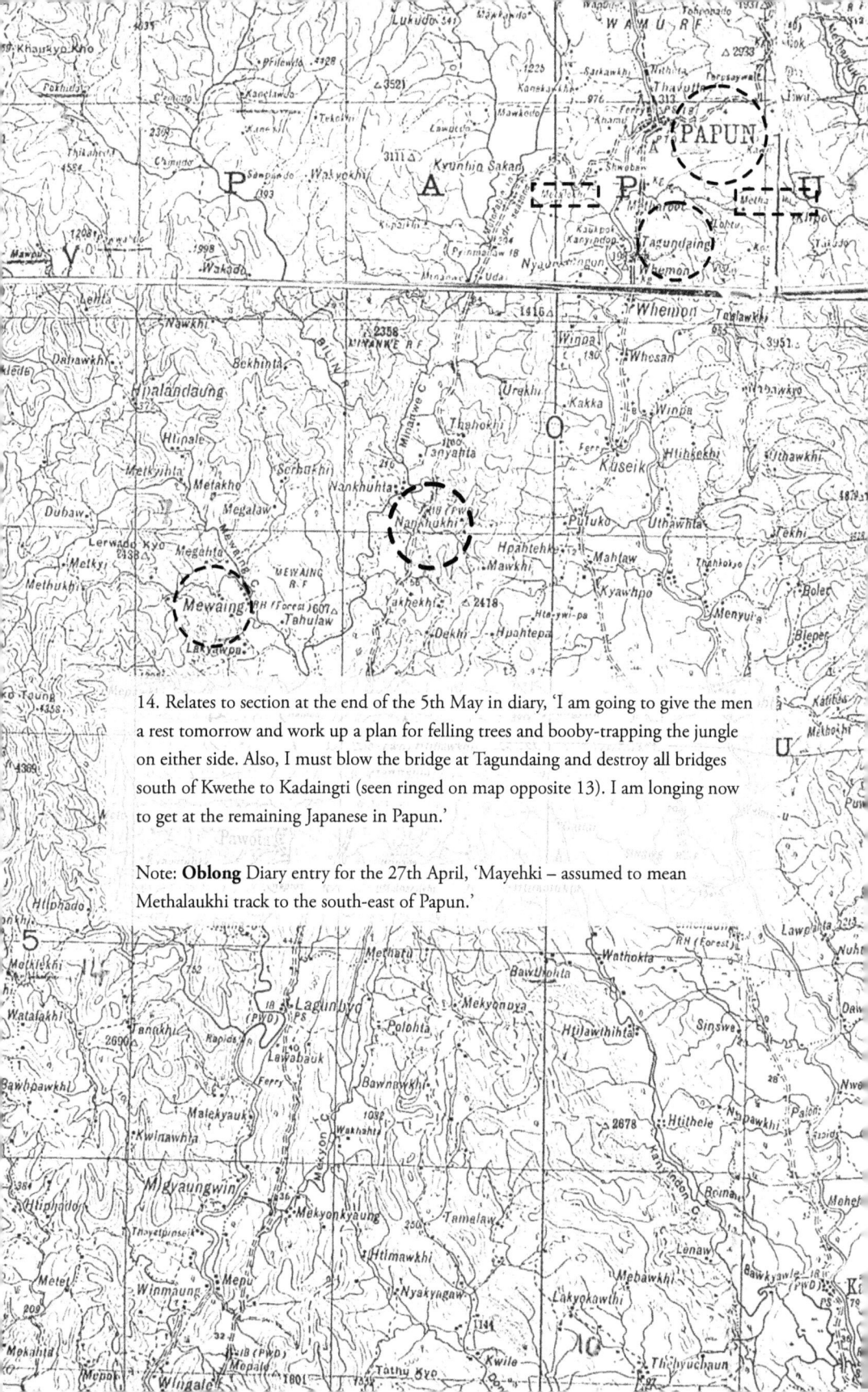

14. Relates to section at the end of the 5th May in diary, 'I am going to give the men a rest tomorrow and work up a plan for felling trees and booby-trapping the jungle on either side. Also, I must blow the bridge at Tagundaing and destroy all bridges south of Kwethe to Kadaingti (seen ringed on map opposite 13). I am longing now to get at the remaining Japanese in Papun.'

Note: **Oblong** Diary entry for the 27th April, 'Mayehki – assumed to mean Methalaukhi track to the south-east of Papun.'

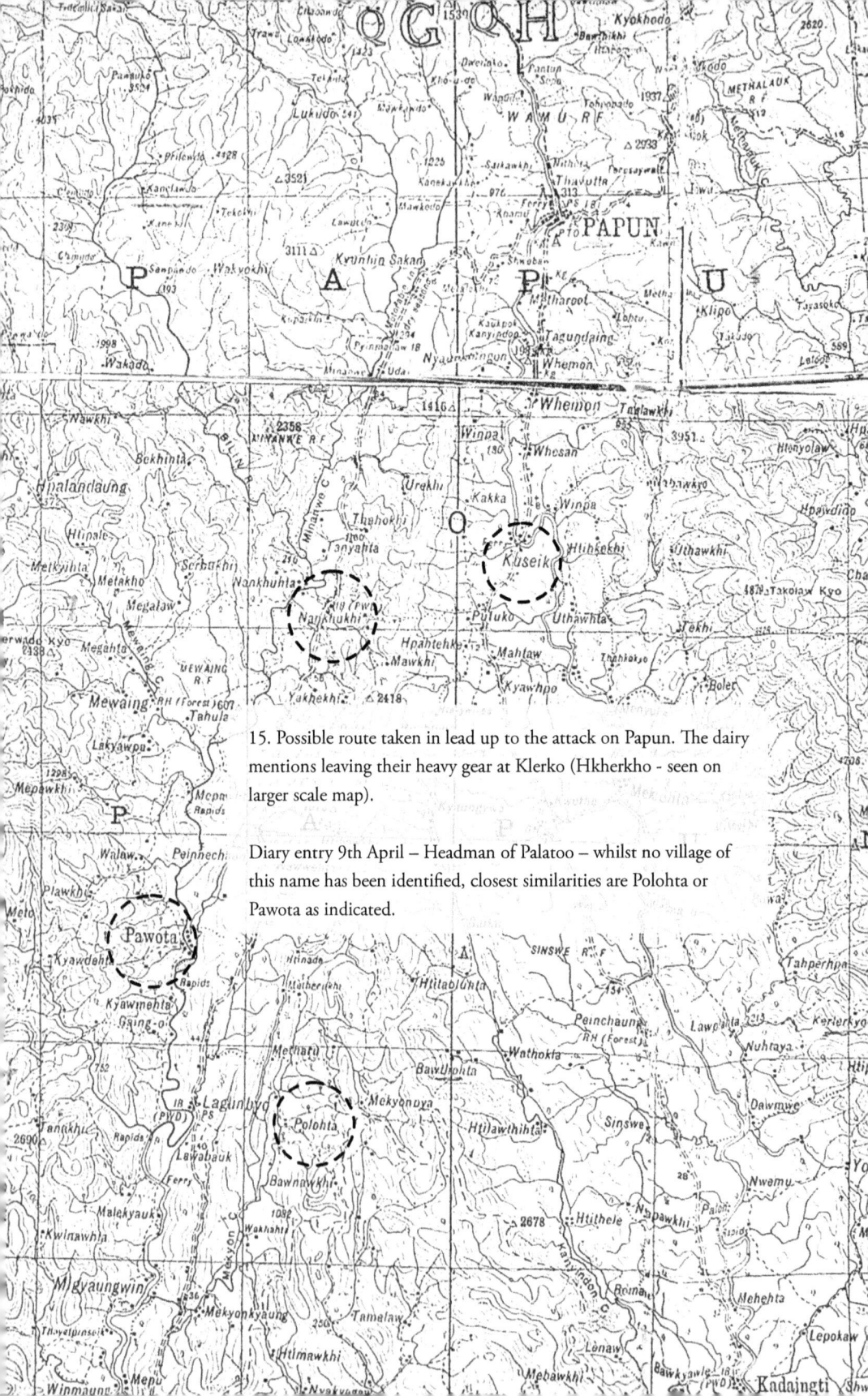

15. Possible route taken in lead up to the attack on Papun. The dairy mentions leaving their heavy gear at Klerko (Hkherkho - seen on larger scale map).

Diary entry 9th April – Headman of Palatoo – whilst no village of this name has been identified, closest similarities are Polohta or Pawota as indicated.

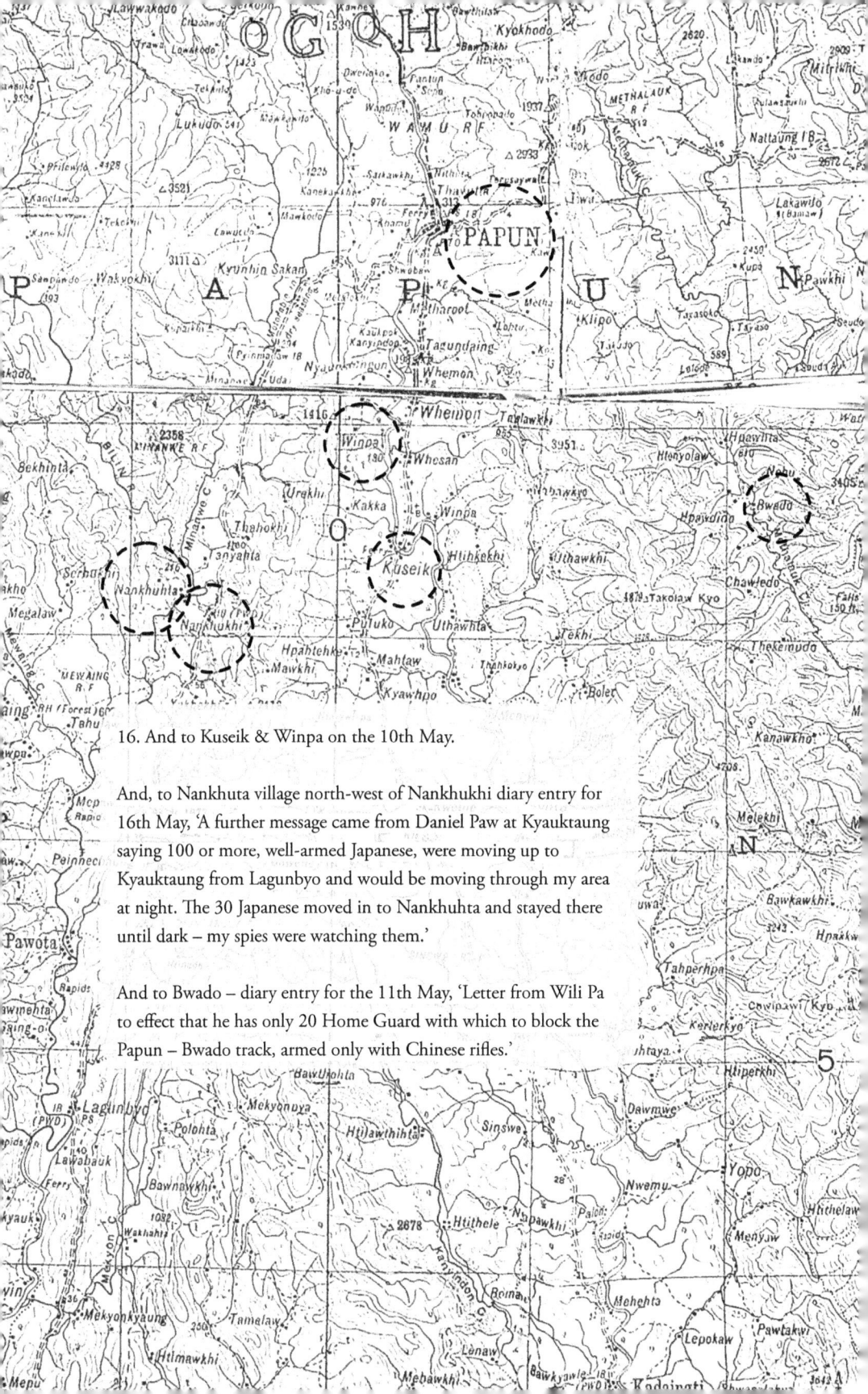

16. And to Kuseik & Winpa on the 10th May.

And, to Nankhuta village north-west of Nankhukhi diary entry for 16th May, 'A further message came from Daniel Paw at Kyauktaung saying 100 or more, well-armed Japanese, were moving up to Kyauktaung from Lagunbyo and would be moving through my area at night. The 30 Japanese moved in to Nankhuhta and stayed there until dark – my spies were watching them.'

And to Bwado – diary entry for the 11th May, 'Letter from Wili Pa to effect that he has only 20 Home Guard with which to block the Papun – Bwado track, armed only with Chinese rifles.'

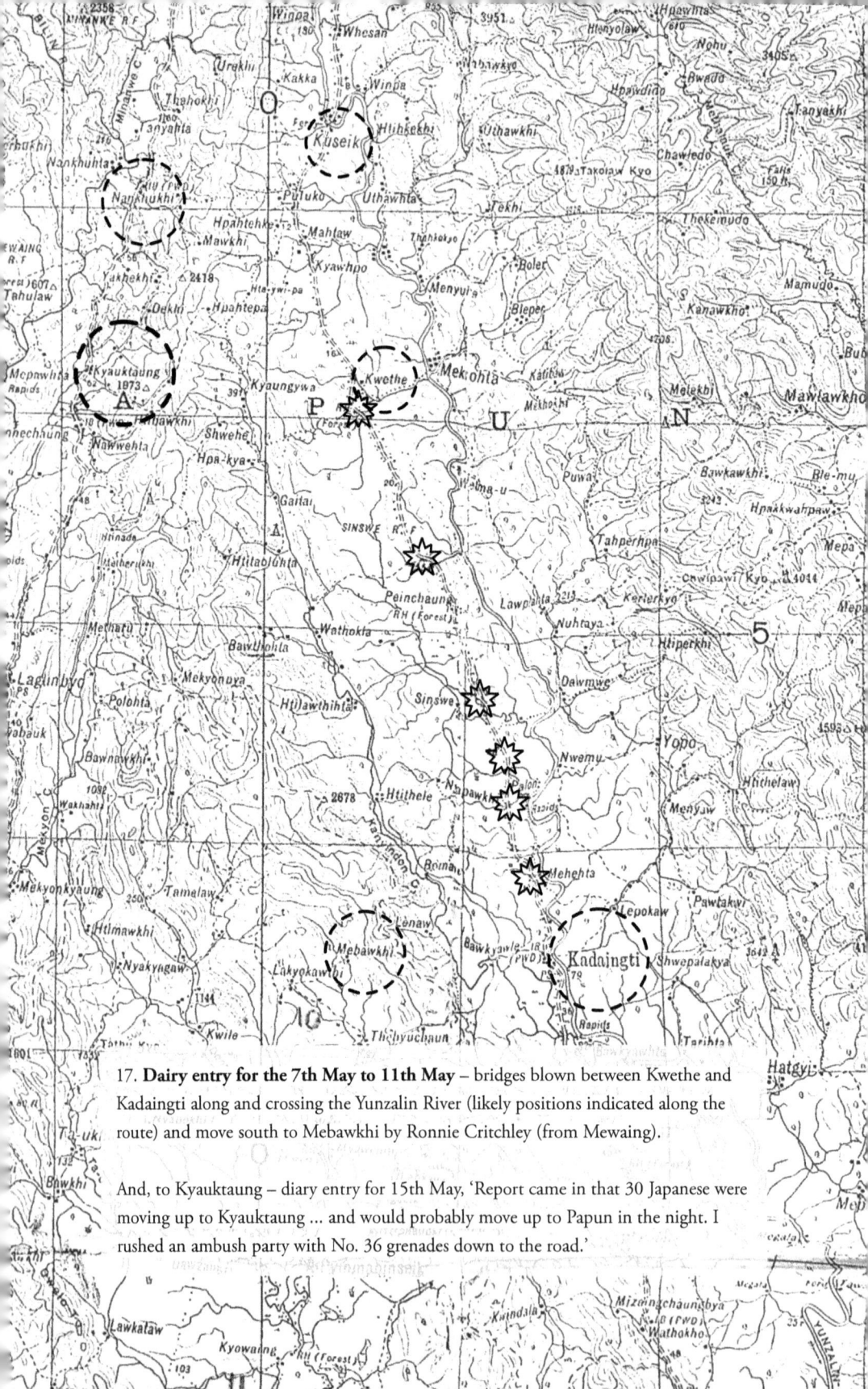

17. **Dairy entry for the 7th May to 11th May** – bridges blown between Kwethe and Kadaingti along and crossing the Yunzalin River (likely positions indicated along the route) and move south to Mebawkhi by Ronnie Critchley (from Mewaing).

And, to Kyauktaung – diary entry for 15th May, 'Report came in that 30 Japanese were moving up to Kyauktaung ... and would probably move up to Papun in the night. I rushed an ambush party with No. 36 grenades down to the road.'

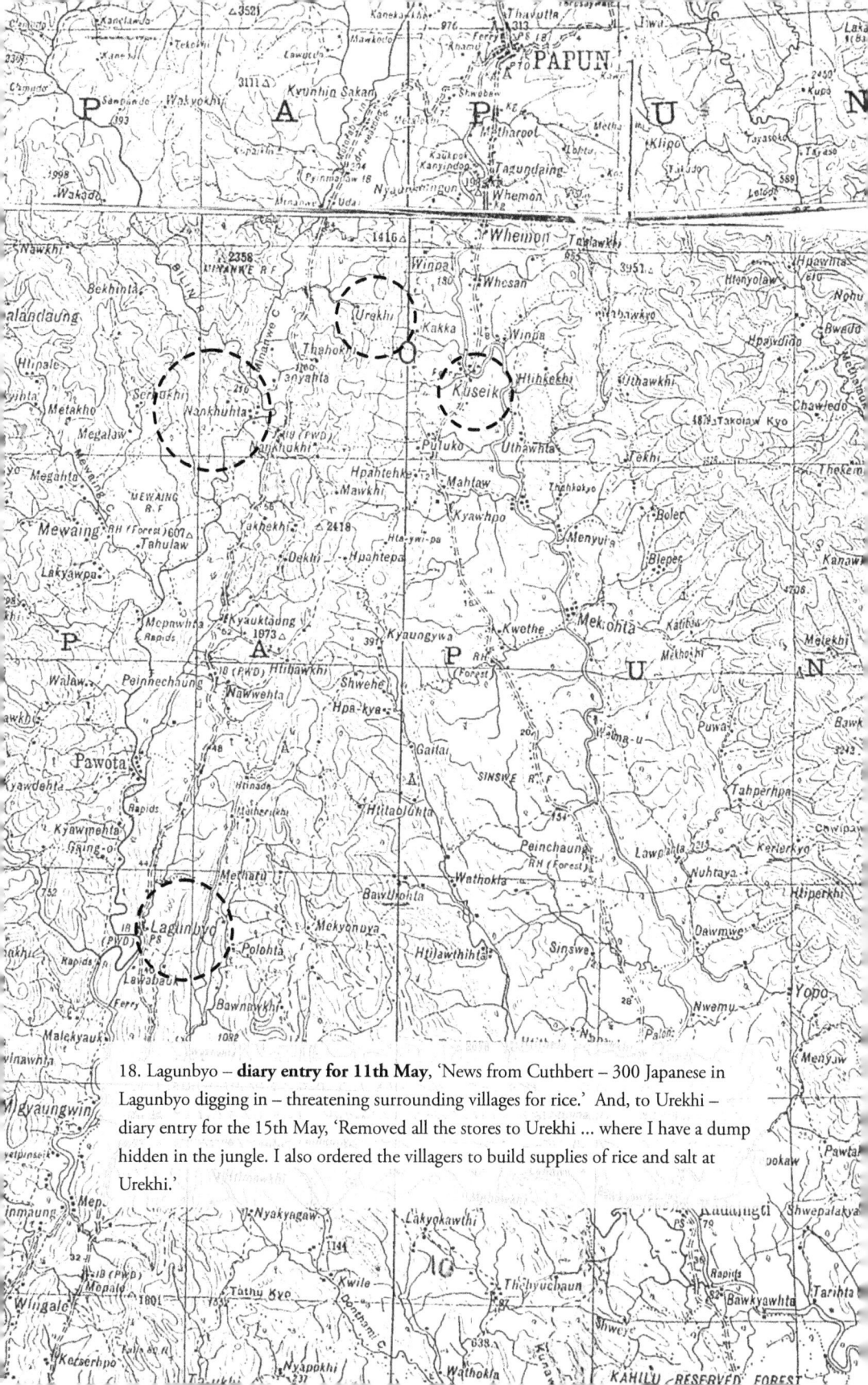

18. Lagunbyo – **diary entry for 11th May**, 'News from Cuthbert – 300 Japanese in Lagunbyo digging in – threatening surrounding villages for rice.' And, to Urekhi – diary entry for the 15th May, 'Removed all the stores to Urekhi ... where I have a dump hidden in the jungle. I also ordered the villagers to build supplies of rice and salt at Urekhi.'

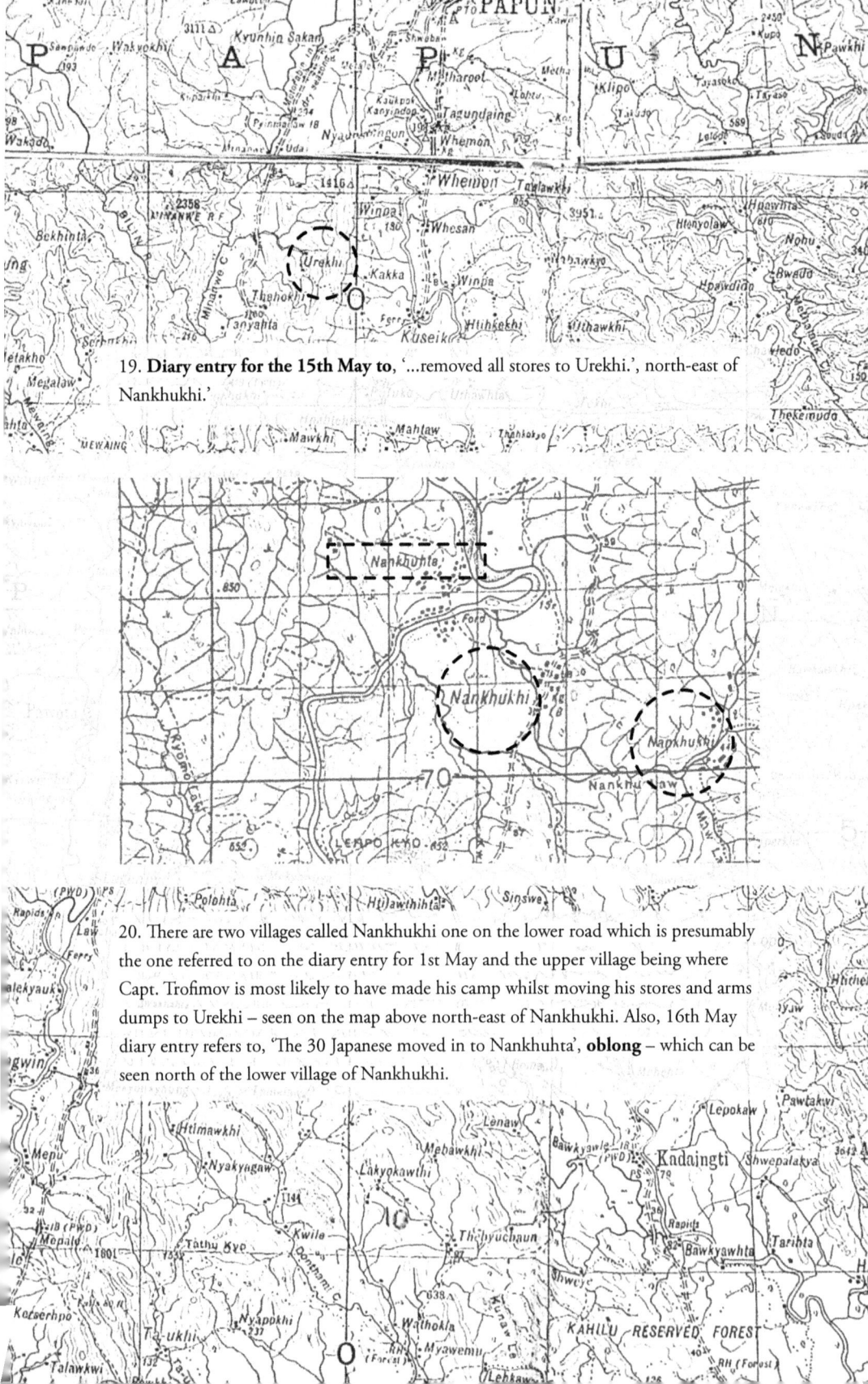

19. **Diary entry for the 15th May to**, '...removed all stores to Urekhi.', north-east of Nankhukhi.'

20. There are two villages called Nankhukhi one on the lower road which is presumably the one referred to on the diary entry for 1st May and the upper village being where Capt. Trofimov is most likely to have made his camp whilst moving his stores and arms dumps to Urekhi – seen on the map above north-east of Nankhukhi. Also, 16th May diary entry refers to, 'The 30 Japanese moved in to Nankhuhta', **oblong** – which can be seen north of the lower village of Nankhukhi.

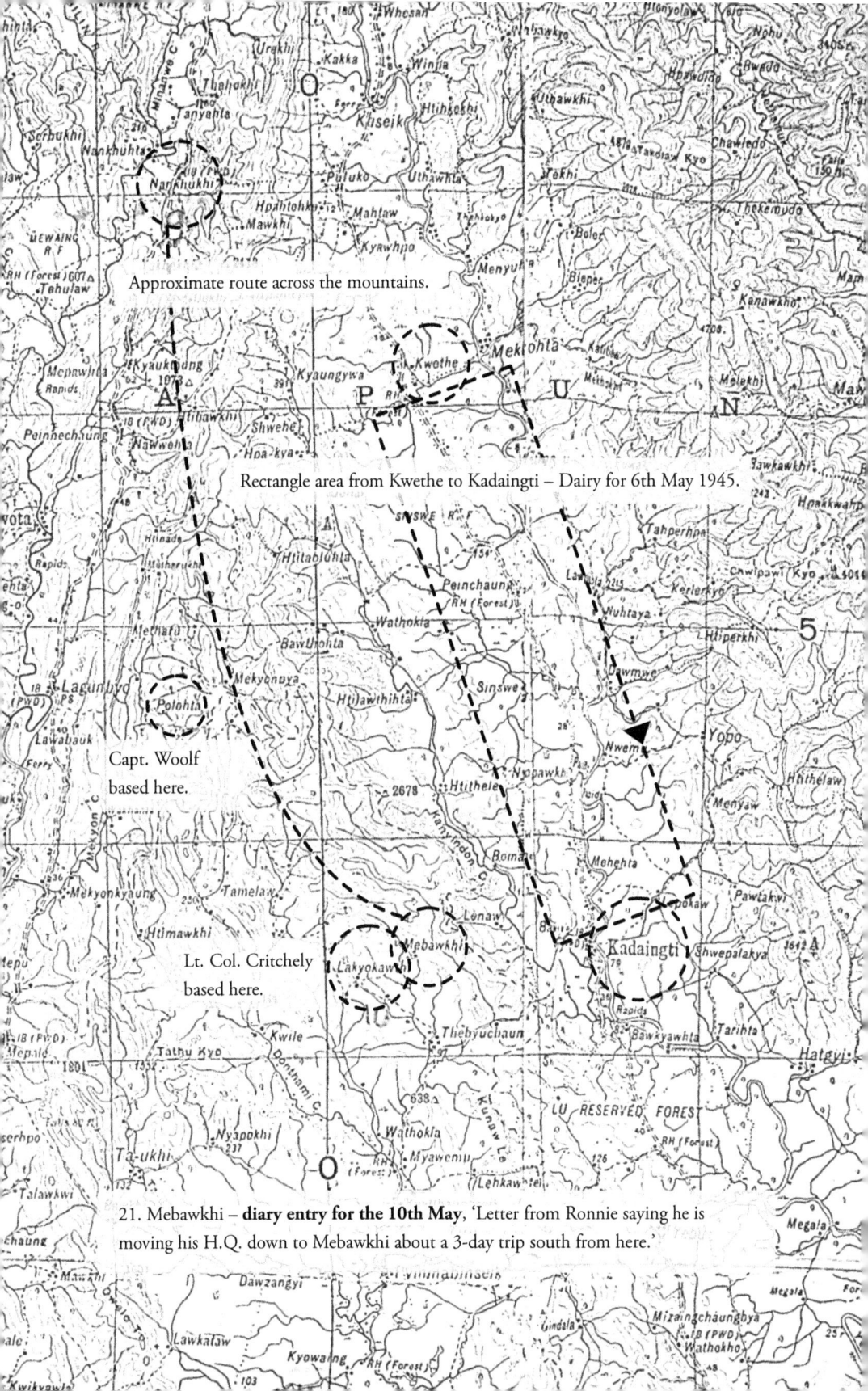

21. Mebawkhi – **diary entry for the 10th May**, 'Letter from Ronnie saying he is moving his H.Q. down to Mebawkhi about a 3-day trip south from here.'

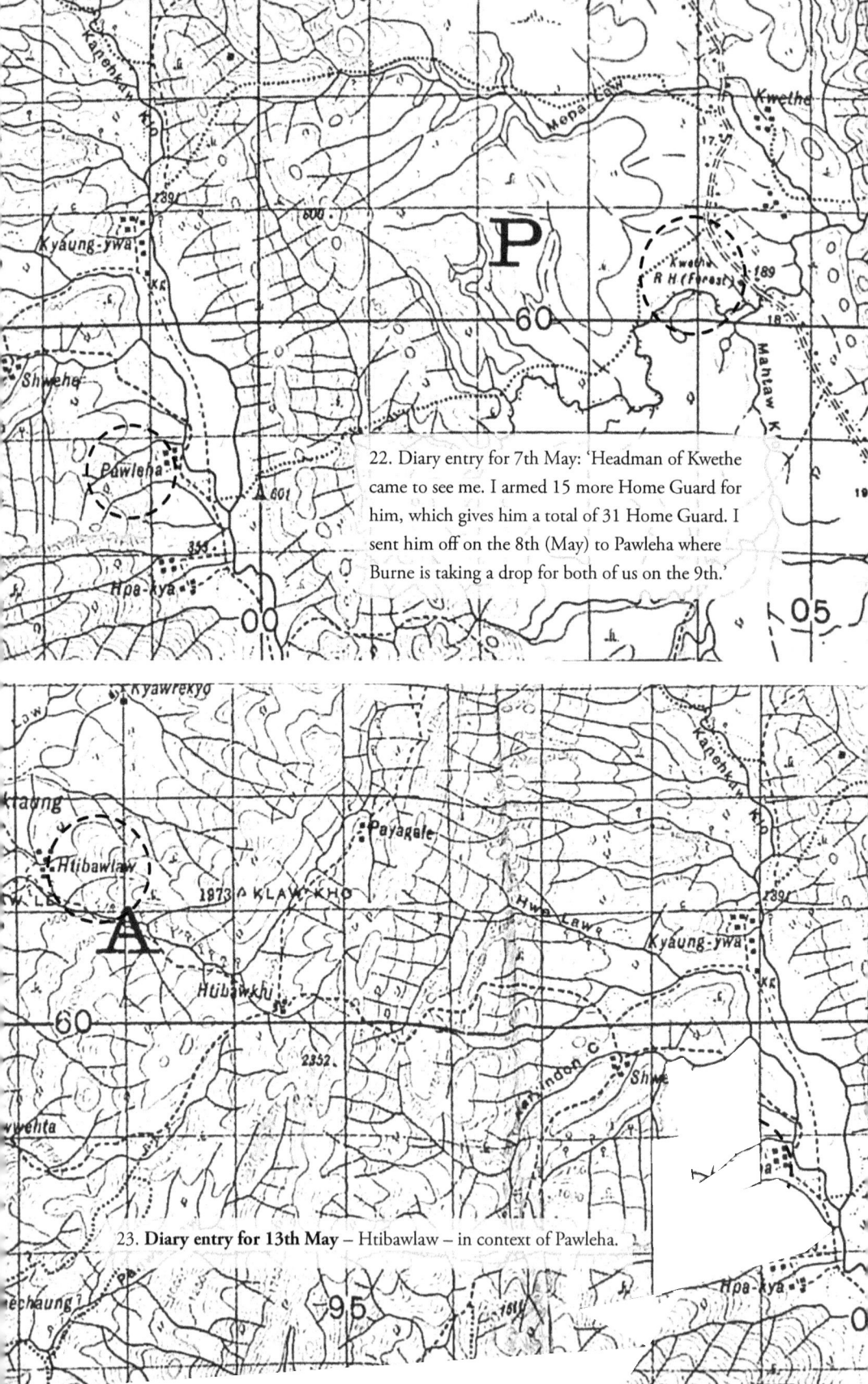

22. Diary entry for 7th May: 'Headman of Kwethe came to see me. I armed 15 more Home Guard for him, which gives him a total of 31 Home Guard. I sent him off on the 8th (May) to Pawleha where Burne is taking a drop for both of us on the 9th.'

23. **Diary entry for 13th May** – Htibawlaw – in context of Pawleha.

24. Capt. Trofimov's move south from his camp at Nankhukhi southwards towards where Lt. Col. Ronnie Critchley is based at Lakyokawthi.

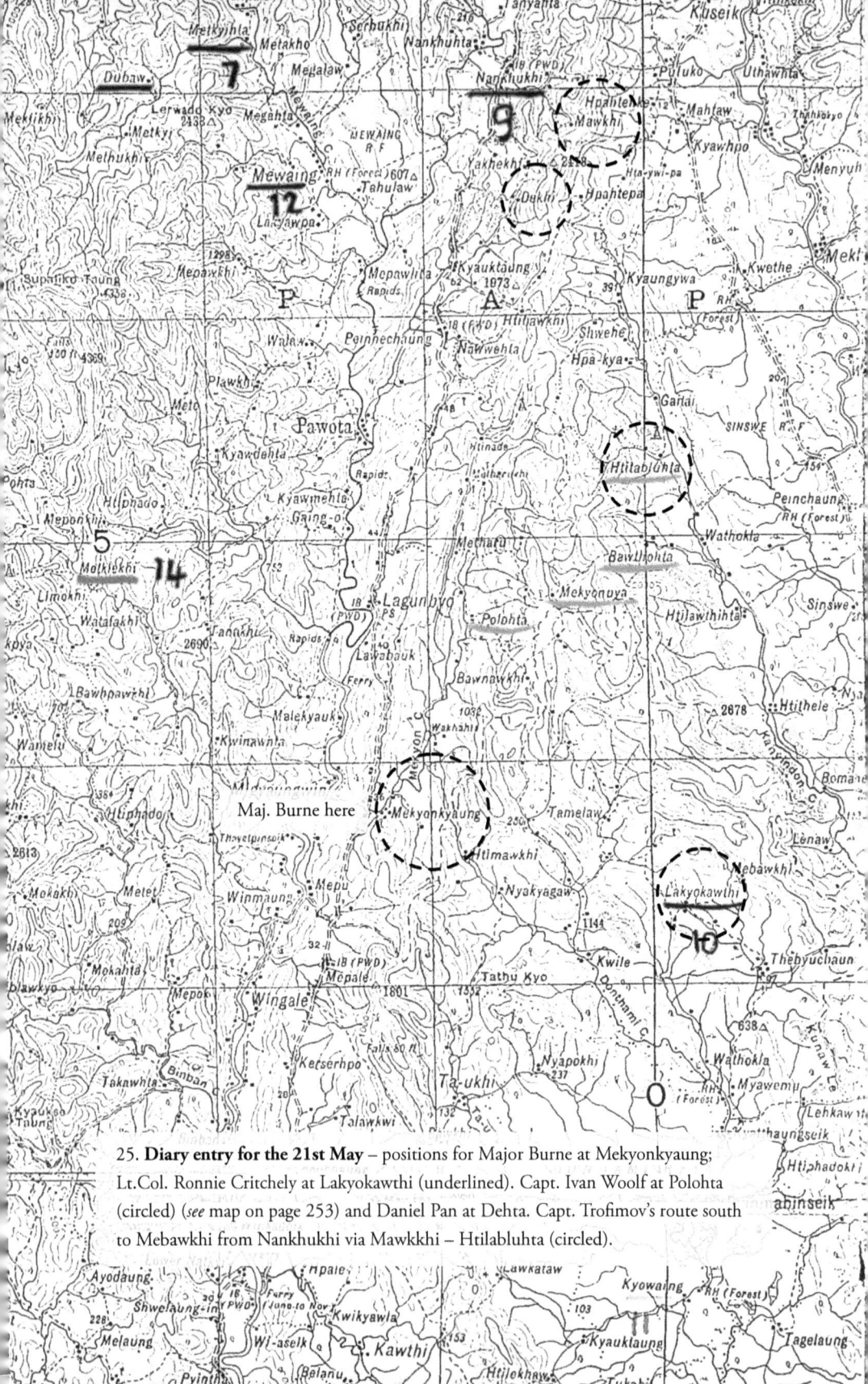

25. **Diary entry for the 21st May** – positions for Major Burne at Mekyonkyaung; Lt.Col. Ronnie Critchely at Lakyokawthi (underlined). Capt. Ivan Woolf at Polohta (circled) (*see* map on page 253) and Daniel Pan at Dehta. Capt. Trofimov's route south to Mebawkhi from Nankhukhi via Mawkkhi – Htilabluhta (circled).

26. Kamamaung – during Capt. Trofimov's de-brief in Rangoon on the 3rd June – as a Japanese stronghold – south of their last position at Lakyokawthi before departure for Calcutta via Rangoon.

27. 3rd June – de-brief in Rangoon to Lagunbyo as another Japanese stronghold.

28. The route back north via Htinade (27th June) through Walaw – Mewaing to Metakho.

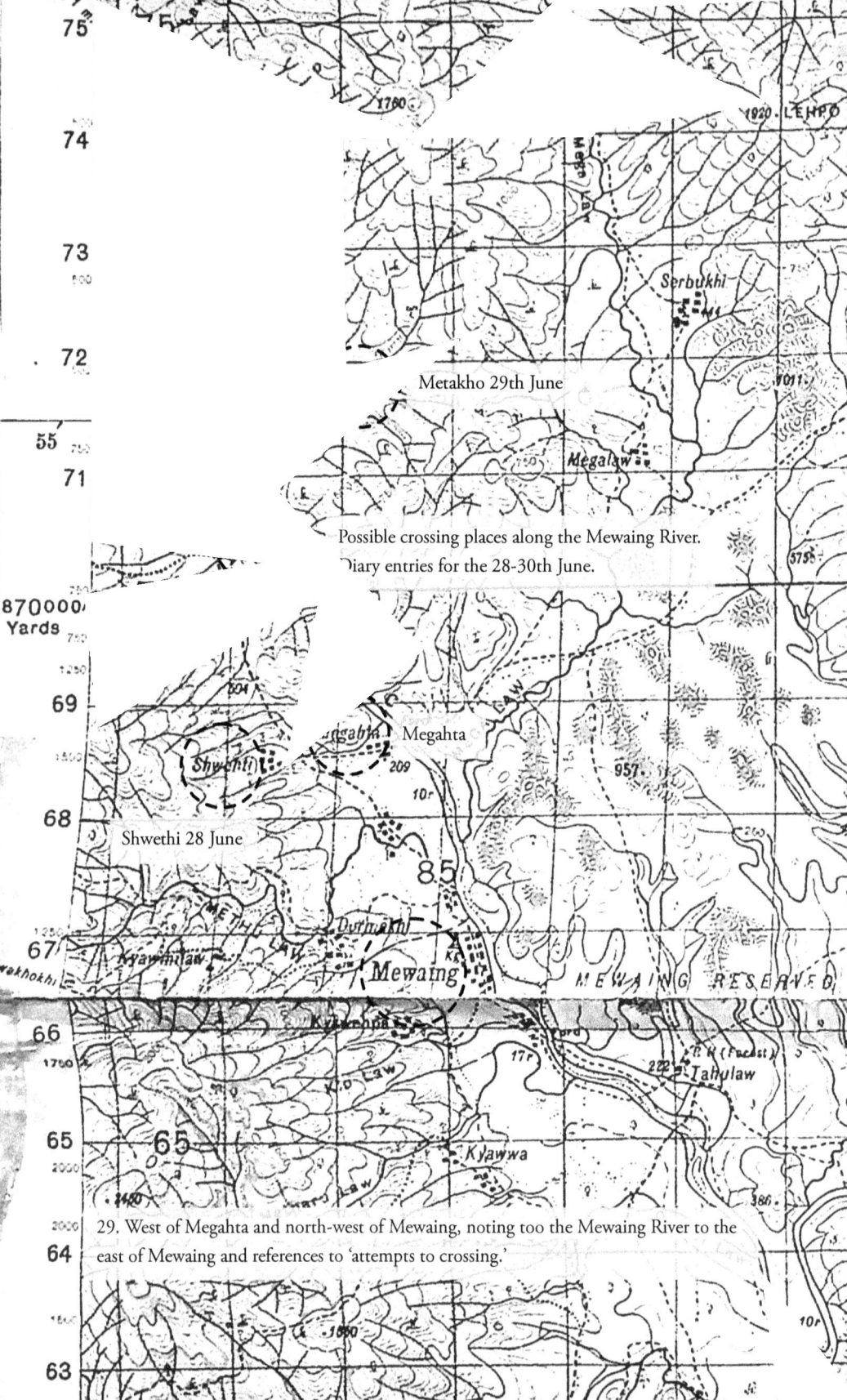

Possible crossing places along the Mewaing River. Diary entries for the 28-30th June.

29. West of Megahta and north-west of Mewaing, noting too the Mewaing River to the east of Mewaing and references to 'attempts to crossing.'

32. **Diary Entry for the 26th July**, 'Shwegyin-Shanywa-Wingale-Bilin-Thaton; one of the Japanese routes of retreat from the advancing British XIV Army.'

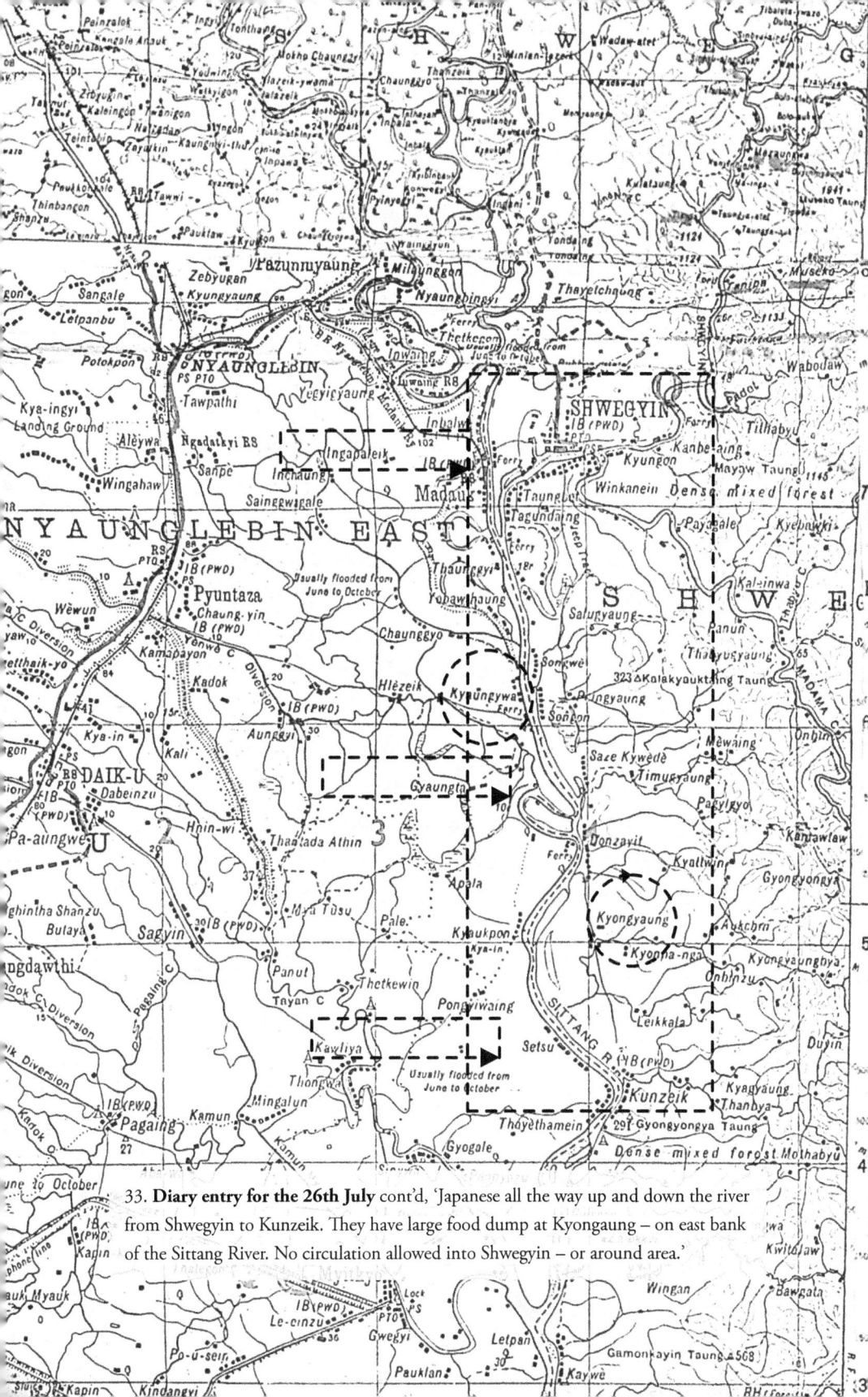

33. **Diary entry for the 26th July** cont'd, 'Japanese all the way up and down the river from Shwegyin to Kunzeik. They have large food dump at Kyongaung – on east bank of the Sittang River. No circulation allowed into Shwegyin – or around area.'

34. **Diary entry for the 6th August** – Padet Chaung tributary to the Sittang River.

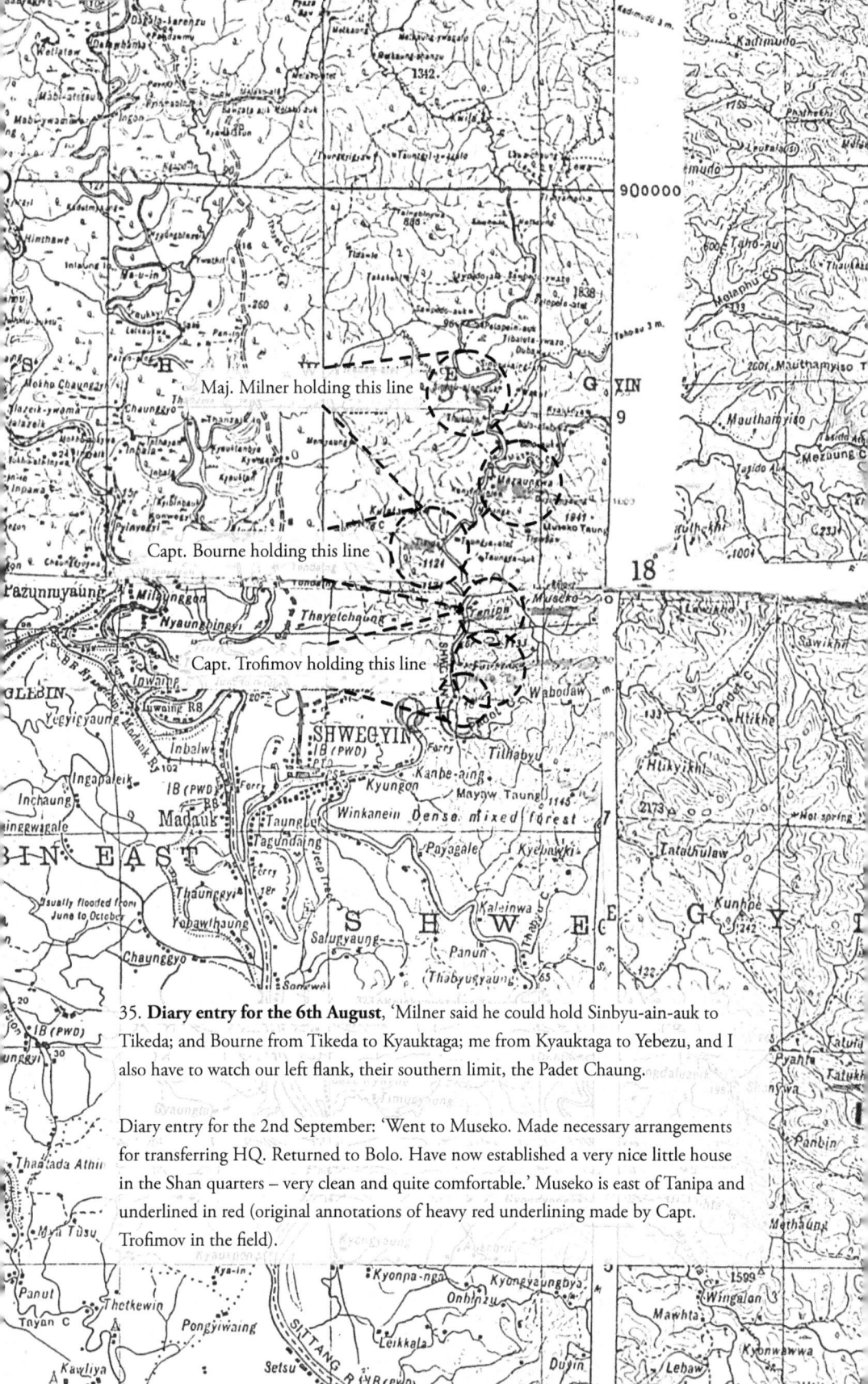

35. **Diary entry for the 6th August**, 'Milner said he could hold Sinbyu-ain-auk to Tikeda; and Bourne from Tikeda to Kyauktaga; me from Kyauktaga to Yebezu, and I also have to watch our left flank, their southern limit, the Padet Chaung.'

Diary entry for the 2nd September: 'Went to Museko. Made necessary arrangements for transferring HQ. Returned to Bolo. Have now established a very nice little house in the Shan quarters – very clean and quite comfortable.' Museko is east of Tanipa and underlined in red (original annotations of heavy red underlining made by Capt. Trofimov in the field).

Appendix I

Codenamed "Guy": With the Jedburghs in France June–August 1944

(The following paper was written by "Trof" probably in the 1990s. It has been edited to provide a detailed personal narrative of his time and activities in France, with some of the very brief details he gives of his life and military career before 1944 being included in the introduction to this book. His comments on the Burma campaign have been incorporated (where useful) into his diary for 1945.)

I had my first interview in London for the Special Forces on the 13th to 19th January 1944, to be followed by a series of tests at various addresses in and around London.

Soon afterwards, having successfully passed the tests, I joined the Special Forces and proceeded to Milton Hall at Peterborough, where there was a training school for Jedburghs (known as Jeds).

There followed an intensive period of training covering every aspect of guerrilla warfare, comprising sabotage, use of explosives, enemy identifications, military operations, silent killing techniques, organisation of networks, dropping zone drill, wireless telegraphy, Morse code, parachute training, training on Eureka and two-way S-phone larynx sets.[1]

Because of my earlier training in Signals, the wireless and Morse code came very easily to me.

We eventually formed into Jed teams, comprising either an English or American Officer, with one French Officer and a radio operator.

I eventually joined up with two groups comprising Captain Jean Claude, Captain Dreux, Lt. A. Thomas and radio operators Masson and Deschamps.

We were briefed in London, and our role was to destroy enemy lines of communication, pass information on enemy movements and to capture an airport near Rennes (Ile-et-Villaine Department, Brittany) long enough to enable a Lysander plane to bring the French Colonel, who attended the briefing, into France.

The jump took place from a Liberator and the signal over the radio was "le chien de TOTO est gentil".

We were dropped near Courcité (Mayenne Department, Pays de Loire), south of Alencon – and I was dropped some distance away from the DZ (Drop Zone), and finally made contact with a member of the reception committee.

We were dropped in uniform and this caused considerable alarm to the members of the Resistance that we met as clearly we would only be able to move by night and it would be more difficult and hazardous to conceal so many of us by day. It must be remembered that there were no active groups of local resistance in the area at the time; only sedentary members of the Resistance. (NB all contacts with Resistance Groups in Ile-et-Vilaine had been lost since March 1944).

We were taken to a safe house where we spent the night in a barn and the next morning I saw a German wireless detector parked outside the farm. Fortunately, we had not been transmitting and they eventually departed.

The Germans knew there had been a drop the night before, and were checking around the countryside.

We proceeded to Ille-et-Vilaine area by road at night, stopping at pre-arranged safe houses. Progress was very slow as we were in uniform and could only travel in the dead of night, carrying all our equipment.

Eventually we came to a barn in the country and could not go any further as we had no safe house to go to from thence onwards.

After making enquiries with the local Resistance contact I learnt that there was a British agent working in the area, whose code name was Michel (Claude de Baissac?).[2]

I obtained, through our contacts civilian clothes and borrowed a bicycle and went to contact Michel. After the usual checks to identify that I was a genuine British Officer, Michel agreed to accompany me back to meet the rest of the group. We cycled back, passing villages where Germans were frequently sitting outside cafes and throughout Michel never stopped singing in English.

Michel was surprised at our uniforms and stated that the wearing of them would make it progressively difficult to get the group to their objectives as we would clearly be penetrating further and further into an area where the Germans were setting up delaying tactics to enable the main troops to withdraw.

Eventually Michel was able to put us in contact with Lulu (Commandant Petri) who organised our journey from thence forward, but again, always in the dead of night. We eventually reached Gorron (Mayenne Department), and growing anxious at the slow progress we were making, we purchased an old car and set off at night, only to run into a German patrol. We were split up and I was not able to rejoin them so I moved to a nearby safe house – a farm owned by M. et Mme Lochu. I had to conceal myself in a barn for several days, whilst the Germans combed the area, looking for the Resistance members that had been reported by the patrol.

Eventually I made contact with Gendarmes Leray and Plassart of Gorron,[3] and they brought food and took my photograph, and eventually obtained a carte d'Identite' and a 'Carte de Refugie'. Together with a set of suitable shabby clothes through another Resistance contact, Felix Drogoul. From then onwards I became Louis Simon Matte.

I set up a network, using Leray, Plassart and Drogoul, and information started coming through that the American forces had broken through from Avranches, and were moving inland towards Alencon. I set about visiting the area to inspect the German defences, and as they changed their positions at night I had to take a chance and go out at night. Returning from one of these trips I ran into a German patrol on the outskirts of Gorron, but by pretending to be drunk got away with it. I walked right through a German battalion resting by the roadside on my way to a Resistance contact.

During the day I managed to check the positions of the mines the Germans were laying, in particular under one of the bridges on a side road leading into Gorron.

On another occasion there was heavy movement of retreating German troops and I managed, by posing as a farm worker, to get a good look into one of the Red Cross vans parked by the hedge – it was full of ammunition boxes.

Soon afterwards I learnt through my contact with the Gendarmerie that the Americans were approaching Gorron. I took a final look at the German positions from a concealed position and set off across the fields with one of the Gendarmes who had volunteered to accompany me.

We were in luck and made contact with an advancing reconnaissance column of Americans, who were preparing to hit Gorron with heavy artillery gun fire from the heights overlooking the town. After identifying myself I was able to convince them of an alternative side route where the Germans had positioned only minimal machine gun posts.

I went in with the first jeep and after an exchange of rifle fire the Germans beat a hasty retreat to avoid being caught in a trap. The town was liberated with very little damage.

I remained with the Americans until they moved on and then recovered my uniform and in due course was taken (West into Brittany) to rejoin the rest of the group who had established themselves at Combourg (Ille-et-Villaine Department, Brittany). The French Officers of the group were busy recruiting troops with a view to patrolling the countryside around St. Malo, where a garrison of Germans were entrenched, determined to fight to the bitter end (the garrison at St. Malo surrendered on 17th August, although German soldiers on an island off the coast continued to fight on until 2nd September). Throughout the area there were snipers and small pockets of Germans in block houses holding out.

I spent some time retracing our journey with M. Lambert in his charcoal driven car, visiting the safe houses where we had left equipment to lighten our load, and signing papers confirming the names of families that had helped us.

I then made contact with Captain Dubois in St. Malo, and established where some of the Germans were still entrenched. We spent some time flushing out snipers within the town of St. Malo itself and passing information to the American troops.

Eventually the Germans capitulated and we made our way to HQ Second Army, where I passed on as much information as I was able to about retreating German troops. I had some difficulty in convincing HQ that the French Officers with us had dropped into France with me, but eventually, after checking back with Station Charlie we were allowed to proceed back to England on the 22nd August 1944.

After reporting back to our Baker Street HQ and preparing my report, I left the others and returned to Manchester on leave.

[1] *See* earlier note on the Eureka system.

[2] Claude Marie Marc Boucherville de Baissac (1907-1974), DSO and bar, Knight of the Légion d'honneur; Croix de guerre 1939-1945, was already a distinguished and highly experienced agent for SOE when he was dropped in Normandy on the night of 10th-11th February 1944. He had been deployed on operations for the French Section of SOE during 1942 and 1943 before returning to the UK on 16th-17th August 1943 as the Germans began to roll up of the Scientist and Prosper networks. His second mission in lower Normandy was to build up a resistance network that would eventually support Allied forces following their landings on the beaches to the North. Highly effective as an intelligence operative, de Baissac held strong views about most things and was not afraid to share them.

[3] Trofimov's group were ideally placed to assist the advance and to interfere in German attempts to re-inforce their collapsing position in Normandy with the Battle of Falaise 12th-21st August resulting in the death or capture of around 60,000 German soldiers and the loss of a considerable number of armoured fighting vehicles. In working with the resistance around Gorron, Trofimov was probably unaware of the detail of the bigger picture, but he certainly seems to have understood the role and value which they could make to speed the Allied advance. American troops would enter Mayenne on 6th August. Trofimov's account of his experiences during these days makes little reference to the defeat of the German armed forces in Normandy which he was helping to facilitate.

Editor's note: The resistance group around Gorron was formed just in time as on 25th July Allied forces in Normandy had launched Operation Cobra, a drive south by American units located in the West of the Normandy bridgehead with the intention of breaking out of the Bocage country. On 31st July American forces reached Avranches at the base of the Cotentin Peninsula. From here they would sweep westwards into Brittany, and Eastwards towards lower Normandy. Their line of advance would take them into the heart of lower Normandy towards Gorron, Mayenne and Alencon. Indeed, Gorron lay less than 40 miles from Avranches. As the wartime journal of Michel Béchet reveals.

Original unedited photograph.

Appendix II

Post-War Report by Major AAE Trofimov on "Mongoose Green"
(The following report appears to have been provided to SOE/Force 136 by Major Trofimov as part of his debriefing after Operation Character).

General
1. In the initial training period in Ceylon, I consider far too much time was spent on schemes in the jungle, after the first scheme I found the remainder boring. More time should have been spent on subjects like wireless, language classes.
2. I thought our briefing was very clear and thorough, though a little bit optimistic about the possible duration of the operation.

Operations – Phase 1

LAUNCHING
Our party comprised:

> **MAJOR RA CRITCHLEY MC**
> **MAJOR TURRALL MC**
> **MYSELF**
> **SPECIAL GROUP**

1.1. We were dropped into Burma in the Karen mountains at PYAGAWPU. The dropping took place on the 29th February 1945 and consisted of two sorties; the aircraft used were Dakotas.

1.2. The first plane with Major RA Critchley and Major Turrall dropped blind at about 2100 hrs. On landing they were to shine their torches and provide a reception for the second aircraft, in which I was.

1.3. The pilot dropped us at well over 20,000 ft up and approximately three miles from the DZ into very mountainous jungle country.

1.4. By taking note of my position in relation to the DZ whilst coming down, and luck, I managed to find my way to the DZ.

1.5. The first group out of the aircraft, headed by Sgt. Leney were not contacted until several days later.

1.6. We spent the remaining part of the night sleeping comfortably in parachutes on the DZ.

1.7. The DZ was in a long and wide valley, which could be approached quite easily by aircraft, as was proved in subsequent drops taken on it.

1.8. During the following week Major Peacock and Major Poles and their special groups were parachuted into PYAGAWPU. At the same time, we received drops of arms and ammunition, which we handed to the Karens who flocked to PYAGAWPU.

1.9. The levies were then split into three parties, two parties to act as escort to Major Peacock and Major Poles who proceeded north to their respective areas, the remaining party stayed with Major Turrall. Major Critchley and Major Turrall had agreed by this time to spilt their area. Major Turrall to remain in the northern sector and Major Critchley and I to take over the southern sector.

1.10. On the 29th February, Major Critchley and I with Saw Aaron, Saw His Tai (parachutists from Captain McCrindle's party), levies left for PAWLUDO to take drops for Major Turrall. We only had one drop in five days.

1.11. March 5th Major Critchley and I went with our party south to POKHIDO in an attempt to form some idea of the possibilities of recruiting in that area. We did not form a very favourable opinion; the people did not appear to be very keen to take an active part against the Japanese. We returned to PAWLUDO to find Major Turrall had been attacked in the interim by the Japanese and had moved his camp to PAWLUDO. Major Critchley decided to move south again. Major Turrall gave us an ex-Burma Rifles Jemadar and about 20 levies and some spare rifles. We arranged through Major Turrall to take a drop at KAUMUDO on the 18th March on a mountainside Tanya clearing. The drop was to include primarily our wireless and signal plan and arms.

1.12. We arrived at LEKAWDO where we made our first training camp. Training started immediately. Major Critchley went south to SAWUKHI to try and make contacts for our area, as we had none at all.

1.13. My task was to receive the first drop at KAUMUDO, establish communications with Calcutta and arrange for further drops of arms and equipment. I was made responsible for recruiting, arming, organising and training mobiles.

1.14. The drop on the 18th March, though in an extremely difficult place, was successful, but we did not recover the package containing the wireless for immediate use, only the wireless package for storage with an uncharged battery. This meant I was not able to come up on the 20th as laid down on the Sked plan. When I eventually did come up, I received Calcutta, but they could not get me.

1.15. Major Critchley returned on the 22nd, having contacted Marshal Shwi, an educated Karen personality at SAWUKHI. At this time Major Critchley had a very badly poisoned foot and some trouble with his eye.

1.16. On the 23rd March I moved camp to KAUMUDO to be nearer the DZ.

1.17. Volunteers were coming in daily. My strength was now about 100.

1.18. As I had not yet established communications with Calcutta, Major Critchley sent Havildar Harry to contact Major Turrall and send a message requesting a drop of arms, equipment, money, medical stores and food, also informing Calcutta that I was on the air. However, on the 28th March, I established communications with Calcutta.

1.19. I took several drops of arms, equipment and food on the KAUMUDO DZ. I kept asking for large supplies of carbines as I consider this to be ideal weapon for mobiles. I issued Home Guards with rifles.

1.20. On the 28th March we were informed of the formation of MONGOOSE AREA with Major Critchley appointed as Area Commander with rank of Lieut. Colonel. In a subsequent message we were informed that MONGOOSE Signal Staff and outstations would be arriving on the 3rd April, which they did guided by Havildar Harry.

1.21. On the 5th April, Lt. Col. Critchley moved the whole party to LOKHI. From here he sent off the outstations to their respective areas and contacts. His HQ and signal staff he established at DUBAW with 50 of my mobiles.

1.22. Together with Major Ford, I proceeded to METKYTHA to take a drop on the 9th (approx.) and establish a large training camp.

1.23. Major C. Burne 2 i/c for MONGOOSE Area and Capt. P. Williams dropped on to the METKYTHA DZ on the 9th April.

1.24. Major Ford and Capt. Williams went off immediately to their area. Major Burne went up to the HQ at DUBAW.

1.25. We were given our D-Day as the 25th April. I was to have 100 mobiles ready armed, equipped and trained by this date, and I was to issue as many Home Guard as possible with rifles. I issued out some 300 rifles to the Home Guard, each man had to fire a few shots and do a short course under my NCO's. I gave 190 rifles to Darlington for his men.

1.26. Owing to the lack of really competent leaders I formed two platoons, each consisting of 50 men split up into 5 sections. One section was a Bren section. I called the platoons "A" and "B" respectively. "A" Platoon was taken over by Lieut. Colonel Critchley with Arran as his Havildar. "B" Platoon was mine with Havildar Harry. All the mobiles were properly equipped and armed with carbines. Every man had to go through a firing course.

1.27. About the 20th April we contacted Arthur TABI, the Township Officer of Papun. He brought with him a sketch plan of Papun (maps, page 244) showing the layout of the town and the disposition of the 300 Japanese Garrison troops he informed us were there. He had "D-Day" postponed to the 28th as we had been having very inclement weather. The attack was to take place at 0630 hrs on the 28th April, it should be proceeded by an air strike from the RAF.

1.28. I feel that we were a little rushed in preparing the plan for the attack, had we had more time I think the attack might have been more successful.

Phase I D-Day

On the evening of the 27th April all levies participating in the attack on Papun were assembled at the rear RV KHLERKHO. Commanding the party was Lt. Col. Critchley, with myself as 2 i/c. Our force comprised 150 mobiles and approximately 250 Home Guards. We had counted on Darlington for 190 men but he had at that time only issued out 80 rifles.

We left KHERKHO at 2200 hrs for Papun, with Darlington's men as guides. When crossing the YUNZALIN river the men in front of me took the wrong turning, so the Colonel was left with approximately half the force. Fortunately, I had a Naik who knew the way, we got into line at 0600 hrs on the east side of the town. At 0635 hrs 6 Spitfires came over and strafed and bombed Papun. We were unfortunately right in the line of their fire and had not been warned of the 200 yards' margin of safety, so that we were well within the danger zone, this had unfortunate effect of unnerving the levies a little. The RAF strike was not effective.

At 0700 hrs we attacked. At the same time to our intense relief Lt. Col. Critchley and his men attacked from the northeast side of the town.

We captured Pagoda and Observation Hills, dominating the town, knocking out an anti-aircraft gun and 2 LMG posts. We advanced on the town and fought a severe battle for 2½ hours. At the end we were driven out again by far superior numbers of automatic arms entrenched all over the town and heavy mortar fire from the west bank. Another party of Japanese got on to the high ground behind and above Pagoda and Observation Hills and machined gunned the whole area.

Many of the mobiles fought very bravely but they scattered and got out of control. The Home Guard with a few exceptions disappeared as soon as the fighting really started.

On Lt. Col. Critchley's orders we withdrew to the rear RV at KHLERKHO.

We killed 36 Japanese, 5 Officers and wounded a large number of Japanese. Our own casualties were:

- 1 Naik killed from my platoon, Naik Morse, an ex-Burma Rifles soldier.
- 1 Naik wounded in my platoon, Naik TUN SHEIN, an ex-Burma Rifles soldier.
- 1 platoon Havildar seriously wounded from Lt. Col. Critchley's platoon, Hav. Saw Aaron. Hav. Aaron was evacuated from the Mewaing airstrip.

The result of this attack was apart from the casualties inflicted the Japanese lived from then on, in the trenches, they doubled their guards and increased the number of sentry posts.

It was evident from the start of the attack that the Japanese had been warned of the RAF attack by the sudden departures of all the Karen Officials including the DC of the town, on the 28th April. Taking no chances, the Japanese had entrenched themselves all over the town in foxholes with their arms, and hence they were not taken completely by surprise. We were never able to actually pin down those responsible for the leakage of the information.

My main criticism is that it was too early on in our operations to take on such a target. We should have waited until we had assessed what could be done with these levies, and given them confidence in themselves, their leaders, and their arms (weaponry) by smaller actions.

Secondly, there were not sufficient officers to control the battle in different sectors. We should have brought over Major Milner with his hard striking force, his mortars and Brens, and made a combined attack. If we had had a 3-inch mortar on both Pagoda and Observation Hills, Papun would have been ours.

Phase II D-Day + 1 Month

Lt. Col. Critchely appointed me Sub Area Commander of the NANK-HUKHI area. My area was as follows:

> Northern boundary a line running east to west through Papun
> Eastern boundary the Salween River
> Western boundary a line north-south through Mewaing
> Southern boundary a line east west through Kwethe

My tasks were as follows:

> Intelligence on Papun and Papun area
> Ambush Japanese on Papun – Bilin Road
> Ambush Japanese on Papun – Kadaingti Road
> To destroy all bridges and lay mines on both these roads
> To report on INA movements coming from the north[1]

I established my HQ at NANHUKHI on the 30th April. As HQ was now at Mewaing I did not take a wireless with me. I arranged that all supplies would be sent up regularly from Mewaing. My force consisted of my mobiles now 70 in strength, Saw Darlington, a Karen and his 190 Home Guard and 74 Local Home Guards. These I employed as follows:

> My mobiles were constantly with me as the main striking force. I also kept 50 of Darlington's men with me. The remainder of Darlington's men I deployed as runners, ambush parties on Papun – Kadaingti Road, harassing parties and on my intelligence network. Of the local Home Guard, 36 were employed as warning posts, sentries for the camp and guides, the remaining 38 were posted up and down the Papun – Bilin Road.

By the 7th May, all bridges on both roads were completely destroyed, mines and booby-traps laid.

On the 11th May, 200 Japanese were reported to be moving down the Papun – Bilin Road. I laid an ambush with 6 Brens and approximately 150 levies. We killed 45 Japanese, which we counted later, and wounded many others, over 50 wounded were reported later by one of my spies down the road. In the counter fire from the Japanese, two of my men were wounded, not too seriously though.

On the 12th May we blew up a bullock cart laden with Japanese weapons and wounded a number of Japanese.

By this time, large numbers of Japanese were beginning to move up and down the Papun – Bilin Road taking every possible anti-ambush precaution and repairing damaged bridges and putting the road back into commission again. I now changed my policy and put in a series of small hit and run ambushes, only killing small numbers, but the cumulative result proved the system effective. These ambushes took place on the 14th, 15th, 16th and 17th May. Our score was now 97 Japanese killed by my mobiles. Meanwhile, I had detached approximately 100 of Darlington's Home Guard to effect daily raids on Papun, they approached from different sides, fired on the Japanese from the mountain sides with an LMG[1] or with rifles and then cleared off. The Japanese would immediately fly to their trenches from which they rarely strayed very far, and retaliated with LMG and mortar fire which they sometimes kept up for as much as two to three hours.

These "Jitter" raids on Papun served the purpose considerably, lowering the morale of the Japanese and of forcing them to expend large quantities of ammunition. Several ambushes were effected by both Darlington's men and the local Home Guard. In many cases they did not stay to count the casualties they inflicted. In one ambush just north of KYUNBIN SAKIN the local Home Guard killed 15 Japanese.

In the Papun – KADAINGTI Road area several raids were carried out on the Japanese by Home Guard plus my men with a Bren, by firing from the west bank at Japanese in villages on the east bank of the YUNZALIN between METHAROOT and KUSEIK.

Arthur Ta Bi, Township Officer of Papun, joined me on the 2nd May and organised a network of spies in and around Papun reporting on all Japanese activities therein, which enabled me to give several static targets to the RAF who promptly effected some very successful strikes on Papun.

On the 19th May we were attacked by a force of well over 1,000 Japanese sent to deal with us at NANKHUKHI. We killed one Japanese but suffered no casualties ourselves. We were able to clear out all our valuable equipment from the area before finally leaving it.

As a parting blow, on the night of the 19th May, a party of my mobiles crept down the road with mines, and blew up a Japanese truck, putting it completely out of action and wounding one Japanese very severely. The known casualties we inflicted on the Japanese in that area, including Home Guard amounted to 113 Japanese killed and we estimate having wounded well over 100 Japanese.

On the 20th May I was recalled by Lt. Col. Critchley to attend a conference at LAKYOKHO in the KYOWAING area, of all Officers in the area, to discuss the change in the situation. After the conference we proceeded to KYOWAING where we remained to give the mobiles a well-earned rest. I was flown out from the strip at KYOWAING and proceeded on leave to Calcutta.

Summary

I really required another Officer to help me at NANKHUKHI, because often when I was away from my HQ mining the road or in an ambush, important information came through and, had I had an Officer with me, it would have been dealt with without any delay.

I made a great mistake in not having a wireless from the very start. I received my wireless and was nominated MONGOOSE GREEN by the Signals Officer Lt. Van Kett on the 15th May. I was not given an operator at the time because there were no available operators. I never had the time to start operating the set. Had I been in contact by wireless with HQ, I would have been able to call for an airstrike on NANKHUKHI and possibly cleared the Japanese temporarily out of the area. I tried to open up but the set was not working.

If I had had some mortars, they would on several occasions have been very useful to drop bombs on to large concentrations of Japanese in villages, but they would have decreased the mobility of my force. The weapon I repeatedly asked for was the grenade discharger cup, but I never got any. This would have been very effective in ambushes for lobbing grenades on to the Japanese coming up behind the ambushed party.

Phase IV – D+1 to D+2

I was flown back to KYOWAING on the 17th June. On the 22nd June Lt. Col. Critchley began to move his platoon, Major C. Burne's platoon and my force to MEWAING, as it was now quite impossible to effect any further attacks on the Japanese in that area on either the PAPUN – BILIN Road or the PAPUN – KADAINGTI roads. The Japanese were now organised and on the alert. They had garrisons of 2-300 Japanese in every important place and regular patrols on either side of the road between these places.

28th June – we arrived at MEWAING. Here I received my new orders and a new area to operate in. I was given Capt. Woolf to operate my wireless and HIS TAY the Karen W/T operator to help him. My area was east of MEKAHTA. My tasks were:

To organise an intelligence network in the area.
To ambush the Japanese when they started using the SHWEGYIN – MEKAHTA – WINGALE tracks.

2nd July – I established my HQ at METKLEKHI. As there was no enemy activity in the area, I started to reorganise my force, disbanding those I had found to be useless and recruiting and training fresh volunteers.

I had acquired from Major Hanna[2] of GIRAFFE party when he left the field in June an ex-Burma Rifles Major and two ex-Burma Rifles Havildars. With these additions I was able to turn out an efficient fighting force.

15th July – My orders were altered to operating on the SHWEGYIN-SHANYWA-MEKAHTA tracks. I was responsible for intelligence on the area SHWEGYIN to KUNZEIK. My contact Saw TUN SHEIN was to help me with this, he was given to me by Major Milner, who also passed on to me 42 Home Guard under an able leader, Saw HTOO.

28th July – I moved my HQ to TATUKHI in anticipation of Japanese movements in the SHANYWA area. HQ gave me orders to prepare a DZ in order to take food and ammunition drops as:

There was no rice or food of any kind to be obtained locally.

My HQ was now too far from MEWAING to be supplied from there and in the event of Japanese movements within my area, long columns of porters would have been seen and compromised the area.

The only possible DZ was an old Tanya up in the mountains in a wide flat valley, which we had to clear. Only one drop was taken on this DZ on the 7th August.

3rd August – Major Milner sent me an urgent message to the effect that he was preventing some 5,000 Japanese from crossing the SHWEGYIN CHAUNG and that he was running out of ammunition and could I come along and help him out. We left the following morning and on the 6th August, I met Major Milner at his HQ at HTILERKLEKHI.

Major Milner asked me to hold the line from KYAUKTAGA to YEBEZU, to be responsible for safeguarding our left flank formed by the PADET CHAUNG and for intelligence on the area south of the PADET CHAUNG to the MADAM CHAUNG and east of the SHWEGYIN CHAUNG.

7th August – I established my troops in the line. I made Captain Woolf responsible for the abovementioned intelligence, also for watching and patrolling the PADET CHAUNG. Major Milner gave us some Home Guard to assist on the PADET CHAUNG.

12th August – The Japanese tried to cross in large numbers at night just south of KYAUKTAGA. We killed 25 of them and wounded many others.

13th August – Japanese made two attempts to cross in large numbers at night – we killed 41 of them.

14th August – Japanese made yet another attempt to cross in large numbers at several places, but the main attempt was at YEBEZU. We killed 35 of them. Captain Bourne had lent me two 2 inch mortars and 3 inch mortar to help me out.

15th August – a further mass attempt to cross was made all along the line. We killed 25 Japanese.

17th August – a very small attempt was made to cross – we killed only 10 Japanese.

Summary

Together with sniping results and daylight kills along the line we killed altogether, including our previous operation in NANKHUKHI, 255 Japanese and estimated that we wounded about 300 Japanese, many of whom died later, owing to lack of medical treatment.

A very useful weapon would have been the grenade discharger cup, but it was still not forthcoming.

Phase V – The Surrender and Winding up Period

The Japanese continued in their attempts to cross the SHWEGYIN CHAUNG up to the 9th September, because they were unaware of the surrender. Later when leaflets were dropped to them, they disbelieved them altogether.

Eventually a Japanese Peace Delegation Officer, Lt. IUCHI of 28th Army HQ MOULMEIN was sent up the west bank of the SHWEGYIN

CHAUNG with orders to contact us and then contact and inform all Japanese parties in the area of the surrender and tell them to proceed to SHWEGYIN.

I contacted Lt. IUCHI at KYAUKTAGA on the 9th September and sent him up to MEZAUNGWA to try and contact Japanese there. From there onwards Major Milner took over.

12th September – Moved my HQ to BOLO where Major Milner had his new HQ next to the airstrip, he had made there.

15th September – withdrew my mobiles from the line to BOLO

19th September – paid off all my men.

21st September – Major Hood flew into the airstrip at BOLO and gave me permission to disband my mobiles. I handed over all my accounts to him there. My arms I handed in to Major Milner's armoury.

Awards

From my platoon I have recommended the following men for decorations for extreme bravery in action against the enemy:

Jemadar HARRY (ex-Burma Rifles Havildar)
Naik MAW GAY
Naik AG WIN

Air Ops

I indicated approximately 15 air targets; upon nine of these the RAF effected very successful strikes. I was not present on all the occasions and am therefore only able to report results. The largest and most effective strike I had was at YEBEZU in August when ninety 500 lbs bombs were dropped only 70 yards away on the east bank was very accurate.

One strike I had on PAPUN was very effective. They destroyed the Pagoda and all the houses on the west bank. The Pagoda was being used as a rice dump and armoury; the houses were accommodating the Japanese at night.

Later when I reported large concentrations of Japanese on the west bank, the RAF strafed and bombed several villages on the PAPUN – KADAINGTI Road between PAPUN and KUSEIK, which were full of Japanese, they killed and wounded a large number of them.

The only close support action I witnessed was when we attacked PAPUN on the 28th April. The attack was preceded by strafing and bombing by six Spitfires. The strafing was insufficient, and the bombs were very small and were dropped in fields.

Supply Drops

In the drops I took, only Liberators and Dakotas were used. In the initial stages I favoured the Liberator drops as it drops all its load in one run, whereas the Dakota would do anything up to 12 runs, thereby drawing attention to an area.

The DZs at PYAGAWPU and PAWLUDO will be reported on by the HYENA group.

At KAUMUDO the DZ was a difficult one approximately 3,000 ft up on a mountainside, a Tanya clearing. I took several drops here and all were successful.

At METKYHTA there was a very good DZ in the wide long MEWAING valley. Only low hills flanked it. The ground was paddy. On this DZ we started daylight drops. We had personnel dropped to this DZ.

At TATUKHI the DZ was a very difficult one to find. It was up in the mountains in a wide long valley. An old Tanya which we cleared. Only one drop was taken on this DZ but it was successful.

Part III – "Q"

The jungle boot we were issued with at ME 25 was ideal footwear prior to the monsoon rains, but it does not wear for very long. Unfortunately, it was two months before any replacements were dropped to us in the way of clothing.

The cotton shirts we were issued with wore out very quickly and did not stand up to the wear and tear.

The angora shirt is, in my estimation, the ideal thing to wear.

Shorts were not issued and these I found to be necessary. Climbing mountain tracks in long trousers in hot sticky weather is unhealthy and uncomfortable.

Supplies Dropped

In nearly every drop during the first four months of operations several toothbrushes and bars of shaving soap were included, but not once did we receive any toothpaste. Soap should have been dropped regularly and in large quantities as in order to keep the levies clean and free from skin troubles we issued them with soap when we had it in stock.

Rations
It was not until July that we received any variety in the food.

Dehydrated vegetables should have been dropped throughout the operation.

For the levies and considering the nature of their work, extras should have been dropped regularly e.g. large quantities of fish powder, tinned fish, dhal, dehydrated meat and curry powder.

Arms
The supply of arms was very good, though there was a marked tendency to waste valuable space by including in almost every drop of arms at least two containers of stens, a weapon for which I had very little use.

Ammunition
In the main plenty of .303 was supplied but very little carbine ammunition by comparison to our actual requirements.

Clothing
Lack of imagination was used when trousers and boots were dropped to us. In the case of boots, they would invariably be all size 9 or all size 6. We constantly asked for boots to be dropped is sizes varying from 6 to 8 with a small percentage of 5s and 9s.

Trousers were usually dropped that would fit only a 6 ft. 4 in tall individual.

Shirts and shorts required replacing every two months, many of the mobiles had only one pair of shorts and one shirt to manage with for 4 months.

The above suggestions and criticisms affect only a small part of the supplies. Altogether we have had many excellent drops and many useful items were dropped that we thought were invaluable.

Conditions of Stores
Supplies were packed, overall, very well indeed. The arms were all free from rust and with a few exceptions were in good working order.

Out of every ten stens, I found at least four would not work due to mechanical defects. Several rifles had no extractor springs. The only container with which I find real fault is the WC 26 carbine container. It is far too overloaded. I have seen 5 WC 26 containers empty their contents into the air. At the moment the parachute develops, the weight inside the container forces the bottom off the container.

Signals

In the first place, when Lt. Colonel Critchley and I formed MONGOOSE area, we had no wireless operator. I was not conversant with the B.2 and had considerable difficulty in establishing communications. I would pick up Calcutta quite clearly on QSA[3] 5 but they, for the first 6 days, reported nothing heard from me.

In our initial training more time should have been spent studying and operating the B.2 in case of emergency in the field, when, as in my case, the Officer must operate the set.

Steam generators had one big fault; the washers issued for them had no wear at all.

Report dated 27th September 1945:

Prepared by Major AAE Trofimov
Sub Area Commander
MONGOOSE / Character Operation

---

[1] INA – assumed to be 'Intelligence Network Areas'

LMG – Light Machine Gun

DZ - Drop Zone

NCO – Non-commissioned Officer

HQ – Head Quarters

RV – rendezvous

RAF – Royal Air Force

[2] https://soeinburma.com/?s=%27Hanna%27 (accessed 27th April 2023)

[3] The QSA code and QRK code are interrelated and complementary signal reporting codes for use in wireless telegraphy (Morse code).

Appendix III

Liberation By Saw M. Shwin, BA, BIL Superintendent, Shwegyin Karen School, Shwegyin, Burma (17th July 1946)[1]

(*The following is a particularly intriguing account of the development of the Karen guerrilla force by the Superintendent of the Karen School at Shwegyin. That town had seen fighting between Burmans and Karens during the British withdrawal in 1942 and Saw M. Shwin was later tortured by the Japanese along with many other Karen citizens of Shwegyin as they tried to encourage/force the Karen to see themselves as 'Hill Burman'. The essay appears to have been drawn up for the purposes of soliciting contact, and a response in kind, by the officers of Operation Character. Given the on-going negotiations about the decolonisation of Burma, and the fate of the minorities within it, during 1946 this attempt to reach out to former British officers may have been for political as well as more narrowly historical purposes. In any case, the recording of the struggles of the Karen during the war could contribute to the further development of their self-consciousness and confidence as people in pressing their political claims during the negotiations for self-determination. On August 1947 the Karen National Union, backed by the Karen National Defence Organisation, and armed with many of the arms delivered by Force 136, declared independence from both the British and the Burmese. An insurgency against Burman rule had begun the previous month and it remains on-going to this day.*)

On the 19th March 1945, Saw M. Shwin who confined himself to his solitary abode at Patakee was told to meet a foreign stranger near Hsawookee. On the outskirt of the village he saw a shirtless, unshaven, and weird looking Britisher sitting in the shades with some Karens. He introduced himself as Major RA Critchley who became the Commanding Officer of the Mongoose Group, a fortnight afterwards when he was promoted to Lt. Colonel on the 2nd April. After explaining his mission, they had a discussion which resulted in the extension of the Spider's activities in the Shwegyin Hill Tracts. The news of the arrival of the "white grandpa" was passed on secretly from village to village and the Karens jumped for joy and gratification when they heard that the long-expected liberators had returned at last.

In fact, Major Turrall, Major Critchley, and Captain Trofimov were the first group to land at Pgagawpu, Salween District, on the 20th February (1945). After issuing out hundreds of rifles to the Karen Home Guards who came enthusiastically in great numbers every day, and organising Levies, Major Critchley and Captain Trofimov came south to Perkeeder with Saw Aaron, Saw Harry, Saw His, Saw His. Teh and 5 Levies, leaving Major Turrall at Pgagawpu (Pyagawpu). It was then that Major Critchley crossed over to Shwegyin Township making contact with Saw M. Shwin and other Karen elders.

The Mongoose Area comprised a line running through Shwegyin to Papun as northern boundary, Belin as southern boundary, Salween as eastern, and Sittang western. The Mongoose Party which was parachuted in near Pgagawpu (Pyagawpu) on the 26th March, joined Colonel Critchley on the 3rd April, where the outstations were given their contacts and areas to proceed to. The Mongoose Group was distributed to operate in their respective areas as follows:

Colonel RA Critchley	:	Commanding Officer - with him
Captain Trofimov		
Major FS Milner	:	Shwegyin Township north and north-east with
Captain T Bourne	:	Headquarters at Sauthehkee and afterwards at
Sergeant Leney	:	Bolo
Major TP Lucas	:	Shwegyin Township south and south-east and
Captain Clark	:	Bilin with H.Q. at Htipadoe near Panate
Captain Pearce	:	(18th April – 30th May) Pete Atet (31st May-
Captain Sankey	:	7th June).
Major Ford	:	Large area next to Mewaing
Captain Williams	:	
W/T Operator	:	

When Colonel Critchley and Captain Trofimov shifted to Mewaing and established a large training camp at Mekyitah, Major C. Burne was dropped into Mekyitah on the 2nd April to be 2nd i/c to Colonel

Critchley. He was stationed at the Colonel's HQ at Dubaw where another training camp was set up.

Each group was assigned the following duties; firstly, to set up an intelligence network in the area concerned and thereby giving targets to the RAF, secondly, to form trained groups of men as mobile groups who would fight where required (many ex-Burma Rifles were enlisted); and, thirdly, to form static groups armed with rifles and to dislocate the enemy withdrawals.

During the early stages of the organisation and formation of mobile and static groups, difficulties of considerable magnitude were involved as the work could not be carried out openly due to the presence of the Japanese spies and frequent visits of the JMP.

While not doubting that the Allies, on account of their superiority of war machines and man power would one day recapture Burma, the Karens were still indecisive and uncertain regarding the maturity of time to throw in the full weight of their support, for tragically experiences of the past had taught them to be alert, cautious and thoughtful. The savageness and barbarism of mental and physical tortures still remained fresh in the memory of the victims. However, the Mongoose Officers and their Karen supporters carried on their clandestine duties with patience, care and caution until success crowned their efforts.

After enlisting the support and assistance of Saw Morris, a Karen leader of Hteetoemukee Village, Major Milner and his group moved down to his village to effect the abovementioned duties, and he stayed there for over a fortnight before he moved further down to Sauthehkee, which became his headquarters.

Within a month mobile troops numbering 150 approximately, were collected and trained. After receiving instructions in the use, care, handling and purport of various modern weapons, they were taught the primary principles and methods of guerrilla warfare. They were armed with carbines, mortars large and small, rifles, Sten guns, and grenades. Many platoons and section commanders were ex-Burma Rifles. There was no time train the Home Guards. They learnt to make use of the weapons through their partially trained comrades who were always willing to help them.

At the close of April before the Levies were thoroughly trained, the villagers brought the news that the Japanese, being routed by the 14th Army in Upper Burma, had started to withdraw from the plains and Kyaukkyi through the Shwegyin Hill Tracts. Waves of enemy withdrawals of considerable strength, ranging between 200 to 2,000 men, penetrated through the thinly populated Karen villages. As the Japanese retreated through various jungle tracks, Major Milner, the directing chief of the area, was compelled to post his men scatteringly in various small sections to block important tracks and to harass the enemy with a floating platoon to accord assistance, whenever required, to their comrades engaging in action. Both mobile and static groups co-operated and made several successful attempts to ambush and give surprise attacks to the retreating enemy. These men were normally led by the Major himself and Captain Bourne. Over three weeks these Officers and the Karens were very busy fighting the Japanese and thereby hampering their orderly retreat at Sauthehkee, Htipanwe, Sauthehtah, Hsawookee and Hsawootah. During the first phase of the campaign in May, 86 Japanese were killed and many more were believed to have been injured by Major Milner's Group with only two casualties on their side. The villagers had to act as scouts and guides.

To return to the work of Colonel Critchley and Major Trofimov. In the corresponding period they established a large training camp at Mekyitah. Captain Trofimov was also responsible for the training of 100 Levies drawn largely from Mewaing Circle for taking drops and arming Home Guards. More than 400 rifles were issued to Village Home Guards, 190 of which were given to Darlington for his men before the 28th April, which was 'D' Day for the Mongoose Group and, therefore the training was to be completed by that date.

One of the most brilliant and astounding accomplishments ever achieved by the Mongoose Group was when Colonel Critchley and Captain Trofimov in an attack on Papun on the 28th April 1945. Early in the morning at 6.30 am after receiving instructions for detail action and taking positions, a small force of 150 mobile soldiers and Levies, 200 Home Guards of Mewaing and 80 more men belonging to Saw Darlington, assaulted Papun. Though it was a fight against overwhelming odds as more than 1,000 trained Japanese were then concentrated at Papun, the first typical offensive, in obedience to the order, was initiated and it was in this arena that the two British Officers and the Karens were showing their mettle. Being inexperienced freshers in the art of warfare, the Karens, who could be relied on their bravery alone, depended mainly on the ingenuity, directing abilities and manoeuvring tactics of the Colonel and Captain Trofimov, who led them from quarter to quarter of the town with indomitable courage and will. It was in Papun that the Karen fighters had the opportunity to witness with admiration the worth and fine qualities of these two Britishers, who had henceforth earned for themselves the fascinating oriental names of "military ogres" and the invention of this rare name was justified when Captain Trofimov was decorated with the MC and was promoted to Major shortly afterwards. The Karens were struck with awe and bewilderment when the Colonel who refused to take cover stood up giving orders to his men with his memorable stick, taking grave risk of being killed as his august body presented a conspicuous target to the foe. The assault was successful for a short time and it was the best which could be expected of amateurs to measure their strength with crack troops. Major Trofimov, describing the operation asserted, "the enemy was warned about us and consequently was waiting for us. Pagoda and Observation hills were captured, and the east bank was held by us for 2½ hours. We then had to withdraw owing to the superior number of automatic weapons firing at us." The Colonel and a few Karens were the last group to vacate Papun, holding their positions until they were certain that the main body of the attacking force had safely retreated. In this section 37 Japanese were definitely known to be killed, plenty more injured and disabled with one killed and two wounded on the part of the attackers.

The whole party then moved back to Mewaing. Major Trofimov, with his party (platoon), was given the task of operating from Nankhukii on Papun-Bilin Road and on Papun-Kadaingti Road. His southern boundary was a line east and west through Nankhukii. They operated quite successfully up to the 19th May, killing altogether in ambushes 98 Japanese. They were forced out of the area by the Japanese. Major Trofimov was assisted by Saw Arthur Tahbi, Township Officer, Papun, Darlington and his 190 men, and Nankhukii Home Guards, which numbered 74. They kept up harassing roads leading to Papun which forced the Japanese to live in the trenches and to expend a great amount of ammunition. They blew up one truck and one bullock cart.

Colonel Critchley meanwhile had established his headquarters at Shweti from which he directed operations. An aerodrome had been made at Mewaing. The Colonel then moved over the Bilin River down to Pawlewa and thence down to Laykyokhoti, where Major Trofimov rejoined him about the 25th May.

The Colonel received drops and made many dumps throughout the area around Kyowaing. The Japanese in the neighbourhood began to organise themselves and prepared to rid Kyowaing area of British elements. On account of the onset of the Monsoon, offensive action could not be carried out in a large scale. The Colonel found it to be more desirable to vacate Kyowaing and to shift his headquarters and Major

Trofimov's platoon back to Mewaing area. After this Colonel Critchley, in obedience to the "stand-by" order from the High Command, established himself at Mewaing, training his men and adding recruits.

On the 23rd May, Major Milner was ordered to transfer to Mewaing to take over the area from Colonel Critchley, who moved over to Kyowaing to operate on the Papun-Bilin Road. Major Milner by that time had increased his Home Guard to approximately 400 strong and it was felt that with that number of guns the Karens could block the tracks and thereby protect the villages. Major Milner was, therefore, free to operate anywhere in the Mewaing area and harass the Japanese. These tactics proved to be successful and effective. In one village attack at Pawota his group accounted for 51 Japanese out of a total of 64.

Here at Mewaing many more Karens from different places came over to join as levies and Home Guards and, therefore, Major Milner was very busy issuing out arms, training the recruits and sending patrols to surprise the Japanese. In addition to these, he had to take drops, to establish dumps, and to improve the runway of the aerodrome. Many more huts had to be built to accord accommodation to the levies and Captain Bourne was mostly responsible for the creation of these jungle lodges.

The Karen, sometimes, felt annoyed when they were repeatedly told by their British Officers to capture some Japanese alive. To the Karens, on account of obvious reasons, a Japanese was a vile vermin which deserved no sympathy and mercy. It was their burning desire to kill the Japanese never to spare any one of them if they could help. However, just to oblige their superiors, Section Commander Tun Pe and Pein Shwe once attempted to catch two Japanese on Guard in a small bamboo hut. He and his section surrounded the outpost and waited until they were positive that the guards were asleep. Tun Pe and Pein Shwe then groped stealthily in the dark into the hut and suddenly fell on the sleeping men seizing them by the hands ordering them at the same time to throw up their arms in surrender. The Nipponese who did not have the term "surrender" in their vocabulary refused to do so and instead they put up stiff resistance. In close grips like this the Japanese stood a better chance to overcome the Karens by employing their jujitsu method in the struggle. At the same time Tun Pe explained to them in Japanese (for Tun Pe could speak Japanese) that it was useless to resist arrest as the place was surrounded by his men. They wrestled for a time and knowing that the guards would soon have the upper hand, the Karens were compelled to shoot at the legs of their antagonists to render them powerless for resistance. Though seriously wounded, the Japanese were still obstinate and unsubmissive. They had to be killed.

Major TP Lucas' Group: At the end of the first week of April, Major Lucas with his staff and more than 30 native soldiers consisting mainly of Burmese parachutists and a few Karen Levies, left Major Milner's party at Kawkee and proceeded to the area allotted to them going through Patakee, Htipadoe, and Ubokchaung. On the way Major TP Lucas, Captain Clark, and Captain Pearce paid a short visit to Saw M. Shwin, who made arrangements to facilitate their journey to Panate. Saw Hubert Shwin and Saw Htoo, for safety's sake, guided the party through the Karen villages, taking necessary precautions on the way. It was the first time for the Karens in that area to see white faces after their 4 year's absence. The villagers on the way, children and parents alike clustered around the strangers and out of curiosity took a good look with 'gaping' mouths at the 'white brothers'. The Karens had been told that the Britishers did not take pains like the Japanese Officers; they always made their subordinates to do the heavy and unpleasant work while they themselves did only light jobs. But this notion exploded when Major Lucas himself carried a heavy load of more than 30 viss[2] in weight, which an average Karen could not even lift, for several days and nights continuously through slippery sliding slopes and treacherous tracks. No natives were more surprised and impressed than the incredulous Karens.

At Htipadoe near Panate an impromptu organisation was made, and a few Karen Levies were enlisted, and 50 Home Guards armed. An air strip was also made at Woolf to receive drops and to enable small aircrafts to land. The air strip was used until it was taken by the Japanese in the middle of July.

Major Lucas' intellectual attainments, as a British educationalist (University lecturer), ranked high in the estimation of his comrades and acquaintances. This intellectual giant showed tact, sympathy and understanding in his various undertakings. Besides organising and intelligence duties his most important task was to blow up bridges and thereby to dislocate enemy supply transportation and communication, and to destroy trucks and railway bogies.

On the 1st May, Major Lucas and party derailed one train and 6 carriages near Kyaitko station. It was estimated that 20 Japanese were killed and (others) wounded. Captain Clark's section also did splendid work. In the month of May his section took action against enemy movement along Mokpalin-Bilin Road and Bilin-Natkyi Road. Generally, he worked in conjunction with the Burma Defence Army of the locality. Between 60 and 120 Japanese were accounted for, in addition to 6 three-ton lorries destroyed, and 10 other automobiles full of ammunition shot up by small arms.

The intelligence section also did their work magnificently. Through their information, several important targets were bombed and strafed, seriously impairing transportation and troop concentration. At one time Major Lucas' party was almost surrounded by the Japanese and they managed to escape narrowly through the help of some Burmese soldiers belonging to the BDA. When Major Lucas was forced to give up Woolf he established himself at Melpo, where he stationed his headquarters.

Captain Clark stated, no doubt with thankful appreciation, that the following Karen personalities (personnel) rendered magnificent services to Major Lucas' party:

Name and Village
Headman Ko Tai: Yewe Auk
Karen Hpongyi U Kyaw Aye: Melpo
Headman Shwe Htit: Megadi
Saw Tun Yin: Hteenyana
Gangawbwint: Methana
Headman of Woolf(reported killed by Japanese) Saw Hubert Shwin: Patakee

At a later stage, Lt. Saw Sankey, who was promoted to Captain afterwards, joined Major Lucas. It was he who was responsible for the employment of more members of the Karen Levies and the training and improvement of their fitness and efficiency. Admittedly, the Karens in his area were unintelligent, unenlightened, ignorant and irresponsive. As they got fed up with war, economic stringency, and unforgettable sufferings, they wanted to remain aloof. Furthermore, it was extremely difficult to communicate with them, especially influential elders, as many of their villages were either burnt down or occupied by the Nipponese and therefore, they had to hide scatteringly in the forests. At Winkan and Zalokkyi, the villagers were terrorised, more than 40 Karens were killed by the Japanese and later on by the BDA and 10 spinsters kidnapped and raped. However, Saw Sankey, despite the various handicaps, through patience and perseverance managed to overcome the difficulties marring his way to recruit the Levies. He displayed organising abilities by collecting not less than 160 Levies within a month for post-war operation, if permissible. Being a powerful organiser praise was due to him and he deserved official recognition of his valuable services, which should surely find its correct place in the Karen military annals.

The civil condition of the villagers involved with the Japanese withdrawal zone in Major Lucas's area could be described as most deplorable. Beginning from the 1st May, the villages between Shwegyin and Sittang, and Yewe Auk and all the villages further south between the Kyaikto Pagoda Hills and the road, were overrun by the retreating Japanese troops. The majority of the villages victimised were rendered uninhabitable as they were reduced to a state of utter destruction and desolation. The houses and rice barns were either burnt down or utilised by the starving Japanese. The victims were mostly shelter less, foodless and clothingless (without shelter, food and clothing). Many also were unable to cultivate their Taungyas[3] and plough their paddy fields. Captain Clark, therefore, wrote: "the greatest need at present is rice and next to that is clothing".

On the 25th July, the Japanese in Pegu Yoma who were cut off in May from their main army in retreat started, in desperation, the breakout. Apparently, many of them were killed by the soldiers of the 12th Army who were posted all along the Railway line. This corridor break-through episode was of historical importance. Approximately 20,000 men, officially quoted, were involved.

At Inbala Village, on the Sittang River in Shwegyin Township, the Karen Home Guards, 40 in number, under the command of Headman Saw Po Kya Aye, an ex-soldier who saw active service in Mesopotamia in the 1914-18 World War, displayed gallantry and fighting stamina for some days in attempting to prevent the Japanese to cross batch by batch, the swollen Sittang River. The Japanese were ingenious enough to improvise rafts made mostly of reeds and leaves. As they were rowing slowly across the river in their hastily built miniature rafts, they were greeted with a volley of shots by the Home Guards who were armed with Sten Guns, .303 rifles, and carbines. After the first discharge, many rafts men disappeared under water and were therefore understood to have been mortally wounded. The Karens fired until they had exhausted their ammunition supply. The Nipponese then rowed across the Sittang River in great numbers, the undaunted Karens charged them with bayonets and dahs. It was a fierce hand to hand fight. After killing 37 Japanese they had to run away as they were hopelessly outnumbered by the invaders who succeeded in shooting down two Home Guards.

On the morrow when they received reinforcement of ammunition supply from the British Officers at Nyaunglebin, the Karens, who had fled from the village, renewed the fight. They guarded strategical points and from their posts they could fire at the Japanese at will. Sometimes, the fight took place in the field at close quarters and some Karens were grazed by the enemy bullets. The Home Guards believed that the Japanese could not hit them as they were too exhausted to aim accurately. Many Karen fighters were good shots. Before the retreats terminated, which took place at frequent intervals, the fighters defended their villages, held their posts and they were praised by the British Army Officers (Yorkshire?) of Nyaunglebin, who came over to do the same work, for their bravery and keenness in the fight. The Karens believed that more than 500 Japanese were killed by their group, 150 or so of whom were shot down by Headman Po Kya Aye alone, who was a crack shot. The villagers said that as a rule Po Kya Aye never missed a running foe within shooting range with his carbine. The Karens collected as war trophies numerous Japanese uniforms with decorations of stars and lines, and war gear such as rifles, pistols, mortars, swords, helmets, grenades, ammunition and so on, which were consequently submitted to the officers concerned. Po Kya Aye and his men were attached to Major Milner and, therefore, the credit went to Major Milner as well, who should justly be proud of them.

Being forewarned about the impending breakout, Major Milner and his group were sent back from Mewaing to Shwegyin Township by the Colonel on the 29th July. It appeared that the Major was thrilled to return to the old hunting ground to do good work. Before his arrival at Mezaungwa, the Japanese who had succeeded in crossing the Sittang River at different sectors and later on Kyaukkyi River, appeared on the right bank of the Shwegyin Chaung opposite to Mezaungwa, Hsinbyuaing, Kyauknaga and Tanaypah. Since May, on account of various minor successes, the morale of the Karens in the area on the whole was pretty high. Some spies were executed under the order of the Area Commander, and undesirable elements and local 'bad hats', irrespective of race and creed, were quietly removed. The term 'Spider', when mentioned, electrified friends and well-wishers with magical effects, whereas it was a terror for hostile persons.

With no Britishers among them, the Karen Home Guards, under the command of Saw Aung Sein opened fire at the invaders on the other side of the Chaung attempting to cross. They kept on firing continuously in the afternoon of the 30th July, and throughout the night. The Karens were determined to defend their homes and families, and they gave good account of themselves. The fight went on with indefinite results in great excitement. The villages behind the fighting line were kept, with intense feeling of anxiety, in suspense. At this critical moment, to the great joy and relief of the defenders, the earnestly-expected reinforcements arrived. The news of the arrival of Major Milner and his men acted like a tonic to the exhausted Home Guards.

The duties of the directing Chief were, firstly, to keep the Japanese in the narrow corridor between Kyaukkyi-Shwegyin Road, and the Shwegyin River, thus making it easy for the RAF to bomb and machine-gun the enemy; secondly, to prevent the Japanese from crossing the river and making contact with their troops farther south who came apparently, to the rescue; and thirdly, to protect all of the villages on the east bank.

To accomplish the above tasks, the whole east bank of the Chaung from Padetchaungwa to Lewa was to be manned and roughly fortified. The man power at that time at the disposal of the Major was insufficient for the gigantic task as the line to be defended was a mighty long one extending more than 25 miles. Mobile and static troops were posted along the lengthy line with the order to shoot on sight and prevent the enemy crossing the Chaung. Beginning from the 5th August, the Japanese numbering approximately 5,000, were more aggressive in their attempt to cross Lewa, Peinpin, Hsinbyuaing, Teketah, Tanaypah, Kyauknaga and Yebinsu. The task was too tremendous for Major Milner's fighters. More men were urgently required.

At the close of July, Major Trofimov was detailed to cover tracks leading from Shwegyin to Wingalon and Mekahtah, to ambush the Japanese, if they started retreating across the mountains to Wingalon and then down to Bilin. Therefore, to be close to the tracks, Major Trofimov took his platoon to Toethukhee, which was intended to be his headquarters. He made some dumps at Toethukhee and Htipadokee. Before he could scarcely settle down, Major Trofimov was ordered to march to Meseekee to assist Major Milner in the defence of the important line. He was given the task to hold the line between Kyauknaga and Yabinsu and to cover up the Padet Chaung in case the enemy tried to outflank the defending force.

Captain Woolf 2 i/c to Major Trofimov, was responsible for the intelligence in the area south of Padet Chaung.

On the 5th August, Colonel Critchley's platoon also came over from Mewaing to bridge in the gaps in the northern section of the Chaung. Captain Clark was in charge of this platoon and the Home Guards in that sector. The detail arrangement for the defence line was thus complete with the total strength of 250 mobile troops with 32 machine guns, 10 mortars, and a number of rifles and carbines. The Home Guards were called in to participate in the fight and approximately 300 came to the line. Thus trenches were dotted at short distances, roughly 50 yards apart, throughout the line from end to end.

The fight was actually one-sided killing in this theatre of war. The Japanese cut down bamboo in great number and converted then to rafts on land. They carried down each raft to the river, one at a time. When they rowed across the Chaung, which was only 100 yards at its widest part, they offered excellent targets to the defenders. The Karens, who had long waited for this opportunity, shot at the enemy with gusto. When machine-gunned, the raftmen stood no chance of escape. Daily scores, even hundreds at times, of them were massacred. Though the Japanese returned the shots, they could not hit the defenders who took shelter in their trenches.

When this daring method of crossing by rafts railed, another tactic was adopted. The clever Japanese invented a peculiar chair like structure with bamboo or plantain trees, donned with leaves, which enabled him, when used, to keep his body under water with his nose up to breathe through a short bamboo pipe. With these simple, but curious and ingenious crafts, the Japanese floated themselves down the river with the hope to deceive the defenders. The Karens were duped for a time. When the Karens knew about it afterwards, they shot at everything afloat – logs, bamboo, reeds, bushes and even leaves. Nothing pleased the Karens better for having the privilege and chance to shoot. The Officers allowed them to do so because any amount of ammunition required for the purpose could be dropped by the RAF. Besides shooting the enemy, the defenders bagged also 4 buffaloes, 7 sambars, 17 wild pigs, 24 barking deers and a host of birds of all species, with and without the knowledge of the Officers, which served as appetising food for them.

The Chaung became a battlefield. The fight went on in high spirit. Shots were exchanged day and night. The mortar section was indeed the rowdiest of the whole crowd. The continuous banging of guns and rifles, the booming of mortar shots and shells, which could be heard miles away – though deafening – helped to heighten the morale of the villagers behind the line. The Japanese were tricked into believing that the line was powerfully defended, and they attempted, without success, several times to find out the weak spots.

The defenders had considerable amount of difficulty and discomfort. The Guards had to sit up in the muddy trenches overnight. Though the

Guards were changed at intervals, the night-watchers, even when relieved, could not sleep as they were attacked vigorously by myriads of mosquitoes. Numerous leeches also caused a great deal of nuisance. Sometime, food supply did not reach them in time, and they went without food for a day or two.

A few scores of Japanese succeeded in crossing the river at night, and not one of them who landed was at large. Only four prisoners were taken as the Japanese refused to be captured alive. The Japanese were thus hemmed-in between the road and the river. Cornered in the narrow corridor, the Japanese offered easy targets to the RAF personnel who bombed and strafed the hastily built camps with devastating effects every day. If there was no air support, the defenders might have been in a very unpleasant predicament. More than 500 Japanese, the patrols reported, were believed to have been killed by the RAF.

The Officers and men of this theatre, both the Mongoose Group and the RAF, could justly be proud of the part played by them in this great history of the Karens. One of the most marvellous and brilliant chapters of this war was written on the banks of the Shwegyin Chaung. The defenders had fought with steady courage and endurance. To them as well to others who bore this share in bringing about the victory, the gratitude of the liberated Karens was due.

In this campaign the medical and food supply services had added yet another glorious page to the splendid record throughout the operation. Supplies of food and ammunition were dropped almost daily at Bolo and Sauthehkee. Without adequate ammunition supply the Karens would have been entirely at the mercy of the invaders. The credit went to the RAF which had provided supplies and amenities without which successful campaign would have been impossible.

Though the Japanese succeeded in occupying Shwegyin for three days after the breakout before they were driven out from the town on the 2nd of August by the British troops who held the town thereafter, they could never succeed in breaking up the east bank defence line. The defence line would forever be known by Karen posterity as the unbreakable 'torres vedras'[4] and the brilliant operation along the line would be certainly described as the most glorious achievement of historic importance on a military point of view, ever accomplished by the Mongoose Group of Force 136. It would never be forgotten that the name of Major Milner, CO of the area, was automatically linked together this historic line, as he was the controlling Chief who was responsible, to his credit which thereafter enhanced his already high prestige and reputation for the detail plans, strategy, and direction of the entire campaign in this battle zone.

Winding up the operation, Major Milner wrote: "The Karens since 29th July have killed or by allowing the RAF concentrated targets have caused more than 1250 Japanese to be killed. Our own losses in this period have been 4 killed and 3 wounded." Roughly speaking, the Mongoose Group had killed Japanese at the rate of more than 100 to 1 (300 to 1?).

Among the Karens, above all others, Major Milner had depended on Saw Morris Say, the leader of the area, in the course of the operation. Two persons of different nationalities could have never paired more successfully than Major Milner and Saw Morris. Saw Morris Say and Mrs. Morris Say (*nee* Thramu Bee Bay) (photos, pages 199 and 335) dedicated their services for the great cause. They not only placed their 15 elephants at the disposal of the major and other Officers, but also had to advance funds from their own pockets, at times, at the early part of the campaign to speed up the organisation and the formation of the troops. In addition, in April, and part of May, they had to feed the recruits at first with their own rice and later with rice and edibles collected from Sauthehkee and villages nearby. No doubt at a later stage the troops were provided with everything required in food and other things such as medical supplies, uniforms, arms and ammunition. Without the help of Saw Morris the success of Major Milner's work would have been a farce. Other Karen personalities such as Saw Po Kya Aye, Saw Aung Sein, Saw Tah Wah, Saw Johnnie and Saw Mya Kya, also rendered substantial services. The spirit of brotherhood which had bound the British Officers and native troops altogether, was exemplary. The Officers worked together in excellent comradeship as brothers of the same profession and there was no distinction between superiors and subordinates in time of action.

The Mongoose Officers who liberated the Karens had not come as masters but as the sincere helpers of the people of Burma. Never did they assume air of superiority over the Karens who could not help appreciating when the liberators gentlemanly overlooked the ignorance, bluntness, shyness, timidity and ugliness of the Karens.

The Karens are no good as pupils of character study, but they sometimes attempt to do so. Finding it difficult to pronounce English names they invented names for them according to the characteristics, if not the eccentricity, discovered in each Officer. For example:

CAPTAIN BOURNE:[5] was called 'Pa-ma-dai' – which means 'Mr Tentmaker', because wherever he went he asked the Karens to make bamboo huts for troop accommodation.

MAJOR TROFIMOV: was referred to as 'Pa-gaw-koe' – which means 'red-haired'.

CAPTAIN CLARK's name was 'Htaw-ka-su' – for his long beard and whiskers. After the operation, when he shaved, the Karens took him to be a new man as he looked younger.

MAJOR LUCAS: was known as 'Pa-pa-yaw' – 'Pa' means 'Mr.' and 'Payaw' means 'Burmese' because he had under him more than a score of Burmese parachutists. No other Officer had Burmese soldiers with them.

MAJOR MILNER: was talked about as 'a gentleman who never swears'. He never used rough words towards the Karens. The attribute is a distinction which the Karens regard as a high honour. The Karens generally dislike to be sworn at. He is sometimes referred to as 'Pa Bren Gun' on account of his complete mastery over this favourite weapon of his which he always employed, always standing, with incredible accuracy and speed – a feat rarely accomplished by fighters.

CAPTAIN WOOLF: was popularly called 'Htaw-na-dai' – or 'Pa-oo-pee' – which means 'Mr. Long-nose' or 'Mr. Piper' respectively. He was called 'Mr. Piper' because the Karens always found him killing time playing melodious tunes on his pipe, his leg punctuating time.

SERGEANT LENEY: was popularly known as 'Hteelerklaykee Headman' – because he was teased with a spinster of the village and was told that if he married the maid he would be Headman of the village.

COLONEL RA CRITCHLEY: was popularly referred to as 'Baw-naw-taut' – which means 'Walking stick' as he always used his memorable staff (comparable to that of Mr. Churchill's cigar, Mr. Chamberlain's umbrella, and Mr. Attlee's pipe), to support him while travelling and to direct his men in action. His other name, seldom used, was 'The aerodrome maker' – because, to him, the work seemed to be a necessary hobby.

The Karens deeply regretted the fact that Colonel Critchley had to return to England prematurely before the work was over to undergo an eye operation. He failed to see through the finishing touches of the whole operation. Though he appeared to be impressionless to a negligent observer, he was indeed the directing genius behind the entire successful campaign, for the forces behind him were mysteriously unfathomable. Acute, resourceful, ingenious and wilful. He possessed an athletic body (6ft. 3in. in his socks) which truly presents British manhood and power of endurance. With about 20 years of military experience behind him, he was indeed an expert in guerrilla warfare, for he had proved it through his stainless army career at the Chin Hills, Kachin Hills and the Karen Hills. The Karens, idolising him, would always remember him as a great friend, an inspiring leader, nay, the 'Pioneer-Liberator' of the Shwegyin-Mewaing hill inhabitants.

The Karens were lucky in having an able and popular substitute in the person of Major Hood, who was given the honour to become the Commanding Officer of the Mongoose Group in place of the redoubtable Colonel Critchley. He would be equally popular and masterful if he were given the same opportunity to do so. He was known by the Karens as a comedian and whenever they had concerts and entertainments, they mimicked him singing 'Suzanna a funnyful man'. His nickname is the 'Comic Singer'.

Another group of worker whose co-operation and contribution towards the success of the Mongoose group and the other groups of the hill guerrillas, unknown and unseen to the liberated natives, deserved high praise. They were the office-bearers serving in the Rangoon Headquarters of Force 136. They carried on their duties faithfully and conscientiously at Rangoon, 125 miles or more away from the Mongoose Area. They were a marvellous lot, truly representing British humanity and imperishable services of self-sacrifice. Tribute ought to be paid particularly to Major King (Lt. Colonel now), the chief Officer who sat in his office chair at Rangoon to work for his comrades and fellowmen far away on the hills. He devoted his time and energy with earnestness also to post-war reconstruction for the people of Burma. He was a silent worker, usually reserved, but sure and true.

The writer apologises to Major Burns, Major Ford, Captain Williams, Captain Ohn Pe and other Officers whose activities are not described and recorded here due to the shortness of time to collect facts and figures from them.

The war is over, but not the work of the Mongoose group, particularly the Karen elders. The end of the war ushers a host of other wars such as, war against poverty, war against starvation, against crime, against ignorance, against diseases, against immorality and against other evils.

This blunt statement might sound paradoxical, but it is true and unrebuttable. The spiritual conflict steps into the shoes of the physical conflict. The war has been won at a record-breaking cost. So would the peace be won. Immediate return of pre-war normal conditions is not readily forthcoming. The place cannot be flooded at once with supplies and clothing, an item that is seriously short – something must be done; it has been done and will be done, so are the assurances.

Regarding the political status of the Karens, they want to be still under the control of the British Government. They realise that she is the only power to give them freedom, peace and security. To avoid the possibility of separation from the mother colony when Burma has a right to secede from the Commonwealth of Nations by the decision of the Dominion status government which will be granted in future as promised by the British parliament in 'His Majesty's Statement of Policy' dated May 1946, under the control of the Governor with the same form of administration exercised in pre-war days and with definite scheme for reconstruction and systematic development. The writer will never forget the repeated assurances of Lt. Colonel King, and Mr. HNC Stevenson (now Director of the Frontier Areas), that fair treatment should and would be given to the Karens for the services and loyalty exhibited by the Karens, particularly the hillmen during the war. They earnestly wish and believe that Officers of Force 136 would see that a separate Karen area be conceded to the hill Karens as promised.

The Officers concerned are earnestly requested to improve upon the essay, to send in their respective accounts to contribute towards the completion of the liberation history of the Shwegyin-Mewaing Karens.

---

[1] *See* also Saw M. Shwin, 'The Shwegyin Karens', TNA: HS1/11.

[2] **Editor's note**: 30 viss is approximately 49 Kilograms.

[3] This was a system of land use developed by the British in Burma in the nineteenth century. It involved land being cleared for the purpose of raising crops over one or more years. Tree seedlings of commercially desirable species are also planted so that after many years a commercial harvest of timber can be taken from the plot. *See* Nicholas Menzies, "Three Hundred Years of Taungya: A Sustainable System of Forestry in South China." *Human Ecology*, vol. 16, no. 4, Springer, 1988, pp.361–76.

[4] The Lines of Torres Vedras were lines of forts and other military defences built in secrecy to defend Lisbon during the Peninsular War.

Original unedited photograph. "Pagoda" with Kya, my faithful orderly. Kya joined me three days after I dropped onto Pyagawpu and remained with me throughout the whole of the operation. A grand little chap! – always happy – taught him to sing several English and French songs. Kya had tears in his eyes when I eventually left the field. I will never forget Kya for his devotion to me under every circumstance.

Editor's Note:
'Apart from those personnel that are highlighted in editor's footnotes herein, many of the SOE Officers and personnel and Karens mentioned in this Liberation report by Saw M. Schwin feature in Maj. Trofimov's diaries and several can be seen within the photo albums.'

Appendix IV

Karen Platoon Lists – Pay (March–September 1945)

Rank: RFM[1] *Name*: **Palai Say** *Village*: Law Bu Dar *Service*: Mar-Sep *Final Pay + Gratuity*: 180 RS + 60

Rank: RFM *Name*: **MgPe HAI** *Village*: Tha Hawki *Service*: Apr-Sep *Final Pay + Gratuity*: 150 RS + 60

Rank: RFM *Name*: **Tun Yin Paw** *Village*: Walaw Klo *Service*: Apr-Sep *Final Pay + Gratuity*: 150 RS + 60

Rank: RFM *Name*: **Shwe Theiw** *Village*: Tha Haw Ki *Service*: Apr-Sep *Final Pay + Gratuity*: 150 RS + 60

Rank: RFM *Name*: **Baw Na** *Village*: Wa aMi Day *Service*: Apr-Sep *Final Pay + Gratuity*: 150 RS + 60

Rank: RFM *Name*: **Hla Bu** *Village*: Wa Ka Say *Service*: May-Sep *Final Pay + Gratuity*: 120 RS + 60

Rank: RFM *Name*: **Shwe Mya** *Village*: Tha Baw *Service*: Mar-Sep *Final Pay + Gratuity*: 150 RS + 60

Rank: RFM *Name*: **Aung Gy**i *Village*: Hti Ya Ki *Service*: Mar-Sep *Final Pay + Gratuity*: 180 RS + 60

Rank: RFM *Name*: **Pashwe** *Village*: Medakota *Service*: Apr-Sep *Final Pay + Gratuity*: 150 RS + 60

Rank: RFM *Name*: **Mya Paw** *Village*: Shwe Hti *Service*: Apr-Sep *Final Pay + Gratuity*: 150 RS + 60

Rank: RFM *Name*: **Mg Ye Hai** *Village*: Pla Pli Ki *Service*: Mar-Sep *Final Pay + Gratuity*: 180 RS + 60

Rank: RFM *Name*: **Shwe Hai** *Village*: Pahbayookwi *Service*: Apr-Sep *Final Pay + Gratuity*: 150 RS + 60

---

[1] Rifleman

Appendix IV

Rank: RFM *Name*: **Dangar Bahardn** *Village*: Nepale *Service*: May-Sep *Final Pay + Gratuity*: 120 RS + 60

Rank: RFM *Name*: **Palai Bu** *Village*: Maw Da Kodar *Service*: Apr-Sep *Final Pay + Gratuity*: 150 RS + 60

Rank: RFM *Name*: **Saw Bu Lay** *Village*: Yakayki *Service*: Apr-Sep *Final Pay + Gratuity*: 150 RS + 60

Rank: RFM *Name*: **Thi Po** *Village*: Pabayookwi *Service*: Apr-Sep *Final Pay + Gratuity*: 150 RS + 60

Rank: RFM *Name*: **Chan Tha** *Village*: Nankhu Khi *Service*: Apr-Sep *Final Pay + Gratuity*: 150 RS + 60

Rank: RFM *Name*: **Pasawho** *Village*: Hti Kayhta *Service*: Apr-Sep *Final Pay + Gratuity*: 150 RS + 60

Rank: RFM *Name*: **Nga Baw** *Village*: Hti Kayhta *Service*: Aug-Sep *Final Pay + Gratuity*: 30 RS + 10

Rank: RFM *Name*: **Pantha Say** *Village*: Hti Kayhta *Service*: Aug-Sep *Final Pay + Gratuity*: 30 RS + 10

Rank: RFM *Name*: **Mg Nyunt** *Village*: Kyauk Taw *Service*: Aug-Sep *Final Pay + Gratuity*: 30 RS + 10

Rank: RFM *Name*: **Seingadon** *Village*: Kyauk Taw *Service*: Aug-Sep *Final Pay + Gratuity*: 30 RS + 10

Rank: RFM *Name*: **Nga Kywet** *Village*: Kyauk Taw *Service*: Aug-Sep *Final Pay + Gratuity*: 30 RS + 10

Rank: RFM *Name*: **Pah Kyawna** *Village*: Shwe Chaungwa *Service*: Aug-Sep *Final Pay + Gratuity*: 30 RS + 10

Rank: RFM *Name*: **Pahmawlu** *Village*: Ohn Bin *Service*: Aug-Sep *Final Pay + Gratuity*: 30 RS + 10

Rank: RFM *Name*: **Tun Yin** *Village*: Paine Ywa *Service*: Aug-Sep *Final Pay + Gratuity*: 30 RS + 10

Rank: RFM *Name*: **Kya Shwe** *Village*: Maw Pun *Service*: Aug-Sep *Final Pay + Gratuity*: 30 RS + 10

Rank: RFM *Name*: **Pohla** *Village*: Tathwita *Service*: Aug-Sep *Final Pay + Gratuity*: 30 RS + 10

Rank: JEM *Name*: **Harry** *Village*: Thaton *Service*: With Seagrim as Havildar Jun-43-Feb 44 *Previous Pay*: 450 RS

Rank: Jemadar *Name*: **Harry** *Village*: Thaton *Service*: Feb-Sep *Final Pay + Gratuity*: 500 RS + 240

Rank: Hav/Maj *Name*: **James** *Village*: Shwe Daw *Service*: Apr-Sep *Final Pay + Gratuity*: 300 RS + 120

Rank: Hav *Name*: **Kyagaing** *Village*: Shwe Daw *Service*: Apr-Sep *Final Pay + Gratuity*: 225 RS + 90

Rank: Hav *Name*: **Saw Byu** *Village*: Shwe Daw *Service*: Apr-Sep *Final Pay + Gratuity*: 225 RS + 90

Rank: NK *Name*: **May Gay** *Village*: Hti Mu Ki *Service*: Feb-Sep *Previous Pay*: 38 RS *Final Pay + Gratuity*: 228 RS + 76

Rank: NK *Name*: **Mg Mu** *Village*: Kawhai *Service*: Feb-Sep *Previous Pay*: 38 RS *Final Pay + Gratuity*: 228 RS + 76

Rank: NK *Name*: **Ag Win** *Village*: Lar Mu Hti *Service*: Feb-Sep *Previous Pay*: 38 RS *Final Pay + Gratuity*: 228 RS + 76

Rank: NK *Name*: **Lha Twe** *Village*: Maw Lu *Service*: May-Sep *Final Pay + Gratuity*: 153 RS + 76

Rank: NK *Name*: **Wa Taw** *Village*: Dapawdar *Service*: Feb-Sep *Previous Pay*: 38 RS *Final Pay + Gratuity*: 228 RS + 76

Rank: L/NK *Name*: **Gu Hai** *Village*: Lai Kaw Dar *Service*: Mar-Sep *Final Pay + Gratuity*: 204 RS + 68

Rank: L/NK *Name*: **Lha Htoo** *Village*: Taw Par Daw *Service*: Mar-Sep *Final Pay + Gratuity*: 204 RS + 68

Rank: L/NK *Name*: **Ag Htoo** *Village*: Walawklo *Service*: Apr-Sep *Final Pay + Gratuity*: 170 RS + 68

Rank: L/NK *Name*: **Paha** *Village*: Sawmita *Service*: Apr-Sep *Final Pay + Gratuity*: 170 RS + 68

Rank: L/NK *Name*: **Ka Mu** *Village*: Lar e Dar *Service*: Mar-Sep *Final Pay + Gratuity*: 204 RS + 68

Rank: Rfm *Name*: **Kya Shwe** *Village*: Shweti *Service*: Apr-Sep *Final Pay + Gratuity*: 150 RS + 60

Rank: RFM *Name*: **Pame** say *Village*: Lerwakodar *Service*: Apr-Sep *Final Pay + Gratuity*: 150 RS + 60

Rank: RFM *Name*: **Ba Pyu** *Village*: Maw They Dar *Service*: Apr-Sep *Final Pay + Gratuity*: 150 RS + 60

Appendix IV

Rank: RFM *Name*: **Panamu** *Village*: Maw They Dar *Service*: Apr-Sep *Final Pay + Gratuity*: 150 RS + 60

Rank: RFM *Name*: **Mg Toe** *Village*: Kyauktalone *Service*: Apr-Sep *Final Pay + Gratuity*: 150 RS + 60

Rank: RFM *Name*: **Pu Yoo** *Village*: Nganetpya *Service*: Apr-Sep *Final Pay + Gratuity*: 150 RS + 60

Rank: RFM *Name*: **Kya Kin** *Village*: Nan Kho Hta *Service*: Apr-Sep *Final Pay + Gratuity*: 150 RS + 60

Rank: RFM *Name*: **Nya Paw** *Village*: Ka Ne Lurdar *Service*: Mar-Sep *Final Pay + Gratuity*: 180 RS + 60

Rank: RFM *Name*: **Kyawhtoo** *Village*: Larwakodar *Service*: Apr-Sep *Final Pay + Gratuity*: 150 RS + 60

Rank: RFM *Name*: **Plawdi** *Village*: Sawklodo *Service*: May-Sep *Final Pay + Gratuity*: 120 RS + 60

Rank: RFM *Name*: **Aye Mg** *Village*: Shwe Hti *Service*: Apr-Sep *Final Pay + Gratuity*: 150 RS + 60

Rank: RFM *Name*: **Binkya Min** *Village*: Waneday *Service*: Apr-Sep *Final Pay + Gratuity*: 150 RS + 60

Rank: RFM *Name*: **Mya Po** *Village*: Methekhohta *Service*: Apr-Sep *Final Pay + Gratuity*: 150 RS + 60

Rank: RFM *Name*: **Po Hla** *Village*: Kalawlaw *Service*: Apr-Sep *Final Pay + Gratuity*: 150 RS + 60

Rank: RFM *Name*: **Pa Ba Ah** *Village*: Bawkludar *Service*: Apr-Sep *Final Pay + Gratuity*: 150 RS + 60

Rank: RFM *Name*: **Nari Hai** *Village*: Koparki *Service*: Apr-Sep *Final Pay + Gratuity*: 150 RS + 60

Rank: RFM *Name*: **Morris** *Village*: Saybawlu *Service*: Apr-Sep *Final Pay + Gratuity*: 150 RS + 60

Rank: RFM *Name*: **Basaing** *Village*: Mawni *Service*: July-Sep *Final Pay + Gratuity*: 60 RS + 60

Rank: RFM *Name*: **Saw Me** *Village*: Hti Ko Ki *Service*: Mar-Sep *Previous pay*: 30 RS *Final Pay + Gratuity*: 150 RS + 60

Rank: Orderly *Name*: **Kya Ywet** *Village*: Sawe Dar *Service*: Jul-Sep *Final Pay + Gratuity*: 60 RS + 60

Rank: Orderly *Name*: **San Nyunt** *Village*: Layki *Service*: July-Sep *Final Pay + Gratuity*: 60 RS + 60

Rank: Orderly *Name*: **Tali** *Village*: Talaykawdar *Service*: Mar-Sep *Previous pay*: 30 RS *Final Pay + Gratuity*: 60 RS + 60

Rank: Orderly *Name*: **Padoe** *Village*: Meda Kolaw *Service*: Mar-Sep *Final Pay + Gratuity*: 150 RS + 60

Rank: Orderly *Name*: **Kyh Htoo** *Village*: Pohaihta *Service*: July-Sep *Final Pay + Gratuity*: 60 RS + 60

Rank: Orderly *Name*: **Dadi** *Village*: Nyachawwawhta *Service*: July-Sep *Final Pay + Gratuity*: 60 RS + 60

Rank: Orderly *Name*: **Kyi Ag** *Village*: Po Hai Hta *Service*: July-Sep *Final Pay + Gratuity*: 60 RS + 60

Rank: Orderly *Name*: **Basein** *Village*: Po Hai Hta *Service*: July-Sep *Final Pay + Gratuity*: 60 RS + 60

Rank: Orderly *Name*: **Kya Pe** *Village*: Nya Chawwawhta *Service*: July-Sep *Final Pay + Gratuity*: 60 RS + 60

Rank: Orderly *Name*: **Than Ma** *Village*: Nya Chawwawhta *Service*: July-Sep *Final Pay + Gratuity*: 60 RS + 60

Rank: Orderly *Name*: **Tha Che** *Village*: Banalako *Service*: July-Sep *Final Pay + Gratuity*: 60 RS + 60

Rank: Orderly *Name*: **Thet Pah** *Village*: Kho Pur Ki *Service*: Apr-Sep *Final Pay + Gratuity*: 150 RS + 60

Major Trofimov's 'A' Platoon – Weapons Issue

Name: **Harry** (Jemadar) *Father's Name*: **Mg Taw** *Village*: Thaton *District*: Thaton *Carbine No*. 1343339

Name: **James** (Hav. Maj.) *Father's Name*: **Mya Ohn** *Village*: Shwe Daw *District*: Thaton *Carbine No*. 576708

Name: **Baw Na** *Father's Name*: **Shwe Htoo** *Village*: Wahmiday *District*: Papun *Carbine No*. 1344022

Name: **Kya Gaing** *Father's Name*: **Ah Kya** *Village*: Shwe Daw *District*: Thaton *Carbine No*. 1108755

Name: **Saw Peyu** *Father's Name*: **Kya Me** *Village*: Shwe Daw *District*: Thaton *Carbine No*. 2079854

APPENDIX IV

Name: **Mg Gay** *Father's Name*: **Klu Pah** *Village*: (illegible) Me Khi *District*: Papun *Carbine No.* 1177919

Name: **Kamu** *Father's Name*: **Thay Tha** *Village*: Larg dai *District*: Papun *Carbine No.* -

Name: **Mg Ye Hai** *Father's Name*: **Pow Way** *Village*: Plapliki *District*: Papun *Carbine No.* 6126645

Name: **Pah e Hwe** *Father's Name*: **Aung Gyi** *Village*: Mothakolaw *District*: Papun *Carbine No.* Bren

Name: **Thi Po** *Father's Name*: **Komy** *Village*: Pahbayookwy *District*: Papun *Carbine No.* 13488871

Name: **Pah Kyaw Hwe** *Father's Name*: **Aung Htoo** *Village*: Hitkayta *District*: Shwe Gin *Carbine No.* 1335469

Name: **Shwe Etya** *Father's Name*: **Mg San** *Village*: Tha Baw *District*: Papun *Carbine No.* 1079839

Name: **Shwe Hai** *Father's Name*: **Ko Ba Hai** *Village*: Pahbayookyi *District*: Papun *Carbine No.* 1069374

Name: **Pah Ahn** *Father's Name*: **Mg Aye** *Village*: Yah Kay Ki *District*: Papun *Carbine No.* 1113347

Name: **Mya** *Father's Name*: **Pah Lo** *Village*: Shwe Hti *District*: Papun *Carbine No.* 1346847

Name: **Hla Htoo** *Father's Name*: **Bru Pah** *Village*: Bau Bwi Dar *District*: Papun *Carbine No.* 3293382

Name: **Bin Kha Min** *Father's Name*: **PHH Htoo** *Village*: Wa Me Day *District*: Papun *Carbine No.* 5592082

Name: **Pa Ba Ah** *Father's Name*: **Ah Paw** *Village*: Baw Lu Dar *District*: Papun *Carbine No.* 5553312

Name: **Po Hla** *Father's Name*: **Lei Tse** *Village*: Ka law law *District*: Papun *Carbine No.* 2490322

Name: **Mya Po** *Father's Name*: **Pah Kway** *Village*: Mgu Thakota *District*: Papun *Carbine No.* Bren

Name: **Mg Toe** *Father's Name*: **Tha Aung** *Village*: Kyauktalone *District*: Papun *Carbine No.* 61097(last 2 numbers illegible)

Name: **Ba Shing** *Father's Name*: **Shwe Gu** *Village*: Kyauktalone *District*: NyaungLay Bin *Carbine No.* 1029307

Name: **Aung Shwin** *Father's Name*: **Mya lay** *Village*: Htiyakki *District*: Taungoo *Carbine No.* 216430

Name: **Nya Paw** *Father's Name*: (illegible) *Village*: Kane Lar Dar *District*: Papun *Carbine No.* (illegible)

Name: **Pa Lai Bu** *Father's Name*: **Hay Thaw** *Village*: Maw Dakodar *District*: Papun *Carbine No.* 2487496

Name: **Kyaw Htoo II** *Father's Name*: **Mg U** *Village*: Po Hai Ta *District*: Papun *Carbine No.* 2484767

Name: **Da Di** *Father's Name*: **May Hai** *Village*: Nya Chawawta *District*: Papun *Carbine No.* 5580794

Name: **Kyin Mg** *Father's Name*: **Po Mg** *Village*: Pohai Ta *District*: Papun *Carbine No.* 1004271

Name: **Ba Sem** *Father's Name*: **Kyaw Ku** *Village*: Pohai Ta *District*: Papun *Carbine No.* 1345285

Name: **Kya Pe** *Father's Name*: **U Kyan** *Village*: Nya Chawawta *District*: Papun *Carbine No.* 5592430

Name: **Dhan Ma** *Father's Name*: **Tun U** *Village*: Nya Chawawta *District*: Papun *Carbine No.* 1330478

Name: **Dha Che** *Father's Name*: **Tun Yin** *Village*: Banaloko *District*: Papun *Carbine No.* 1335644

Name: **Mg Byaw** *Father's Name*: **Pah Klawwa** *Village*: Hti Kay Hta *District*: Shwe Kym *Carbine No.* 1075300

Name: **Pah Tha Say** *Father's Name*: **Mawkya E** *Village*: Hti Kay Hta *District*: Shwe Kym *Carbine No.* 1085528

Name: **Kya Kim** *Father's Name*: **Cherry** *Village*: Saw Di Ta *District*: Papun *Carbine No.* 1341939

Name: **Sein Gadon** *Father's Name*: **Sam Shun** *Village*: Kyaula Tan *District*: Shwe Kym *Carbine No.* 5567883

Name: **Mg Nyunt** *Father's Name*: **Mg Tay** *Village*: Kyaula Tan *District*: Shwe Kym *Carbine No.* 6141359

Name: **Po Kywet** *Father's Name*: **Po Thaw** *Village*: Kyaula Tan *District*: Shwe Kym *Carbine No.* 5591532

Name: **Po Hta** *Father's Name*: **Pyo Tha** *Village*: Ta Thwita *District*: Shwe Kym *Carbine No.* 1265346

Name: (illegible) **yin** *Father's Name*: **Po dauk** *Village*: Paine ywa *District*: Shwe Kym *Carbine No.* 1251579

Name: (missing) *Father's Name*: **Mg Lewe** *Village*: Ohn B(torn)ywa *District*: Shwe Kym *Carbine No.* 5593424

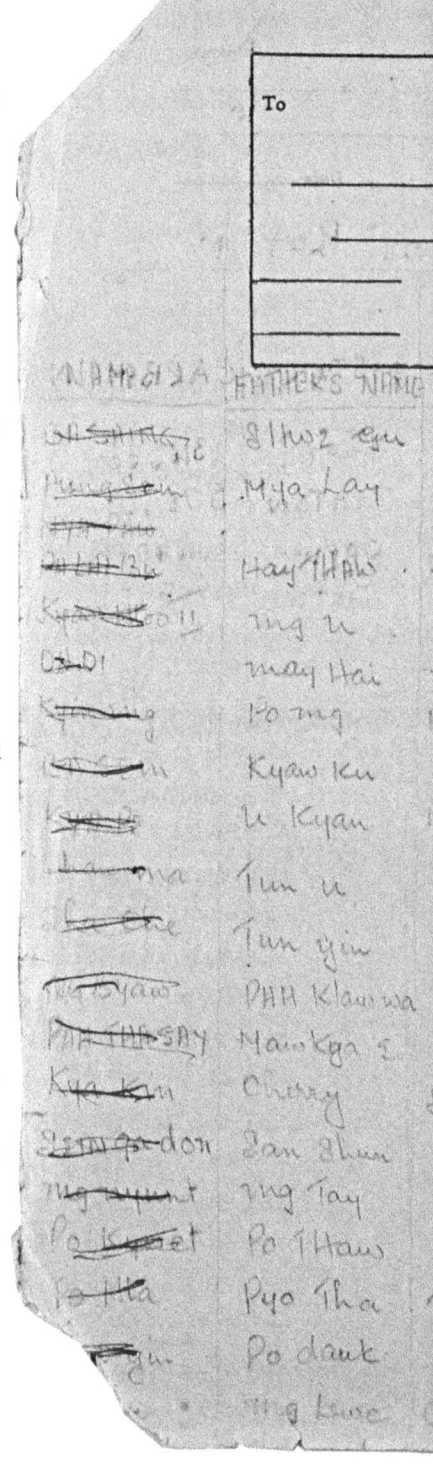

'B' Platoon

No. 1 Name **Harry**
No. 2 Name **James**
No. 3 Name **Wa Taw**
No. 4 Name **Kya Yinet**
No. 5 Name **Baw Na**
No. 6 Name **Pah Lai Say**
No. 7 Name **Nya Paw**
No. 8 Name **Morris**
No. 9 Name **Kya Htoo II**
No. 10 Name **Kya Gaing**
No. 11 Name **Mg Gay**
No. 12 Name **Mg Ye Hai**
No. 13 Name **Ka Mu**
No. 14 Name **Pah Chwe**
No. 15 Name **Thi Po**
No. 16 Name **Pah Kyaw Hue**
No. 17 Name **Shwe Mya**
No. 18 Name **Chwe Hai**
No. 19 Name **Pah Min**
No. 20 Name **Mya Paw**
No. 21 Name **Mg Mu**
No. 22 Name **Hla Htoo**
No. 23 Name **Bin Kya Min**
No. 24 Name **Pah Ba Ah**
No. 25 Name **Po Hla**
No. 26 Name **Mya Po**
No. 27 Name **Mg Toe**
No. 28 Name **Pu Yoo**
No. 29 Name **San Nywnt**
No. 30 Name **Klaw Lei**
No. 31 Name **Dan Gai Bah Hardur**
No. 32 Name **Aung Win**
No. 33 Name **Gu Hai**
No. 34 Name **Ba Pyu**
No. 35 Name **Kya Htoo I**
No. 36 Name **Pah Mi Say**
No. 37 Name **Pah Toe**
No. 38 Name **Kya Shwe**
No. 39 Name **Pah Dwai**
No. 40 Name **Aye Mg**
No. 41 Name **Saw Thi**
No. 42 Name **Saw Dali**
No. 43 Name **Aung Sein**
No. 44 Name **Hla Thwe**
No. 45 Name **Aung Too**
No. 46 Name **Pah Ha**
No. 47 Name **Htoo Yin Paw**
No. 48 Name **Mg Pe Hai**
No. 49 Name **Thet Pah**
No. 50 Name **Shwe Thein**
No. 51 Name **Pah Lai Mu**
No. 52 Name **Na Ri Hai**
No. 53 Name **Saw Hlh Bu**
No. 54 Name **Ba Saing**
No. 55 Name **Saw Byu**
No. 56 Name **Pah Lai Bu**
No. 57 Name **Kyn Mg** 9th July 1945
No. 58 Name **Kya Pe** 9th July 1945
No. 59 Name **Da Di** 9th July 1945
No. 60 Name **Than Ma** 9th July 1945
No. 61 Name **Basein** 9th July 1945
No. 62 Name **Mg Tha Che** 9th July 1945

Mosko Recruit

No. 1 Name **Nga Byaw** 8th August 1945
No. 2 Name **Pah Tha** Say 8th August 1945

Appendix V

Letter to Girlfriend in England (Unposted), 6th March 1945, Describing Parachute Drop into Burma

March 6th 1945 Karen Mountains

Darling – I am writing a letter I don't suppose I shall ever be able to post to you. But should you ever receive it you will realise that I am thinking of you & wondering – hopefully wondering whether when I get out of this show you will be waiting for me – but it is an awful lot to expect of a gal – to wait even though she is not hearing from her lover. I will try shortly and briefly to describe what has happened to me up to date.

On the 20th of Feb I wrote my last letter to you – that afternoon I emplaned together with a Sergeant and several Burmans – of a group which was to afford me protection whilst I began my work.

It is the old story repeated. Major Ronnie Critchley & self, comprise a Jed team attached to a special group of Burmans under the command of a Major Turrall For our protection.

Ronnie has set off on an earlier plane with Turrall – they were to drop blind & then put up the lights to bring us in.

Our particular mission was to arm & train the Karen mountain men to guerrilla warfare & give all possible intelligence on our area.

The journey in the plane was long and damnably cold – it was to be a new experience for me as I was to do a door jump – the plane being a Dakota. We arrived over the dropping zone at about 10pm: My turn to jump – I stood at the door looking out – a firm grip on either side of the door. It was a queer sensation – I felt quite cool & collected – I looked down & saw the lights – Something was wrong we were too high – too late, the red light – I braced myself, the green light a mighty leap into space, the rushing of air, a pull on my shoulders & there I was suspended at about 2500ft above a vast jungle. I looked up to see if the others had followed. I saw the shadows of their parachutes pull away. I then realised what a lousy trick the pilot had played on us – instead of going in low & dropping us about 800 ft – the wretched fellow had been scared of his own skin as there were a few hills around the group & had dropped us a at 2500ft – we had not a chance. Anyhow, I had at lest 4 mins in the air as there was a strong upward whirl of wind – I oscillated terribly – I was weak with trying to pull on the guide ropes in a vain attempt to guide myself to the lights. But there was no hope – the lights on the ground were at least two miles away & I was drifting away from them. With a tightening of my stomach I realised I was going to fall in dense jungle – the last 100 ft went like a whirlwind – with a yell I hit the top of the trees – there was a crashing sound – branches lashed my body – something struck me across the face, and then I was lying in a tangled mess amongst the broken branches – warm blood trickling down from the gash in my face. My heart was pounding – I did not move – all was silent and dark around me, a silence that is enhanced by the loneliness of being alone in a vast jungle.

My thoughts as I lay there turned to my last jump in France, than also I was dropped too high & miles away from the ground I should have landed on.

I began to try and untangle myself – it was difficult as all of us had jumped with masses of equipment and our carbine. Once free I breathed a sigh of relief, for apart from bruises on my face, I was intact.

I took a pace forward & to my horror fell head first down a precipice about 30ft deep. The fall knocked the wind out of me – I felt stunned – I groped around for my pack & found my torch – all around me was dense jungle with thick undergrowth. It was dangerous to move as I seemed to be on a mountain with a sheer gradient. Painfully & laboriously I clambered back up to my parachute. I tried to get it down from the trees but it was caught too fast in the trees.

I started to move up the mountain side – it was hard going –

eventually I arrived at the top – then by some stroke of fate I came across a jungle track, my heart leaped for joy – it was bound to lead somewhere. I reckoned that I was South of the ground so I moved North, after 30 minutes or so – I came to a clearing on my right & there on the other side of the valley was a light slowly moving about in the jungle. I realised immediately it must be one of my men. I climbed on to a knoll & shone my torch – after about one hour some Burmese boys clambered up to me. They were pleased to find me – one of them explained that he had landed in a tree.

I regained the track and kept on going – suddenly I heard a noise in the bushes – I shone my torch and there was a terrified Burman. I had now three out of the four that had followed me out of the plane.

At this point I came to a T junction, a good mountain track running E to West. I got my map out – I eventually decided to go West. Fate again was with me, after about an hour's march down the steep mountainside I suddenly came upon a clearing in a long valley – I immediately knew this must be the place. I proceeded warily as I did not know if there were any Japanese in the area. Suddenly I spotted some lights. I went to them & was met by Major Turrall & Ronnie, they were thrilled & amazed to see me. They had seen our parachutes miles away & had not expected to see us for days.

They informed me that they had not seen the Sgt & his men drop from my plane.

They showed me a stream & I drank cool water & had my wound dressed, and then I settled down and slept in a silk parachute tired & weary but happy – a new adventure lay ahead of me.

APPENDIX V

Original unedited photograph. A Dakota drop at Bolo airstrip.

Appendix VI

Itinerary of Character/'Mongoose' Operations from February 1945 to September 1945 in the Karen Mountains

February

Date: 11th Feb *Itinerary of movements*: Left Horana via Trinco for Ceylon
Date: 12-15th Feb *Itinerary of movements*: Arrival in Calcutta

Date: 16th Feb *Itinerary of movements*: Moved to camp at Jessore

Date: 19th Feb *Itinerary of movements*: Jessore aerodrome

Date: 20th Feb *Itinerary of movements*: Take off time 5.30 pm TOT 10.00pm, maps illustrated from page 230 to 265

Date: 20th Feb *Itinerary of movements*: Parachuted into operated DZ near *Village*: PYAGAWPU

Date: 21st Feb *Itinerary of movements*: Moved off to safe rendezvous 3 miles away to SE near *Village*: PAWLAWDO

Date: 24th Feb *Itinerary of movements*: Established 'lovely camp by the riverside' near *Village*: PAWLAWDO

Date: 25th Feb *Itinerary of movements*: Japanese building food stores between Papun & Shwegyin and building reserves at Kawludo, Kemapyu & Mawchi. Also mention of Japanese concentration at Kyakye. *See* these three locations on the map relative to Character/Mongoose Area

March

Date: 2nd Mar *Itinerary of movements*: Moved off to village of Pawlawdo. Note DZ awkwardly placed in deep valley but camp 'in a pleasant little spot – a glen nestling in a deep valley ... on a bend in the river' *Village*: PAWLAWDO *See* larger scale maps for possible locations

Date: 10th Mar *Itinerary of movements*: Set off to Kaumudo arriving at 6.0 pm (probably not until 12th March as diary details journey made via 4,000ft mountain then crossing the Bilin River on the 11th March and up the other side on route to Lekawdo on the 11th March and then onto Kaumudo) – Moved to recce' Levy potential recruits *Village*: Set off on journey to KAUMUDO via Lekawdo

Date: 11th Mar *Itinerary of movements*: Note diary reference of Japanese 'three-way thrust from Papun – Shwegyin and Kawludo closing in on Pyagawpu'. Camped in a valley in dense jungle after crossing the Bilin River on to its south side *Village*: *See* copy taken from original silk map of this area with these towns/villages highlighted relative to location of PYAGAWPU

Date: 12th Mar *Itinerary of movements*: Early start Arrived at Lekawdo at around 3.00 pm. Had feast then set off to Kaumudo around 3.00 pm *Village*: LEKAWDO

Date: 12th Mar *Itinerary of movements*: Arrived at Kaumudo at around 6.00 pm

Date: 13th Mar *Itinerary of movements*: Proceeded to village of Pokhido (but found that Karens too frightened to join), so set off back to Kaumudo *Village*: POKHIDO

Date: 13th Mar *Itinerary of movements*: Returned to *Village*: KAUMUDO

Date: 14th Mar *Itinerary of movements*: Set off back to Pawlawdo (via DOHEDO) through Lekawdo then crossed the Bilin River and made camp on the other side of the 4,000ft mountain on the other side *Village*: LEKAWDO

Date: 15th Mar *Itinerary of movements*: Arrived at *Village*: PAWLAWDO

Date: 16th Mar *Itinerary of movements*: Return journey to Kaumudo (route as before) over 4,00ft mountain, crossed the Bilin River and camped on the other side. Indicated possible crossing points

Date: 17th Mar *Itinerary of movements*: Trek through jungle arriving at Lekawdo at around noon. Japanese movement so arranged with guide move to hideout: 'It is right up on the southern side of the Bilin River about 3500 feet up. It overlooks the valley of the Bilin and to the north the Pyagawpu valley' *Village*: Near Lekawdo mountain hideout overlooking the Bilin and the Pyagawpu valley

Date: 18th Mar *Itinerary of movements*: Then Capt. Trofimov set off south to set up DZ & training camp just north of Kaumudo; whilst Ronnie Critchley took party to Thauthekhi *Village*: KAUMUDO – area to the north to establish a DZ Presume that camp remained in previous hideout position as above

Date: 24th Mar *Itinerary of movements*: Moved to new camp above Kaumudo – probably closer to DZ *Village*: KAUMUDO – dairy note '… right up on hillside, lovely stream …'

April

Date: 5th Apr *Itinerary of movements*: Moved off to new camp for Ronnie Critchley at Lokhi *Village*: LOKHI

Date: 8th Apr *Itinerary of movements:* Accompanied Capt. Ford to Leklede via Khauchi *Village:* LEKLEDE

Date: 9th Apr *Itinerary of movements:* Arrived at and organized DZ *Village:* METKYHTA

Date: 11th Apr *Itinerary of movements:* Colonel Critchley moved his camp to – prior to attack on Papun *Village:* DUBAW

Date: 25th Apr *Itinerary of movements:* Capt. Trofimov set off for (en-route to attack PAPUN) *Village:* TAHULAW (near Mewaing)

Date: 25th Apr *Itinerary of movements:* At midnight of 25th set off for *Village:* NANKHUKHI

Date: 26th Apr *Itinerary of movements:* Crossed over on track leading to BawBaw *Village:* BAWBAW

Date: 27th Apr *Itinerary of movements:* Then to (where we left all our heavy packs) *Village:* HKLERKO

Date: 28th Apr *Itinerary of movements:* And on to (attack) Papun. Refer to hand drawn maps for details of the attack by Capt. Trofimov, Colonel Critchley and Darlington's Platoons *Village:* PAPUN

Date: 29th Apr *Itinerary of movements:* After the attack returned via Hkhlerko after crossing the Yunzalin River then to BawBaw camped overnight *Village:* KLERKO (Crossing Yunzalin River) & BAWBAW

Date: 30th Apr *Itinerary of movements:* Then on to *Village:* NANKHUKHI

Date: 30th Apr *Itinerary of movements:* And onwards to rest house at – stayed overnight *Village:* TAHULAW

May

Date: 1st May *Itinerary of movements:* Then moved to my new Area at Nankhukhi: – this new area encompasses south of Papun between the Bilin & Kadaingti roads to Nankhukhi and Kwethe *Village:* NANKHUKHI

Date: 5th May *Itinerary of movements:* Ambush parties operating 2 miles south of Nankhukhi *Village:* South of NANKHUKHI

Date: 7th May *Itinerary of movements:* Plans to blow up bridge at Tagundaing *Village:* TAGUNDAING

Date: 10th May *Itinerary of movements:* Letter from Ronnie Critchley that he is moving his camp to Mebawkhi *Village:* MEBAWKHI

Date: 11th May *Itinerary of movements:* Japanese making 3 main Garrisons and supply places – Papun, Lagunbyo (map right of No. 14) and Lower Natkyi *Village:* PAPUN-LAGUNBYO-Lower NATKYI

Date: 13th May *Itinerary of movements*: Maj. Burne moving to Lagunbyo – East of map ref 14 and south of it. Saw Daniel Pan at Htibawlaw is to be our link. (*see* location on large scale map [ref. 922/614) *Village*: LAGUNBYO HTIBAWLAW

Date: 15th May *Itinerary of movements*: Moved stores and dumps to Urekhi – *Village*: UREKHI

Date: 15th May *Itinerary of movements*: Report came in that 30 Japanese were moving up to Kyauktaung (south of map ref. 9) *Village*: KYAUKTAUNG

Date: 16th May *Itinerary of movements*: A further message came from Daniel Paw at Kyauktaung saying 100 or more, well-armed Japanese, were moving up to Kyauktaung from Lagunbyo and would be moving through my area at night. The 30 Japanese moved in to Nankhuhta *Village*: Japanese movements up to Kyauktaung from Lagunbyo through to Nankhuhta

Date: 16th May *Itinerary of movements*: Japanese were leaving Papun for Kuseik *Village*: KUSEIK

Date: 17th May *Itinerary of movements*: At 1 am. a report came in to say a bus has arrived in Nankhuhta. Reports came in that 300-400 Japanese concentrating in area south of Papun from Metharoot (south of Papun) down to Kuseik. *Village*: Japanese moving from Metharoot – south of Papun down to Kuseik

Date: 19th May *Itinerary of movements*: Tanyahta: 'We then heard sounds of shooting coming up from our north side. We proceeded slowly up to our Tanya(hta) retreat – the one I had thought bloody' *Village*: TANYAHTA

Date: 20th May *Itinerary of movements*: Set off to jungle site at Mawkhi: 'Sent Wattaw off with 25 men to Urekhi to bring over some food stores. As soon as he arrives, I will move off – to Mawkhi – one of my men knows the way. We …(must) be careful crossing the Nankhukhi – Bawbaw track. All morning nearby sounds of shooting coming from the village below (assumed to mean the lower Nankhukhi Village [map ref. 938/712) and that Trofimov's base camp is near the upper Nankhukhi Village.' *Village*: MAWKHI (SW of Nankhukhi) from Tanyahta

Date: 22th May *Itinerary of movements*: From Mawkhi to Pawleha *Village*: PAWLEHA (large scale map)

Date: 24th May *Itinerary of movements*: Arrived at Htitabluhta *Village*: HTITABLUHTA

Date: 25th May *Itinerary of movements*: And then to Mekyonoya, probably via Bawthohta *Village*: MEKYONOYA

Date: 25th May *Itinerary of movements*: Met up with Colonel Critchley at *Village*: LAKYOKAWTHI

Date: 28th May *Itinerary of movements*: Proceeded south to Kyowaing. map ref. no. 11 (and depart on leave – Calcutta) *Village*: KYOWAING

June

Date: 2nd June *Itinerary of movements*: Taken by Lysander aircraft from Kyowaing airfield via Mewaing to Rangoon *Village*: RANGOON

Date: 3rd June *Itinerary of movements*: De-Brief reference to Kamamaung *Village*: KAMAMAUNG

Date: 5th June *Itinerary of movements*: Left for Calcutta *Village*: CALCUTTA – RANGOON

Date: 16th June *Itinerary of movements*: Return form leave flight from Calcutta to Rangoon and then by air Lysander to Kyowaing (Map Ref. No. 11) *Village*: KYOWAING

Date: 22nd June *Itinerary of movements*: Set off north back to *Village*: LAKYKOKAWTHI

Date: 25th June *Itinerary of movements*: Then to (dreadful march) *Village*: POLOHTA

Date: 27th June *Itinerary of movements*: Moved north to Htinade *Village*: HTINADE

Date: 27th June *Itinerary of movements*: Crossed the Bilin River to *Village*: WALAW

Date: 28th June *Itinerary of movements*: Thence to Camp at *Village*: MEWAING

Date: 28th June *Itinerary of movements*: And north to *Village*: SCHWEHTI

Date: 30th June *Itinerary of movements*: Set off to Metakho *Village*: METAKHO

Date: 30th June *Itinerary of movements*: Then back down to (Shwegyin-Mekahta area) *Village*: MEKAHTA

July

Date: 1st July *Itinerary of movements*: Via *Village*: PLAWKHI

Date: 2nd July *Itinerary of movements*: Established HQ at *Village*: METLEKHI (via THAUTHEKI)

Date: 15th July *Itinerary of movements*: a) Ambushing along the Shanywa – Meyitha – Mekahta track (NW of Mekahta); and b) Ambushing along the Wingalon – Mekahta track (east of Mekahta)

Date: 26th July *Itinerary of movements*: a) Japanese to move form Shwegyin to Shayna, Wingale, Bilin to Thaton – *see* line on map, b) Japanese movements from Shwegyin to Kunzeik and food dump at Kyaungywa

Date: 28th July *Itinerary of movements*: Arrived at camp at Methekhi *Village*: METHEKHI

Date: 29th July *Itinerary of movements*: Reached Tatukhi *Village*: TATUKHI

August

Date: 4th Aug *Itinerary of movements*: Thence to River Shwegyin (set up camp at) *Note*: message in from Col. Critchely 'telling me that he had recommended me for promotion to Major. *Village*: WABODAW

Date: 6th Aug *Itinerary of movements*: Went through to Mesikhi then entrenched along River from *Village*: YEBEZU to KYAUKTAGA

Date: 7th Aug *Itinerary of movements*: Established new HQ at *Village*: MUSEKO

Date: 10th Aug *Itinerary of movements*: Met Colonel Critchley at Tanipa. *Note*: Col Critchely congratulated 'Trof' on the award of the Military Cross – confirmed by the 12th Army *Village*: TANIPA

September

Date: 1st Sep *Itinerary of movements*: Final destination at *Village*: BOLO

Date: 27th Sep *Itinerary of movements*: Left field for Rangoon – Calcutta *Village*: CALCUTTA

321

Appendix VII

These three photo albums were found in the 'Tin Trunk' – compiled by our late father sometime after the war from photos taken during the campaign.

Professional photographs were taken of each page of the three albums. From the digitally saved photos a selection was made by Harry Bennett for more careful restoration by DevonPress, which are included in the photo album section of this book (pages 144-229).

That leaves a considerable number still in their original condition – bearing in mind there were no negatives to be found – and these original, remaining unedited and unrestored photographs are included here to allow the reader to firstly see the complete range that is available within the 'Trofimov' archive but also to compare the quality of the originals with those that have been restored.

Apart from those that were taken early on in the field during the period of training firstly at Ceylon and then at the Jessau camp north-east of Calcutta, all the other photographs within both the restored album sections and these unrestored ones shown here, were taken after Capt. Trofimov's period of leave at the beginning of June 1945 when he was able, with the help of SOEs 'Q' department as described in the third diary during his de-brief in Rangoon and Calcutta, to obtain a Kodak 35 mm camera to assist with the recording of information in the field once he was returned to active duty in the Karen mountains.

Like the original diaries, these photo albums were carefully stored and the captions which appear beneath each herein are taken directly from the original hand-written captions that our father made within each page of each album and which he stored within the Tin Trunk heavily wrapped together for safe keeping.

Taken together, the restored and unrestored photos comprise the full archive of the photographs that Major Trofimov retained from his exploits as part of SOE's Force 136 Operation Character, Area Mongoose during the period from February to September 1945 and substantially within the period post-leave from June to September, as aforesaid. As we allude to both in the introductions to the restored album sections and in the context of the independent 'Liberation report' by Saw M. Shwin that appears in its original text in Appendix III, these photographs help the reader to understand not only the nature of the topography of the Karen mountains and the various logistical challenges that the SOE personnel and Karen forces faced in undertaking these clandestine operations behind enemy lines, but also to identify some of those who appear in the written diaries and indeed the Liberation report within the many photographs that Trof's archive contains. In so doing it helps to bring the narrative to life and, along with the other elements of this book records one SOE agent's activities as a small cog in a complex part of a very special Operation of irregular warfare that helped secure the liberation of Burma in WWII.

(Prepared by the sons of Major Trofimov)

Landing strip at Kyowaing on return to Burma after Capt. Trofimov's leave in Calcutta.

Lt. Col. Critchley on Kyowaing airstrip evacuating party of British Officers to Rangoon. They had been kept on the run by the Japanese and after six weeks had had enough.

Pagoda – before he was taken ill.

My HQ was in a rather comfortable Pungyi Kyaung (Buddhist Church).

Elephants bringing up my stores from Tatukh.

Capt. Ivan Woolf (My 2nd I/C) with Harry and Japanese prisoner.

The Japanese chopped bamboo to make rafts for river crossing.

Boat patrols down the Mezaung Chaung.

Where the Mezaung Chaung joins the Shwegyin Chaung.

The Bolo airstrip not being quite ready, L5s had to be used for our evacuations.

L5 which Lt. Col. Critchley came in by to give us our orders.

Above right After the surrender.

An L5 preparing for take-off.

The first Lysanders coming into our airstrip at Bolo.

Above left Major Milner – Lt. Col. Critchley and an American pilot and taking off.

A Lysander shown ready for take-off on the makeshift bamboo airstrip at the Bolo camp.

Throughout the operation the RAF gave us Air strikes – sometimes in support of an attack – or upon a very large concentration of Japanese. Here is a crater from one of the strikes.

Major (Fred) Milner, Captain Kim Yadov ADC 12th Army, Major Trofimov (Trof).

Mr and Mrs Morris and POKYAE with Major Milner, going out to Rangoon to represent Karens at Government conference.

Nga Paw, my second orderly and Kya, either side of Maj. Trofimov.

Above left Collecting the parachutes from the drop.

Parachutes of supplies being dropped.

And collected into stores.

And above right Bolo airstrip being made with split bamboo to make it an all-weather landing strip.

And below left Leveling the airstrip.

And above left Temporary huts and shelter to the side of the airstrip.

More drops of food and supplies.

The local Karens and Shans collecting the drop to stores.

Air supplies being dropped at the Bolo camp from the distinctive Liberator B24.

Containers being parachuted in from a Dakota.

The sports day, keeping troops fit and occupied pending release form service.

Setting out the high jump.

Above Final parade of Major Milner's, Captain Bourne's and (*below*) Major Trofimov's mobile guerrilla fighters.

The final parade, (*below*) Major Trofimov's 'B' Platoon.

Morris.

Morris – a levy who served with Tr... ...latoon in Mongoose Area throughout the c...

Navigating the swollen river crossing.

The white flags of surrender from the Japanese on the western banks of the Shwegyin river, or its tributary.

Below right Inspecting the Japanese side of the Shwegyin River with Trof's faithful dog named Pagoda after the battle of Papun (Pagoda Hill) seen here in the foreground.

...re before his untimely demise.

A Home Guard, Karen stands on sentry duty.

Major Milner with his orderly in Bolo.

The New Bolo – built by our guerrillas to house the large force of guerrillas we had concentrated here.

Those Karens who fought in the last moments.

The final farewell at Bolo camp.

Guerrillas stand at ease.

Kya and his aunt.

Below right Photograph taken at the Bolo camp before departure from the field.

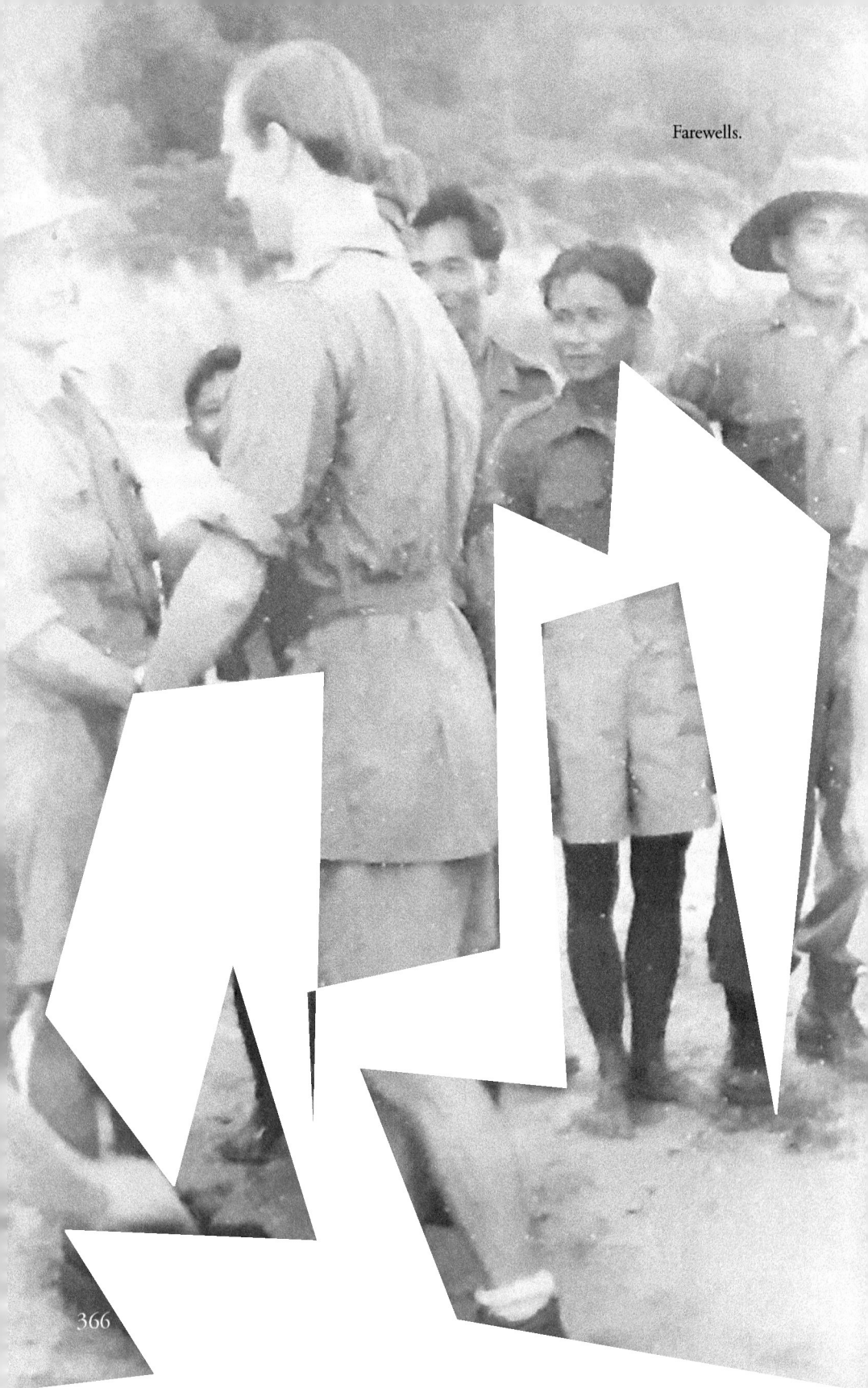

Farewells.

Farewells.

Below right Mothers and sisters of my guerrillas who came to give me a farewell.

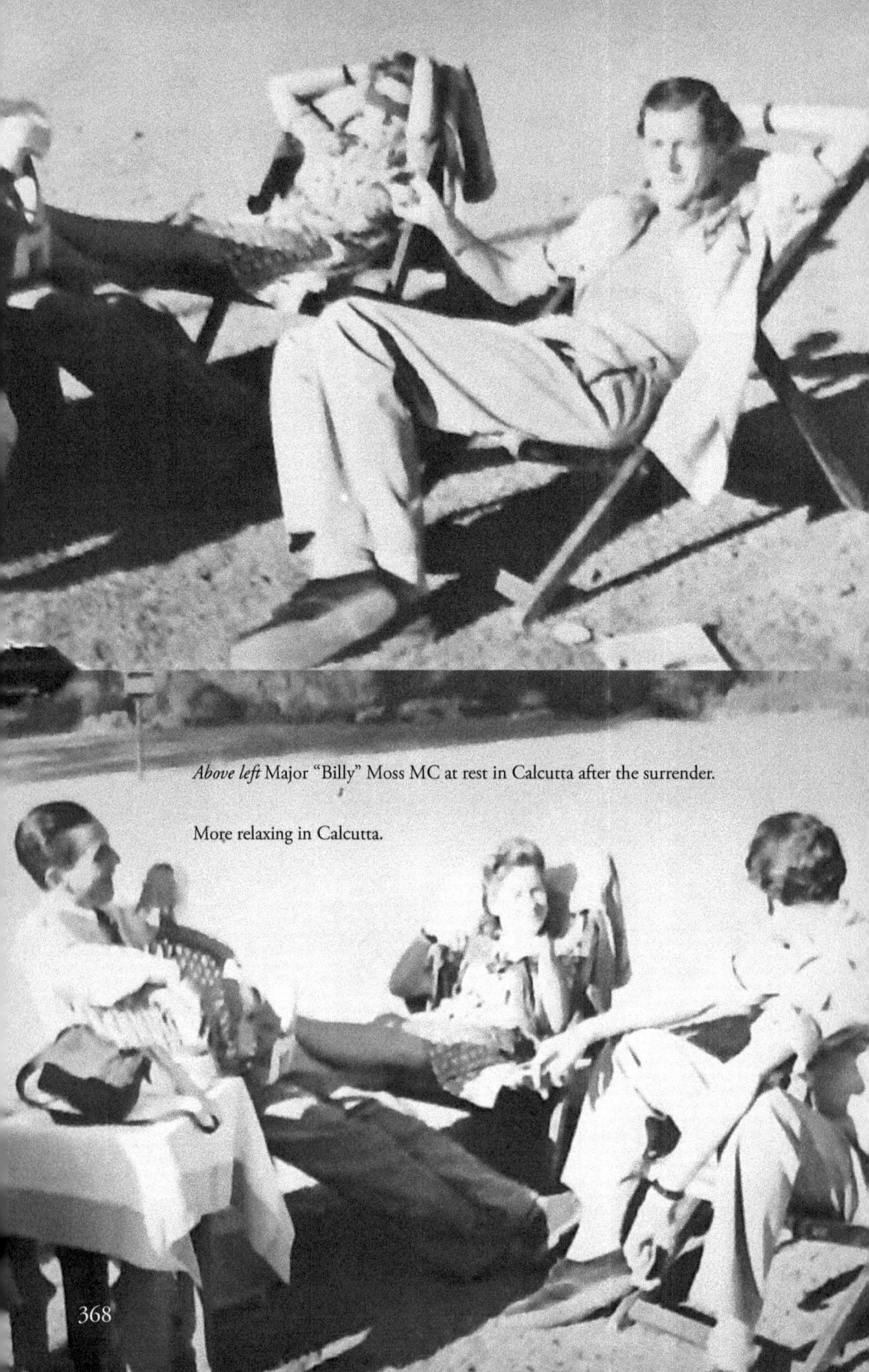

Above left Major "Billy" Moss MC at rest in Calcutta after the surrender.

More relaxing in Calcutta.

Flight Lieutenant Arthur Breen MBE.

Pat O'Brien and Di Turner.

All relaxing.

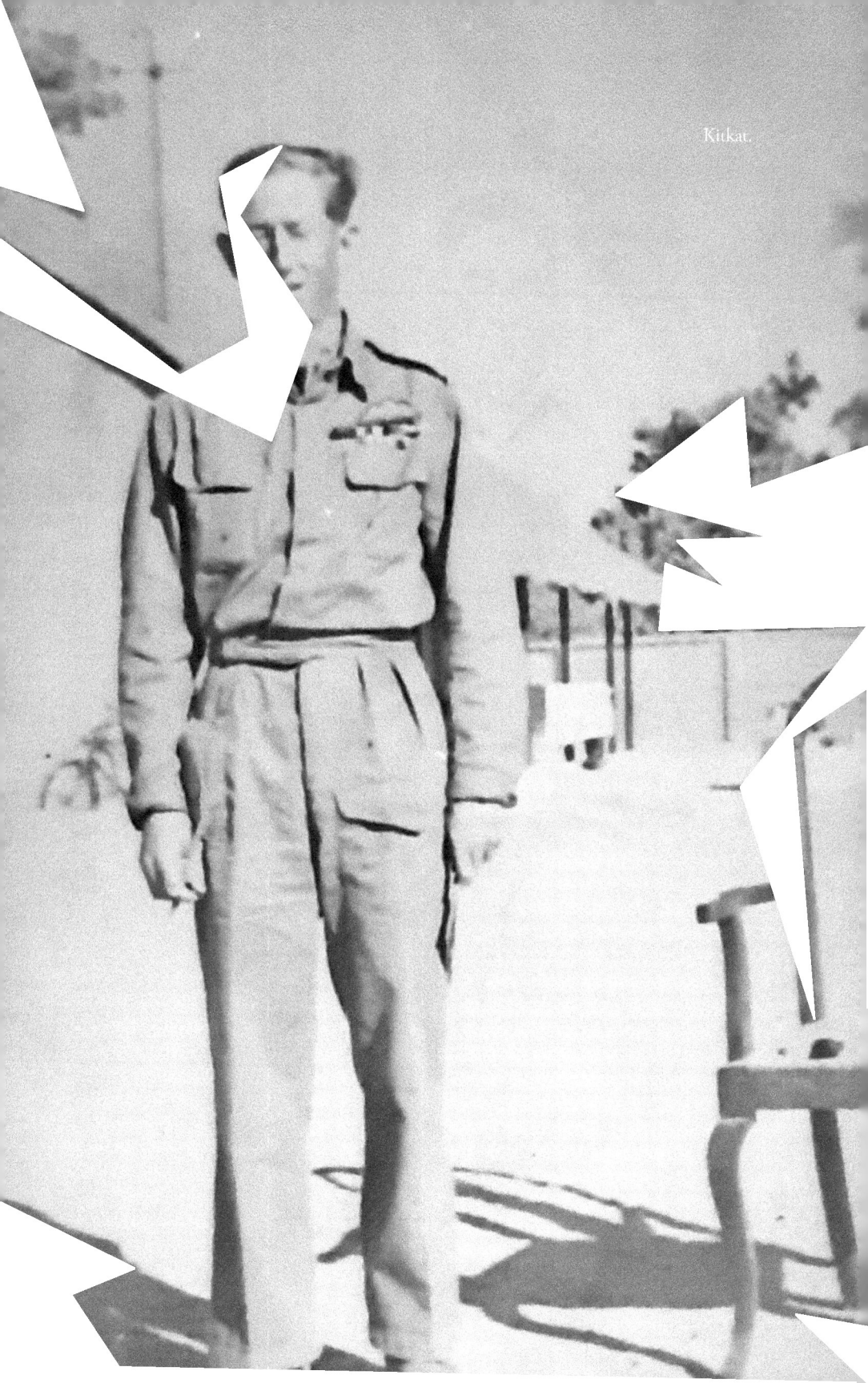
Kitkat.

"Bill" Beatson – Burmese interpreter.

Major Saw Butler MC (diary entry for the 24th February on page 51 and footnote 17).

Appendix VIII

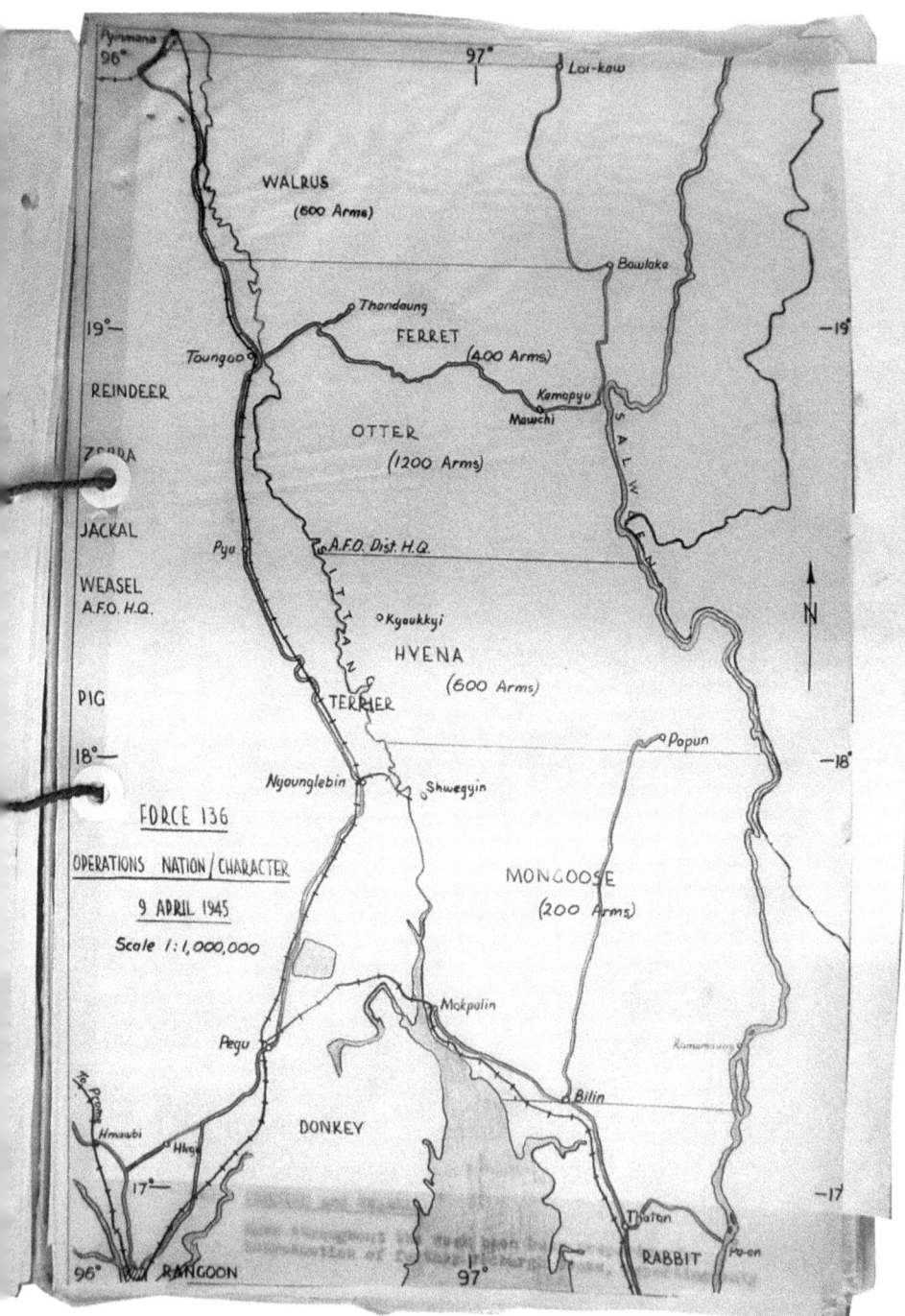

APPENDIX VIII

'Burma all operations (below) and for 'Force 136 Nation | Character' (left) in the period to which this SOE Book refers i.e., 1945 (April). *The Operations of SOE Burma – The Special Operations Executive in Burma 1941-1945* (soeinburma.com)

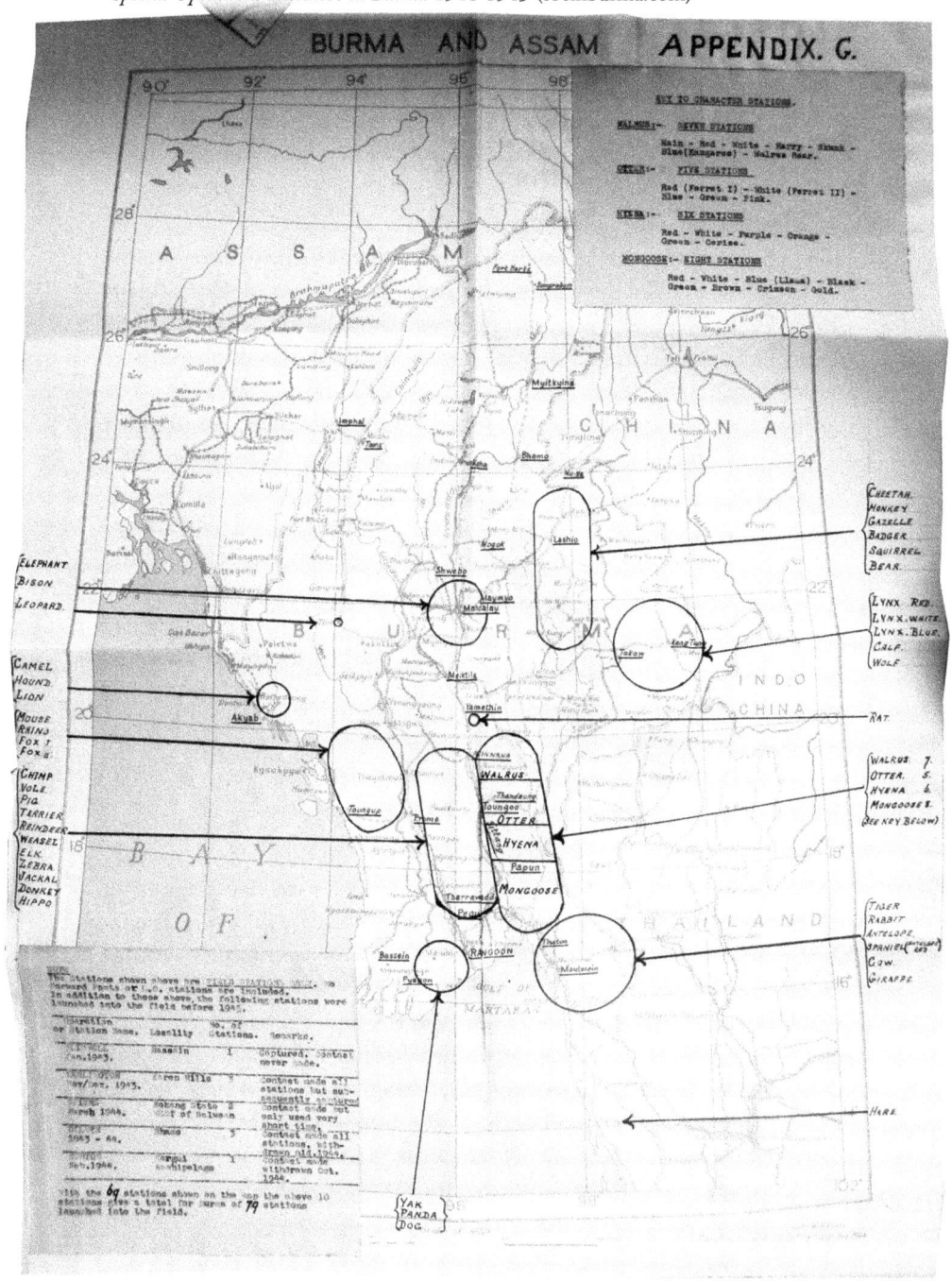

Major AAE Trofimov, MC, Croix de Guerre, Dip. Arch (Manchester) ARIBA

He was born in Manchester on the 7th December 1921 and from the age of 7 to 13 he attended the College du Sacre Coeur, Menton, Cote d'Azur and at Lycee in Nice. He completed his schooling in England at the Queen Elizabeth Grammar School in Ashbourne, Derbyshire and later studied architecture at Manchester University (from 1939) until he joined the Royal Artillery (RA) in 1941. While in the ranks he attended a course at Catterick School of Signals and passed with distinction as a Signals Instructor.

He was commissioned in the RA in September 1943 and joined 148/170 Field Regiment RA at Glynde in Sussex and was subsequently posted to Ireland for training. In one of his post articles, he writes:

> "Shortly afterwards a notice appeared on the board asking for volunteers from anyone with a sound knowledge of French and experience in Signals prepared to work behind enemy lines. I had both qualifications and volunteered on the 30th October 1943."

He was invited to interview in London in January 1944 and then underwent extensive tests in different locations and then at Milton Hall, near Peterborough in 1944 where he underwent extensive training in guerrilla warfare tactics (including sabotage, use of explosives, enemy identifications, military operations, silent killing techniques, organisation of networks, dropping zone drill, wireless telegraphy, morse code, parachute training, training on Eureka and two-way S-Phone larynx sets) under the joint command of the British Special Operations Executive (SOE) and the Special Operations (SO) wing of the American's Office of Strategic Services (OSS) in London. The intention being for selected agents to operate and infiltrate behind enemy lines in advance of and post the Allied Forces D-Day landings under the codename 'Jedburghs' ('Jeds'). These were teams generally of three comprising an English or

American Officer, with one French Officer and a radio operator.

He was dropped behind enemy lines in Brittany (part of Team Guy – SOE) in early July 1944 and subsequently into the Karen Mountains in Burma (as part of SOE's Force 136 – Operation CHARACTER / HEAVY / WOOLF / MONGOOSE) in February 1945. He was awarded the Croix de Guerre for his part in the capture of Gorron, Brittany by the Allied forces and mentioned in despatches, then later for his services in Burma as part of Force 136 Operation Character, Area Mongoose, he was awarded the Military Cross following the attack on Papun, a Japanese garrison stronghold in the Karen mountains; forming part of Force 136 efforts in support of General Sir William Slim's 14th Army advances in early 1945 and specifically deploying guerrilla warfare means to help delay the Japanese sending reinforcements to defend Toungoo after the Allies had recaptured Meiktila, 125 miles to the north in March 1945.

Following the Japanese surrender and SOE's operations disbanded in the field, he held administrative posts at Manipur and Deolali Transit camps until he was released from British Army service in time to re-join the Manchester School of Architecture in the autumn 1946 after spending some time with Resistance friends in Brittany. Shortly after obtaining his diploma in architecture, in October 1949, he joined a firm of Architects in London (Cotton, Ballard, and Blow),[1] eventually becoming a partner and taking over, by mutual consent, their practice in the North-East when he set up in private practice in May 1964.

Throughout his career as an architect, he maintained strong links with France, principally involving former French resistance fighters: In 1954 he met a developer who was interested in acquiring an estate at Le Touquet, which included a hotel, golf courses, and 2,000 acres of pine forest. His plans for the development of this area eventually won official acceptance, with help from some friends from the French Resistance. The plans provided for building sites along cul-de-sacs penetrating into the forest and following the natural contours of the land., to afford maximum privacy to each dwelling with the minimum disturbance to the forest through very strict controls. His achievement was recognized in 1984 when he was made 'Citoyen d'Honneur' of Le Touquet.

Another development overlooking the Cherbourg Peninsula was carried out with the help of the renowned former Resistance leader in Brittany, Commander Louis Petri, who later became the manager of the

---

[1] Cotton, Ballard and Blow | Charles | Saumarez | Smith | (charlessaumarezsmith.com).

completed development with his wife.

He began to wind down his practice in 1979 and moved from Northumberland to Middleton-on-Sea, West Sussex, to make life easier to travel to France for his consultancy work at Le Touquet, around Paris and throughout the north of France as well as representing a developer operating throughout the coastal areas in the south-east of England. He later retired on his 70th birthday in December 1991.

In September 1949 he married Jean (Jean Hope *neé* Halliwell 1930-2008), a freelance model and later interior designer and keen gardener, and they have two sons: Mark and Paul, each of whom are married and have two children. He died on the 6th May 2006 shortly after attending a reunion of the SOE Jedburghs in London attended by one of his sons.

Richard Duckett

Richard is a graduate of the Universities of Essex (BA, 2000) and Reading (MA, 2001), and was awarded a PhD in 2015 by the Open University. He has published two books on the Special Operations Executive in Burma, and continues to lecture widely on the subject. He also maintains a website (www.soeinburma.com) where more of his latest research can be accessed for free. Richard has taught History and Politics since 2004 and is currently employed at Leighton Park School where he is Head of Politics and Assistant Head of Sixth Form.

GH Bennett

Harry is Associate Professor at Plymouth University where he has taught history, including that of the Second World War since 1992. Author of more than 20 volumes on Military, Diplomatic and Political history he has appeared in documentaries on the Second World War as well as historical series such as *Who Do You Think You Are* and *Combat Ships*. He is also a regular contributor to BBC National, Local Radio and to Gem Collector TV.

Clive Bassett Harrington Aviation Museum

Clive Bassett on left receiving Trof's carbine for display at the museum. In the background Harry Verlander[1] – an SOE veteran and Paul Trofimov, youngest son of Trof.

Meeting and getting to know "Trof", initially through the Jedburgh Reunion Association, was very special indeed. Putting on photographic displays and exhibiting examples of wartime items and equipment that they used during their service, for their reunions was an immense pleasure.

Listening to Trof's accounts of his wartime activities and learning more of his role with the Jedburghs in France and his later service in Burma with Force 136 was an immense privilege. Trof also supported our Museum at RAF Harrington, with wonderful donations of his Fairbairn-Sykes 2nd pattern Fighting Knife, American manufactured M1 Carbine and his Binoculars. RAF Harrington was an Airfield in Northamptonshire where the American 801st/492nd Bombardment Group "The Carpetbaggers" were based, flying black painted B-24 Liberator Bombers, especially converted for SOE (Special Operations Executive) and OSS (Office of Strategic Services) operational use.

The Jedburghs were dispatched from a number of different Airfields, both here in the UK and North Africa. 26 Jedburgh teams flew to France from RAF Harrington. A number of Jedburgh family members, including Trof's sons, Mark and Paul, also attended the reunions and although the Association is now disbanded, still keep in contact with each other and ensure the Jedburgh flame is kept alive.

For my part, I was privileged to be made an honorary "Jed" by the veterans themselves and wear with pride on every suitable occasion the Special Force Tie that was presented to me. The Jeds were a quite remarkable and unique organisation, their history, service and sacrifice will never be forgotten.

Clive Bassett is the Chairman and co-Founder of the Harrington Aviation Museum and Society

www.harringtonmuseum.org.uk

Sunnyvale Farm, Off Lamport Road, Northampton NN6 9PF

---

[1] A veteran SOE agent. He was a special friend of my father – his recently published book:

Verlander, H., (2010) *My War in the SOE: Behind Enemy Lines in France and Burma with the Special Operations Executive*, Independent Books.

Index

A
Ag Win, Naik 102, 139, 282, 306

B
Ba Chit, Maj. 90, 91, 103, 111
Bassett, Clive 10, 381–382
BawBaw 90, 101, 318
Bilin (River) 24, 60–62, 76, 81, 90, 92, 123, 290
Bilin Road 79, 81, 83–84, 91, 94–96, 98, 100, 104, 123, 128, 277–278, 280, 290–292
Bissett, Capt. 129–130
Bombay 146
Bourne, Capt. Ted 124
Brenda 117–120, 122, 124, 127, 129–130, 134
Burma rifles 49, 60, 63, 70, 77, 83, 96, 124, 154, 230, 273, 276, 280, 282, 288
Burman 14–15, 25, 51–52, 54, 61, 64, 106, 127, 286, 312, 314
Burne, Maj. Cuthbert 75–78, 80–81, 94–95, 97, 101–102, 104–106, 122–123, 134, 275, 279, 287

C
C Te 91–94
Calcutta 9
Carew, Tom 8

Catterick School of Signals 378
Ceylon 24, 48, 146, 272, 323
Character, Operation 14–15, 24, 27–28, 35–37, 39, 41, 47, 146, 190, 214, 230, 272, 286, 323, 379
Charles, Havildar 59
Chaung 296
Chin Hills 301
Choke, Lt. Kan 13
Clarke, Capt. 131
Claude de Baissac, codename Michel 267
Collins, Nora 129
Craster, Capt. Oswin Edmund 109, 113, 115
Critchley, Col. Ronald A. (Ronnie) 24, 37–38, 47–49, 52, 101, 140, 146, 230–231, 272–276, 279, 285, 286, 287, 288, 289, 290–291, 296, 300–301, 312
Croix de Guerre 19, 23, 48, 378–379
Crosby, Lt. Colonel 'Bing' 116

D
Dakota, (aircraft) 27, 49, 52, 54, 56, 58, 72–73, 78–79, 103, 133, 140, 272, 283, 312
Danyungon (Japanese depositions) 125
Diane 119, 134
Dixon, Joan 108, 127
Dohedo 61, 317

Dreux, Capt. 266

Dubaw 36, 76–78, 230, 274–275, 288, 318

Duron, Capt. André 21

F

FANY's 134

Force 136 14–15, 23–24, 35–37, 39, 41, 46–48, 50, 115, 190, 230, 272, 286, 298, 301–302, 323, 379, 381

Ford, Capt. Dennis 73–76, 105–106, 120–121, 274, 275, 287, 301

G

Gardner, Lt. Col. Ritchie 119

Gavin, codename 22

Gemmel, George 116, 118

Gorron 22–23, 268, 379

Groult, Lt. Roger 21

Gte 124, 130

Gurkha 14, 40, 84

Guthrie, Capt. Duncan Dumbar OBE 48, 51–53

Guy, codename 22–23, 37, 39, 266, 379

H

Hanbury-Tracey, John (Officer at ME 25) 105, 117

Harrington Museum 10–11, 231

Harrington, Maj. 108, 115

Hedley, Maj. John 13

Heiho Tat 25

Hkhlerko 81, 83

Hodgart, Maj. 116

Horana 48, 146

Howell, Lt. Colonel Hugh Warton 118

Htinade 123

Hyena 24, 36, 67, 73, 106, 214, 230, 283

I

Ille-et-Vilaine 267

Imphal 26

Iuchi, Lt. 140–141, 204, 281–282

J

Ja Gain, Havildar 136

Jagha, Havildar 130

James, Havildar Maj. 132–133

Japanese 14, 19, 23–29, 35–37, 50, 52–54, 56–57, 59–62, 64, 76, 78–79, 82–86, 88–89, 91–105, 109, 114, 124–128, 131–141, 204, 208, 231, 273, 275–282, 286, 288–299, 314, 379

Jedburghs 10, 21, 23, 39, 42, 48, 52, 72, 146, 154, 266, 378, 382

Jessore Camp 48

John, Sgt. 117

K

Kachin 14

Kachin Hills 301

Kadaingti 74–75, 90, 94, 96, 115, 277–278, 280, 282, 290, 318

Kamamaung 115, 320

Karen 11, 14–15, 19, 24–29, 35–42, 46–48, 50–56, 59–60, 62–63, 71, 75, 77, 79, 81, 84–86, 90, 92, 106, 114, 123, 128, 132, 135, 146, 154, 166, 208, 214, 222, 230, 273–274, 276–277, 280, 286–294, 297–302, 304, 323

Karen Hills 19, 24–28, 50, 301

385

Karen Mountains 9, 35, 41, 48, 63, 78, 103, 146, 230–231, 272, 312, 316, 323, 379
Kaukpok Road 82
Kaukyi 60
Kaulback, Maj. 105, 108
Kaumudo 59–62, 64–65, 73, 230, 273–274, 283, 317
Kawludo 52, 60
Khauchi 75, 318
Khlerkho 84, 275–276
King, Col. Robin 108, 115, 301–302
Kinmunsakan (Japanese dispositions) 125
Kodak camera 38
Kohima 26
Kunzeik 129
Kuseik 81, 91, 96, 98–100, 102, 278, 282, 319
Kwethe 90, 94, 96, 99, 231, 277, 318
Kya Uway 51, 55, 85–86, 93, 100, 120–122
Kyakgyin 79
Kyauktaga 136–137, 281–282, 321
Kyauktaung 97–98, 319
Kyaungywa 132, 320
Kyunbin Sakan 84

L

Lagunbyo 97–98, 115, 318–319
Lahu 14
Lakyokawthi 36, 102, 121–122, 231
Lekawdo 60–62, 71, 73, 230, 273, 317
Leklede 75, 230
Lenaw 104

Leney, Sgt. 287
Lha Twe 134
Liberator, (aircraft) 10, 27, 52, 54, 56, 58, 72–74, 78–79, 267, 283, 287
Little, Sgt. 49–50
Lockhart, Alan 116
Lokhi 71, 73–75, 274, 317
Loosmore, Sgt. Robert Glyn 39, 76, 129, 131
Lucas, Maj. 15, 129, 292, 293, 294, 300
Lysander (aircraft) 21, 27, 95, 106–109, 114, 120, 139–141, 154, 190, 267

M

Mackenzie, Col. Colin H 13, 38, 40
Madama Cloe Valley 133
Mahtaw 90
Mandalay 26
Maw Gay 77, 85, 87–88, 93, 100, 105–106, 132, 139, 282
Mawchi 52, 128
Mawkhi 101–102, 231, 319
McCrindle, Capt. 273
McLeod, Capt. 50
Meiktila 26, 75, 379
Melaung (Japanese dipositions) 125
Mepawkhi 127
Mepok (Japanese dipositions) 125
Methako 123
Metharoot 100, 278, 319
Metklekhi 125, 166, 280
Metkythia 75
Mewaing 36, 76–77, 80–82, 88, 92, 95, 102, 108, 114, 123, 127, 133, 139, 230–231, 276–277, 279–280, 283, 287, 289–291, 295–296, 301–302, 320

Meyitkhi 130, 132–133

Mg Mu 85–86, 129

Military Cross 19, 137, 379

Milner, Maj. Freddie 15, 73–74, 122, 114, 120–121, 123, 133–137, 139–141, 204, 214, 222, 231, 277, 280–282, 287–289, 291–292, 295–296, 299–300

Milton Hall 20–21, 42, 47–48, 266, 378

Mongoose 14–15, 24–25, 35–36, 38–39, 41, 46, 138, 146, 214, 231, 272, 274–275, 279, 285–289, 298–299, 301, 316, 323, 379

Moore, Lt. 130–131

Moses 83–84, 86–87, 89

Myanmar 19

N

Nankhukhi 76, 81–82, 90–93, 95, 98–101, 103–104, 230–231, 278–279, 281, 318–319

Natkyi 97

Newcastle, HMS 48, 146

Ngapyawdaw 292–293

O

Ohn Pe, Capt. 79, 81–83, 90, 105, 301

Otter 24

P

Pa La Too 76

Padet Chaung 136, 281

Pagoda (dog) 14, 97, 104–108, 114, 118–120, 126, 131–132, 134, 140

Pagoda Hill 82–84, 87–89

Pagoda Hills 294

Palatoo 75, 102

Panate 287, 292

Papun 51, 84, 89, 280, 282

Pawlawdo 52, 316

Pawleha 95, 102–104, 231, 319

Peacock Force 47–48, 52, 146, 230

Peacock, Lt. Col. Edgar 13

Phillyos, Maj. William 117

Plawkhi 124, 132, 320

Po Kaing 94–95

Po The 51

Pokhido 61, 63, 70, 76–77, 273

Poking (new cook) 100

Poles, Maj. William Eustace 51–52, 54, 273

Polohta 102

Porta Rico Club 119

Pungyi 125

Pyagawpu 49, 56–57, 60, 62, 71, 76, 230, 272–273, 283, 287

Q

Queen Elizabeth's Grammar School 8–9, 20, 30

R

Rangoon 14, 26, 108, 114–115, 118–120, 126–127, 134, 138, 140, 156, 160, 198–199, 222, 231, 301, 320–321, 323

Robert Dee, Jemadar 64, 75

Royal Artillery, 148/170 Regiment 20

S

Salween (River) 24, 64, 277, 287

Sankey, Capt. 287

Saturday Club 116

Sauthehkee 287

Saw Aaron 54, 57, 59, 60, 62–64, 69, 82, 85–87, 90, 273, 276, 287

Saw Aung Wain 51

Saw Butler, Maj. 51, 375

Saw Daniel Pan 97–98, 102, 319

Saw Dannier 77

Saw Darlington 79–85, 87, 90–95, 98, 100–101, 104, 275, 277–278, 289–290, 318

Saw Harry 54, 61, 70–71, 82, 98, 133, 287

Saw Harry, Havildar 54, 61, 70, 75, 77, 82, 85, 87, 91, 93–94, 96, 100–101, 114, 124, 127, 130, 139–140, 274–275, 282

Saw His Tai 54, 55, 273

Saw Htoo, Havildar 130, 133, 136, 280, 292

Saw Hubert Shwin 292, 293

Saw Marshall Shwin 14, 40, 286, 287, 302

Saw Maco Gay 51

Saw Ohe Htoo, Mrs 132–133

Saw Sankey, Lt. 129, 293

Seagrim, Maj. Hugh 24, 28, 50, 54, 63

Shan 14, 25, 61, 64, 84, 90, 107, 140, 166, 214

Shepherd, Sgt. 127, 131

Shwe Ma, (Karen cook) 72, 110

Shwegyin 52, 60, 64, 79, 125, 129, 132–141, 204, 280–282, 286–288, 294–296, 298, 301–302

Shwehti 81–82

Simon Matte, Louis 268

Sinbyu-ain-auk 136

Sittang (River) 24, 37, 64, 115, 123, 128–129, 132, 231, 287, 294–295

Sked 57, 64–65, 70–73, 76, 100, 105, 122, 126, 129–130, 274

Slim, General 14, 27

Snelling, F/O 137

Special Operations Executive 8, 10–11, 13–15, 19, 21–24, 26, 27–29, 35–42, 48, 121, 130, 154, 190, 272, 323, 378–380, 382

St. John, Tony 105–107, 122–124, 127, 134

Stevenson, HNC 302

T

Ta Bi, Arthur 92, 98, 278

Tabe, Arthur 139

Tack, Sgt. 54

Tagundaing 94, 318

Tahulaw 81, 90, 230, 318

Tanipa 136, 138, 140, 321

Tatukhi 132–133, 138, 280, 283, 320

Tazi 75

Thadin, Jemadar 83, 90, 122

Thahokhi 100

Thaung Tu 135

Thauthekhi 62, 133, 135, 317

Tollygunge 117–120

Torry, Maj. Saw 13

Toungoo 14

Trinco 48, 146

Trofimov, Maj. Aubrey Alwyn Edgar 9, 13–16, 19–30, 47–49, 59–60, 85–86, 96, 101, 106, 136–137, 146, 166, 204, 214, 222, 230, 266, 272, 285, 287, 289–291, 296, 300, 308, 323, 378, 381–382

Trofimov, Marie (*nee* Woodcock) 20, 70, 113, 129

Tun Shin, Havildar Maj. 75, 87, 88, 131, 132, 134, 135, 280

Turrall, Maj. Rupert Guy 49, 51–53, 55–57, 59, 61, 70, 71, 73, 79, 272–274, 287, 312, 314

U

Urekhi 97, 99, 101, 319

Usher, Sgt. 127

W

Walaw 123

Walrus 24, 36

Wattaw 53, 77, 101–102, 104, 133, 319

Wili Saw 74

Williams, Capt. John Philip 74–76, 106, 108, 110, 114, 275, 287, 301

Winamuang (Japanese dispositions) 125

Wingale 132, 134, 280, 320

Wingalon (Japanese dispositions) 125

Winkadeik (Japanese dispositions) 125

Winpa 96

Wolf, Capt. Ivan 48, 74, 123, 204 281, 296 300

Y

Yadav, Capt. Kim 139, 143

Yakhekhi 91, 100–101

Yebezu 136, 281–282

Young, Maj. 48

Yunzalin 79, 83, 87, 96, 275, 278, 318

PB ISBN 978-1-73944-026-8
HB ISBN 978-1-73944-027-5

Raiding Support Regiment
The Diary of a Special Forces Soldier 1943–1945

GH Bennett

Harry is Associate Professor at Plymouth University where he has taught history, including that of the Second World War since 1992. Author of more than 20 volumes on Military, Diplomatic and Political history he has appeared in documentaries on the Second World War as well as historical series such as *Who Do You Think You Are* and *Combat Ships*. He is also a regular contributor to BBC National, Local Radio and to Gem Collector TV.

The Second World War in Yugoslavia is an area neglected by historians and other commentators. This is perhaps surprising as Yugoslavia was the only country in Europe to be conquered by the Germans and then, later, to free itself solely as a result of guerrilla activity. Other countries had to be liberated by Allied armies. The British played an important role in supporting the activities of Tito's guerrilla army. This is the story of Walter Jones's service and the operations of the Raiding Support Regiment.

A precursor to the modern SAS the Raiding Support Regiment fought alongside the commandos and Tito's partisan in Yugoslavia. Based on the Island of Vis in the Adriatic they provided heavy weapons support to British and partisan forces trying to drive the Germans out of Yugoslavia. Later they served in Albania and Italy. This is a brutally honest account of one man's service with the Regiment and a neglected period of European history. It documents the transformation of a young man into a combat veteran as he witnesses the effects of bombing, the deliberate killing of POWs and partisan savagery against those who transgress the partisan code.